Folkloric Poverty

Folkloric Poverty

Neoliberal Multiculturalism in Mexico

Rebecca Overmyer-Velázquez

The Pennsylvania State University Press
University Park, Pennsylvania

The photographs in this book are by
Rebecca Overmyer-Velázquez.

Library of Congress Cataloging-in-Publication Data

Overmyer-Velázquez, Rebecca, 1966–
Folkloric poverty : neoliberal multiculturalism in Mexico / Rebecca Overmyer-Velazquez.
p.   cm.
Includes bibliographical references and index.
Summary: "Analyzes the crisis indigenous political groups faced in Mexico at the turn of the twenty-first century. Focuses on an indigenous peoples movement in the state of Guerrero that gained unprecedented national and international prominence in the 1990s and yet was defunct by 2002"—Provided by publisher.
ISBN 978-0-271-03657-1 (cloth : alk. paper)
ISBN 978-0-271-03658-8 (pbk. : alk. paper)
1. Indians of Mexico—Mexico—Guerrero (State)—Politics and government.
2. Indians of Mexico—Mexico—Guerrero (State)—Government relations.
3. Indians of Mexico—Mexico—Guerrero (State)—Ethnic identity.
4. Indian activists—Mexico—Guerrero (State)
5. Protest movements—Mexico—Guerrero (State)
6. Guerrero (Mexico : State)—Ethnic relations.
7. Guerrero (Mexico : State)—Social conditions.
8. Guerrero (Mexico : State)—Politics and government.
I. Title.

F1219.1.G93O94 2010
305.800972'73—dc22
2009041368

Copyright © 2010 The Pennsylvania State University
All rights reserved
Printed in the United States of America
Published by The Pennsylvania State University Press
University Park, PA 16802-1003

The Pennsylvania State University Press is a member of the Association of American University Presses.

It is the policy of The Pennsylvania State University Press to use acid-free paper. Publications on uncoated stock satisfy the minimum requirements of American National Standard for Information Sciences—Permanence of Paper for Printed Library Material, ANSI Z39.48–1992.

contents

List of Illustrations vii
Acknowledgments ix
List of Abbreviations xi

Introduction:
The Nationalist Indian in a Neoliberal Age   1

ONE
The Anti-Quincentenary Campaign in Guerrero, Mexico: Indigenous Identity and the Dismantling of the Myth of the Revolution   33

TWO
Indigenista Dreams of the Mexican Indian   59

THREE
Indian Populists: The Indigenous Movement and the Guerrero Council, 1991–2000   89

FOUR
Opportunities and Obstacles: Contextualizing the Guerrero Council's Work in the 1990s   135

Conclusion: The Exhaustion of the Indigenous Movement: What Comes Next?   172

References   191
Index   203

illustrations

MAPS
Mexico, with Guerrero highlighted   23
Official regions of Guerrero   23

PHOTOGRAPHS
Basketball hoop in Cuamanotepec   9
Council leaders before the Mexican flag   12
Martha Sánchez Néstor   24
Meeting participants identify themselves with their fingerprints   62
CCI–Tlapa mural: INI brings education   65
Chilapa market   71
CCI–Tlapa mural: INI brings immunizations   86
Community projects in and around Cuamanotepec   114
Encuentro Intercultural march in Chilpancingo, April 2000   115
Steep mountain milpas in the Montaña region   123
Rancho Nuevo de la Democracia meeting, December 1999   124
Then: old state government building in Chilpancingo, 1999   186
Now: new state government complex outside of Chilpancingo, 2005   187

acknowledgments

This book would not have been possible without the kindness and assistance of many individuals. Above all, I wish to thank the women and men of the Guerrero Council who opened their homes and hearts to me. The time spent with them, throughout the state of Guerrero, formed the basis for my research. I offer the thoughts expressed here with great respect and with the hope that they contribute in some measure to the thoughtful consideration of the rights of indigenous peoples.

I owe a great debt to Avery Gordon and John Foran and Sarah Cline, who were with me from the beginning of my graduate career. As my teachers and mentors, and as good human beings, they consistently balanced ready acceptance of my initiative and ideas with constructive criticism. Their support and encouragement brought me through every rough part of the process and helped lay a solid foundation for this book. I am grateful to my friends and colleagues at Whittier College—sal johnston and Les Howard, in particular—for making sure I had the time to work on this project. I thank the anonymous readers of the manuscript, whose insightful comments improved the final text you have before you. All errors and equivocations are my own.

My partner, Pam, deserves her own prize for enduring me and doing all the extra work that needed to be done when I was too swamped to help; she also produced the maps in this book. Pam and my daughter, Amara, remind me that the life of the mind is always nourished by the love and support of family. My deep thanks to them as well as to my parents, Dan and Estella, my brother, Mark, and my grandmother Bernice.

Finally, fellowships from the University of California Institute on Global Conflict and Cooperation and the Institute for the Study of World Politics made my original research in Mexico possible; a Whittier College Faculty Research Grant supported my follow-up research in 2005. The Centro de

Investigaciones y Estudios Superiores en Antropología Social in Mexico City kindly sponsored me as a visiting researcher in 1999–2000. Parts of the book appeared in earlier versions in the *Berkeley Journal of Sociology* 46 (2002) and *Latin American and Caribbean Ethnic Studies* 2, no. 1 (2007) (http://www.informaworld.com).

abbreviations

ANIPA	Asamblea Nacional Indígena Plural por la Autonomía (Plural National Indigenous Assembly for Autonomy)
CCA	Consejo Comunitario de Abasto (Community Food Council)
CCI	Centro Coordinadora Indigenista (Indigenous Coordination Center)
CDI (Conadepi)	Comisión Nacional para el Desarrollo de los Pueblos Indígenas (National Commission for the Development of Indigenous Peoples)
CETEG	Coordinadora Estatal de Trabajadores de la Educación en Guerrero (Guerrero State Coordinating Committee of Education Workers)
CFE	Comisión Federal de Electricidad (Federal Electricity Commission)
CNC	Confederación Nacional Campesina (National Peasant Federation)
CNDH	Comisión Nacional de Derechos Humanos (National Human Rights Commission)
CNPA	Coordinadora Nacional Plan de Ayala (National Coordinating Committee of the Plan of Ayala)
CNPI	Consejo Nacional de Pueblos Indígenas (National Council of Indigenous Peoples)
CONASUPO	Compañia Nacional de Subsistencias Populares (National Company of Popular Subsistence)
COPLAMAR	Coordinación General del Plan Nacional de Zonas Deprimidas y Grupos Marginados (National Program for Depressed Areas and Marginal Groups)
CPNAB	Consejo de Pueblos Nahuas del Alto Balsas (Council of Nahua Communities of the Upper Balsas)

ENAH	Escuela Nacional de Antropología e Historia (National School of Anthropology and History)
EZLN	Ejército Zapatista de Liberación Nacional (Zapatista National Liberation Army)
FRS	Fondos Regionales de Solidaridad (Regional Solidarity Funds)
ILO	International Labor Organization
INEGI	Instituto Nacional de Estadística y Geografía (National Institute of Statistics and Geography)
INI	Instituto Nacional Indigenista (National Indigenous Institute)
LuzMont	Unión de Ejidos y Comunidades Luz de la Montaña (Light of the Montaña Union of Ejidos and Communities)
MIL	Mujeres Indígenas en Lucha (Indigenous Women in Struggle)
NAFTA	North American Free Trade Agreement
OCESP	Organización de Campesinos Ecologistas de la Sierra de Petatlán y Coyuca de Catalán (Peasant Environmentalist Organization of the Sierra de Petatlán and Coyuca de Catalán)
OCICI	Organización Campesina Independiente de Comunidades Indígenas (Independent Peasant Organization of Indigenous Communities)
OCSS	Organización Campesina de la Sierra del Sur (Peasant Organization of the Sierra del Sur)
OPIM	Organización del Pueblo Indígena Me'phaa (Organization of the Me'phaa Indigenous People)
PAN	Partido Acción Nacional (National Action Party)
PCM	Partido Comunista Mexicano (Communist Party of Mexico)
PNR	Partido Nacional Revolucionario (National Revolutionary Party)
PRD	Partido Revolucionario Democrático (Party of the Democratic Revolution)
PRI	Partido Revolucionario Institucional (Institutional Revolutionary Party)
PRONASOL	Programa Nacional de Solidaridad (National Solidarity Program)

PRT	Partido Revolucionario de Trabajo (Revolutionary Labor Party)
RAP	Región Autónoma Pluriétnica (Pluriethnic Autonomous Region)
SARH	Secretaría de Agricultura y Recursos Hidráulicos (Ministry of Agriculture and Water Resources)
SEDESOL	Secretaría de Desarrollo Social (Ministry of Social Development)
SETAI	Secretaría Técnica de Asuntos Indígenas (Technical Secretariat for Indigenous Affairs)
SNTE	Sindicato Nacional de Trabajadores de la Educación (National Union of Education Workers)
UNAM	Universidad Nacional Autónoma de México (National Autonomous University of Mexico)
UNORCA	Unión Nacional de Organizaciones Regionales Campesinas Autónomas (National Union of Autonomous Regional Peasant Organizations)
UPN	Universidad Pedagógica Nacional (National Pedagogical University)
WGIP	Working Group on Indigenous Populations

INTRODUCTION:
THE NATIONALIST INDIAN IN A NEOLIBERAL AGE

At 10 A.M. on 22 October 1999, the directors of one of Mexico's most prominent national indigenous organizations were scheduled to meet in a conference room at the Legislative Palace in Mexico City to discuss the group's political strategy. With the presidential campaign season about to begin, the directors of the Plural National Indigenous Assembly for Autonomy (Asamblea Nacional Indígena Plural por la Autonomía, or ANIPA) were gathering to debate how the ANIPA could provide Mexico's indigenous peoples with a voice in national policy making. It was not going to be easy.

By 11 A.M., thirty or so men and women (far more men than women) had seated themselves at several tables set up around the room and were visiting with one another. No one seemed in a hurry to start. Once the meeting finally got under way, however, Margarito Ruiz Hernández, a former federal congressman from Chiapas and executive director of the ANIPA, rose to say that both the country and the indigenous movement were in crisis. "We lack the will to make decisions and we haven't been able to create a large national force for change in the country," he lamented. Although the ANIPA was culturally diverse and politically pluralist, there was no place for it in the national dialogue. Julio Atenco Vidal from Veracruz, an Amnesty International prisoner of conscience in 1997, added that the indigenous movement was divided ideologically: whereas some rejected institutional politics and focused only on Chiapas and the Zapatista National Liberation Army (Ejéricito Zapatista de Liberación Nacional, or EZLN), others, like those in the ANIPA, embraced politics as a way to bring the indigenous problem to a larger arena.

In addressing the challenge that free trade, especially the North American Free Trade Agreement (NAFTA), posed to all Mexicans now that they had to compete directly with transnational corporations, a few participants argued that it was not enough to emerge from the crisis in the movement. They had to go beyond indigenous issues. "We have to enlarge our struggle against the capitalist system," said a participant. In general, however, the economy took second place to issues internal to the indigenous movement and its leadership. For one director, the central problem was a lack of professionalization, coordination, institutionalization, and commitment; for another, the problem was precisely the professionalization and urbanization of leaders who had minimal contact with their *pueblos,* their home communities. For Pedro de Jesús Alejandro, a founder of the Guerrero Council 500 Years of Indigenous Resistance (Consejo Guerrerense 500 Años de Resistencia Indígena; hereafter shortened to "council") and other assembly directors, there were clearly differences that mattered within the ANIPA. "Don't think we will all agree. But we can respect and accept these differences," he said hopefully. "Our participation in electoral politics through alliances and coalitions is one way to fight. That doesn't mean we will abandon other forms of struggle." It did mean, however, that they would have to go beyond the ANIPA's traditional focus on regional indigenous autonomy to include issues not specific to Indians.[1] These were all long-standing issues that would not be resolved at this meeting.

The differences within the ANIPA leadership are reflected in the thousands of different indigenous communities that form the heterogeneous basis for the indigenous movement in Mexico. In a meeting held in Oaxaca in late August 2000, academics and indigenous leaders frankly discussed the status of the movement, its relationship to communities, and its future under a new presidential regime (see Sarmiento Silva 2000). The "movement," though present in the communities, in community discussions and relations, was not always visible to outsiders. It continued to be fragmented into regional groups that were largely isolated from one another. Indeed,

---

1. Since 1995, when the group was founded, the ANIPA had favored a regionally based indigenous autonomy that would be "pluriethnic, democratic, and inclusive"—and located in a recognized territory. This would involve the creation of a fourth level of government in addition to the existing national, state, and municipal levels. See Ruiz Hernández 1999.

argued Francisco López Bárcenas of the Center for Human Rights and Indigenous Culture, the movement's "strong community identity . . . favors community autonomy and creates problems for the creation of municipal autonomy and regional autonomy." Conflicts between communities over land posed another serious problem. Whereas in Chiapas, because of the special circumstances there, indigenous people talk about regional autonomy, in a state like Oaxaca, where "there are many agrarian problems, intercommunity conflicts and difficulties with political parties" have divided community loyalties. Reynaldo Miguel García of the University Human Rights Workshop of Oaxaca insisted with others that "it will have to be the communities themselves that provide the solution to the problems [indigenous people face]."

Raúl Gatica of the Popular Indigenous Council of Oaxaca was hopeful that the new political situation—with the long-ruling Institutional Revolutionary Party (Partido Revolucionario Institucional, or PRI) having lost the presidency in July 2000—would make it possible "to transcend local politics" and "to build power that is more regional, statewide" (Sarmiento Silva 2000). All agreeing that there was a lack of indigenous leadership at the state and national levels, they asked how they could join forces to arrive at a national dialogue where distinct positions would be voiced and respected, with the idea to conquer this space for indigenous peoples. For some, the hope lay in strengthening the community base; for others, it lay in the organizations that acted as the vanguard of the movement, providing its leadership and many of its best strategies. Although the movement faced acknowledged risks at both the community and the extracommunity level, it was crucial that both levels be strengthened to advance indigenous demands. In sum, even in August 2000, the "indigenous movement" was not yet a national political force.[2]

---

2. There has been an ongoing discussion in Mexico among indigenous and mestizo intellectuals about the appropriate level of political autonomy for indigenous peoples, with two proposals dominating this discussion: the communal and the regional. In Oaxaca, with its history of relatively autonomous Indian towns that managed to retain their communal lands, a *comunalista* vision of autonomy has the most support (Mattiace 2003, 105–11; Martínez Luna 1993). Comunalistas "insist that the construction of autonomy emerge from the communities and be realized 'from the bottom up'" (Esteva 2003, 268n2). The regional autonomy proposal has been well developed by Tojolobals from Chiapas, whose migration to the Lacandon rainforest in the 1950s allowed them to reconstitute a sense of identity "based on common goals rather than discrete community identities" (Mattiace 2003, 102). For regionalists, the community remains important but autonomy does not end there because "the most important problems that affect Indian peoples transcend the community" (Díaz Polanco 1998, 54; see also Burguete Cal y Mayor 1999). The ANIPA has incorporated both autonomy proposals into its platform for national political reform.

The sentiments expressed at these two different meetings of indigenous leaders are striking, if not surprising. It is to be expected that in a country with as varied an indigenous population as Mexico's—where up to seventy-two different indigenous languages are spoken in a geographically diverse territory and where political party and religious affiliation increasingly matter in even the smallest rural hamlets—there will be important differences among groups representing Indian interests. What is striking is that, in 2000, after almost a decade of unprecedented political, social, and cultural activity by indigenous peoples all over Mexico, its leaders could nevertheless assert that this movement was in "crisis." There was a "bitter feeling about the negligible political movement toward the recognition of indigenous peoples" (Hernández Castillo, Paz, and Sierra 2004, 23). What had happened? Why had the political movement been so limited? *Folkloric Poverty* offers one explanation for the crisis faced by indigenous political groups in Mexico at the turn of the new century.

To do this, it examines the relationship between indigenous peoples and the Mexican state, with a focus on an indigenous peoples movement in the state of Guerrero—the Guerrero Council 500 Years of Indigenous Resistance—during the 1990s. The first decade of the Guerrero Council, from 1990 to 2000, witnessed the rise of a national indigenous movement coincident with the rapid acceleration of free market and political reforms in Mexico. *Folkloric Poverty* assesses the life of this group, defunct since 2002, as representative of an important moment in the political mobilization of indigenous peoples. More broadly, it analyzes the impacts of neoliberal reforms—still very much in effect—on indigenous movements in Mexico today.

The end of the twentieth century was notable for the cultural and political florescence of indigenous peoples in Mexico. The historical conjuncture of the 1992 anti-quincentenary protests against official celebrations of "the encounter of two worlds" and the 1994 neo-Zapatista uprising in Chiapas acted to propel the grievances of indigenous peoples into national consciousness as never before. Local, regional, and national indigenous organizations formed to pursue a variety of causes—legal, economic, cultural, social, and political—to benefit indigenous peoples in all of the country's regions. But these movements emerged within economic and political contexts that shaped not only their character but also their ability to effect the changes they sought. More specifically, I argue that Mexico's neoliberal economic restructuring and a complementary revamped national populism were the necessary economic and political conditions for the emergence of an indigenous movement in Guerrero in the early 1990s.³ On the one hand, these were enabling conditions for the council, granting the group a legitimacy and authority it would not otherwise have had, especially since the neoliberal emphasis on autonomy and self-reliance ("rights") also coincided with emerging indigenous demands for economic and political self-determination. On the other, these conditions placed real material and ideological limits on who indigenous peoples could be and what they could do. In short, the neoliberal moment facilitated the emergence of an "indigenous peoples" movement at the beginning of the decade while contributing significantly to the crisis this movement faced at the end.⁴

Like other indigenous rights movements in Mexico, the Guerrero Council claimed a common citizenship intimately associated with Mexican revolutionary nationalism and affirmed the legitimacy of the Mexican state. This last position clearly distinguished it from the Zapatista National Liberation Army (EZLN) in Chiapas, which has rejected all official government authority in the regions where the EZLN has a strong presence, even though the EZLN remains highly nationalistic. Strong claims to nationalism persist among Mexico's indigenous peoples despite the expansion of international human rights—including uniquely indigenous rights—and a global laissez-faire political economy that together provided the opportunity for the council and other indigenous groups to claim indigenous self-determination. But this opportunity came with significant costs, which included the withdrawal of government programs to promote rural development and small agricultural production, leaving peasant producers unprotected in an increasingly competitive market. In effect, the movement toward new collective or cultural rights for indigenous

---

3. *Nation-state* and *nationalist* as used here refer to the ideological construction of the Mexican "nation," that is, to a culturally and politically defined space and people occupying that space. The terms *state* and *government* refer to the institutions and representatives of governments at the state and federal levels; *government* is sometimes qualified as either *state* or *central/federal government* for the sake of clarity.

4. Kevin Middlebrook and Eduardo Zepeda (2003, 24; emphasis added) described the relationship between neoliberalism and popular movements in this way: "Reducing the state's role in economic affairs contributed to greater pluralism in state-society relations, and it implicitly questioned the legitimacy of the state's long-dominant position vis-à-vis organized social forces. Although it is important not to exaggerate the dimensions of this phenomenon, the resulting change in public expectations may have encouraged the emergence of more densely textured, more autonomous civil society in which interest groups gradually mobilized to demand increased political representation and greater accountability on the part of governmental authorities. *However, this was a contradictory process because, over time, economic restructuring also undermined social structures and organizational networks that had sustained popular mobilizations in earlier periods.*" As discussed in detail below, ideology has also worked contradictorily to promote and undermine indigenous peoples movements.

peoples recognized under international law came at the expense of older social and economic rights.

This was not coincidental. The reduction of social rights in Mexico as a result of free market reforms was in part made possible by the government's conspicuous acknowledgment of international human rights, and indigenous peoples were seen as key beneficiaries of this acknowledgment. As Jane Hindley (1996, 230) points out, "The issue of indigenous rights was effectively harnessed to the . . . project of modernizing the Mexican state and the broader political context of ensuring neoliberal economic restructuring and regime maintenance." Mexico's formal acknowledgment of international human rights in the early 1990s included the creation of the National Human Rights Commission (Comisión Nacional de Derechos Humanos, or CNDH), with official Human Rights Commissions in each state, a new Federal Electoral Institute to monitor elections, the ratification of International Labor Organization Convention 169 on the Rights of Indigenous and Tribal Peoples, and the amendment of Article 4 of the Mexican constitution to recognize the country's "pluricultural" composition. These reforms made a positive international impression and gave the U.S. government a politically defensible reason to sign onto the market reforms initiated by Mexican president Carlos Salinas de Gortari in the North American Free Trade Agreement. The 1993 U.S. State Department Human Rights Report on Mexico, for example, presented a picture of the Mexican government doing all it could to protect human rights despite considerable obstacles; it praised the efforts of the CNDH and noted a decline in rights abuses thanks to "the work of government and nongovernmental human rights agencies and a commitment by the Salinas Administration to prosecute offenders."[5] Indeed, the Mexican government tended to escape any blame for violations of human rights. In the section on discrimination based on race, the report asserted that indigenous groups "remain largely outside the country's political and economic mainstream, a result not of overt governmental discrimination but rather of long-standing patterns of economic and social development."[6] Soon after the Chiapas uprising on 1 January 1994, U.S. State Department officials were quick to defend the Salinas government from charges that it had violated the rights of Maya Indians. "Mexico is a rapidly evolving democracy," asserted Alexander F. Watson, assistant secretary of state

---

5. *Congressional Record,* 29 October 1993, S14663.
6. Ibid., S14667.

for inter-American affairs. "It's pretty clear that what happened in Chiapas has energized this process" (Abrams 1994).

Meanwhile, and to much acclaim, Mexican state populism privileged indigenous peasants and constructed them as independent entrepreneurs. New centralized rural development programs like the Regional Solidarity Funds (Fondos Regionales de Solidaridad) initiated by President Salinas at the beginning of the 1990s specifically targeted these peasants and received the vast majority of government funding for the countryside. This was, as Denise Dresser (1991) notes, a neopopulist solution for neoliberal problems since the government was removing its global social programs and replacing them with targeted programs of reduced scope such as the Regional Solidarity Funds. But the privileged beneficiaries of these new programs were not at all new and had a long history in the populist imaginary of the Mexican state. The peasantry was a key figure in this imaginary, but more important, in the 1990s it was "Indian" as imagined by the dominant national Indian policy, *indigenismo*. The council's leadership was similarly populist in this more specific—and very Mexican revolutionary—form, emphasizing always a particular kind of Indian who was the legitimate bearer of citizenship rights. It is this Indian who represents what I call "folkloric poverty," a widespread notion that Indians are, by tradition, poor, isolated, and community bound.[7]

The Guerrero Council

Having a significant political presence in Guerrero and in the national indigenous movement based in Mexico City, especially in the ANIPA, the Guerrero Council represented the four major ethnic groups of indigenous people in the state: Amuzgos, Mixtecos, Nahuas, and Tlapanecos, who together made up 13 percent of its population and who lived in forty of its eighty-one municipalities (all located in the mountainous eastern part of the state). By 2000, the council had fourteen mostly young, mostly male directors, each representing a particular ethnic group from a different region. Though headquartered in the state capital of Chilpancingo, the council directors spent a good deal of time in their respective regions participating in local politics and acting as liaisons between national development agencies and community members. But it was community leaders,

---

7. I have borrowed and modified "folkloric poverty" from José del Val Blanco, who pointed out to me the "folkloric scenography of poverty" that continues to characterize images of Indians in Mexico.

traveling long distances to the council's offices in Chilpancingo to obtain funding for very specific community projects, who provided the council's main connection to the indigenous communities it represented. And though the council's presence in the state capital served to bring members from different communities into contact with one another, the emphasis was on the pueblo, the local community.

The bulk of the council's work actually took place between pueblos and the state government, channeling government funds to community projects like electrification, road repair, and the construction of piped water systems, latrines, wood stoves, and basketball courts. It was eminently local work to take care of immediate needs. Though the council did not represent all of Guerrero's indigenous communities, that it was able to mobilize community members for highly visible congresses and marches in Chilpancingo, for marches from Guerrero to Mexico City, and for protest roadblocks along the busy Mexico City–Acapulco highway made it a recognized representative of indigenous peoples in their dealings with the state and federal governments. As such, through its advocacy, the council was able to obtain for its community leaders basic infrastructure like electricity and piped water, which they had never had in their villages before.

Populism and Neoliberalism

The expansion of neo-liberal capitalism, which is incorporating large sections of the peasantry . . . into an international industrial reserve army of labour, is being accompanied by a worldwide resurgence of nationalism and a corresponding displacement of socialist ideas by 'new' populist ones. Among other things, this licenses the re-emergence of folkloric variants of reactionary nationalism linked to the agrarian myth.

—TOM BRASS, *Peasants, Populism, and Postmodernism* (2000)

Populism, argues Brass (2000, 2), is "an 'a-political'/'third-way' discourse that is . . . a 'from above' attempt to mobilize the rural grassroots on the basis of the agrarian myth, thereby obtaining support among peasants and farmers opposed to the effects of industrialization, urbanization and capitalist crisis." In modern Mexico, state populism was never at odds with capitalism, which included socialist-style state ownership of industry and strong government paternalism. The agrarian myth, which has both a discourse-for and a discourse-against, informs Mexican state populism and the council leadership's characterization of the indigenous movement. The discourse-for emphasizes rural-based, small-scale production and culture, the "religious/ethnic/national/regional/village/family identities

Basketball is the most popular sport in Guerrero's indigenous communities, second only perhaps to party politics, which are represented here on the post. The backboard documents that this court in Cuamanotepec was made possible thanks to the work of the Guerrero Council.

derived from Nature" (3). The discourse-against opposes urban, large-scale industrialization, finance capital, and bureaucracy (and, I would add, anything or anyone defined as "cosmopolitan" or "intellectual," inevitably linked to an effete foreignness that threatens the nation). "All the latter are perceived as non-indigenous/inauthentic/'alien' internationalisms imposed on an unwilling and mainly rural population" (3).

The advent of neoliberal economic policies in Latin America prompted researchers to examine how populism—generally understood to be an economic project that widely redistributes resources—has survived in the region in an era of shrinking states. This examination has deepened our understanding of populism as a complex phenomenon irreducible to a restricted economic, political, or social definition (Roberts 1996, 2007; Knight 1998; Brienen 2007; Weyland 2001). For example, Alan Knight's definition (1998, 226) of populism as a political "style" that "implies a close bond between political leaders and led" and Kurt Weyland's assertion (2001, 13) that "the populist connection between leaders and followers is based mostly on direct, quasi-personal contact" both leave undetermined the economic and social policies that might follow from such political personalism. We have seen in leaders such as Alberto Fujimori in Peru, Carlos Menem in Argentina, and Carlos Salinas in Mexico how a populist style was quite compatible with an economic policy that withdrew broad support from the poor and working class. As Kenneth Roberts (1996, 88) argues, "There are no clear theoretical or empirical grounds for adopting an essentialist perspective that prioritizes any single property of this multidimensional phenomenon." Brass's emphasis on the cultural dimension of populism—the agrarian myth—reminds us that the expression of this phenomenon is always specific to a particular time and place. Brass draws a clear line between populism, which he argues is always a reformist project of the political right, and socialism/communism, which advocates a systemic, revolutionary change in capitalist relations of production. Populists and now neopopulists, Brass asserts, fundamentally oppose this systemic change and use the agrarian myth to draw peasants away from revolution and toward accommodation and limited resistance. His definition of populism helps explain how in Mexico in the 1990s the central government gave voice to a Mexican agrarian myth and continued old-style clientelist practices that tied peasants to government agencies while implementing policies that eroded the economic and social bases of indigenous peasant life.

An analysis of the Guerrero Council adds to our understanding of populism as a cultural idiom shared by state agents and popular movements within a national historical context. As the agrarian myth, populism becomes hegemonic because it involves the ongoing consent of those subject to government coercion. But hegemony is also a process, in which "power and meaning are contested, legitimated, and redefined at all levels of society" (Mallon 1995, 6). The "state" is hardly monolithic (as a look at indigenismo will show) and popular movements, too, are internally divided, making the hegemonic process always complex and never complete. As a cultural expression, populism is subject to challenge and redefinition even as it works to keep people in line. Indigenous movements, "like all social actors, struggle against dominant political forces at some times and ally themselves with them at others, depending upon the historical and political contexts" (Postero 2004, 192). The council was always in the middle of this push and pull between contestation and legitimation of government power.

Indigenous Peoples and Nation-States

Despite the fact that our grandmothers and grandfathers gave their blood to abolish slavery in the War of Independence, in the War of the Reform, in the Mexican Revolution at the side of our General Emiliano Zapata, and despite the blood offered by our Mayan brothers, those of the "for everyone everything, for us nothing," those of the hidden face of the Zapatista National Liberation Army (EZLN), despite all of this, our rights as indigenous peoples are still neither recognized nor respected.

—GUERRERO COUNCIL 500 Years of Indigenous Resistance, February 2000

All ethnicities need to be understood within the historical context of particular nation-states. Each ethnic group, whether labeled as such or not (there are "invisible ethnics," too), is situated at a particular place in the national narrative of belonging; each place registers a relative degree of citizenship, loyalty, and sacrifice (Williams 1989). Nationalist mythologies of nation building typically insist on a particular "race/class conflation that becomes the ideologically defined 'real producers' of the nation's patrimony" (Williams 1989, 434). Groups considered "ethnic" or "minority," such as indigenous peoples in Mexico, are set in competition with a nation's dominant group to prove "that they too have contributed to the national foundation" (435).

Brackette Williams assumes in her argument that ethnics, as outsiders, want to get inside the dominant national narrative by modifying but not dismantling its criteria of belonging. The black civil rights movement in the United States, for example, and the Guerrero Council were very similar ethnic movements as Williams defines *ethnic,* and not at all like ethnic movements that define themselves in opposition to the nation-state and deny its very legitimacy. For the council, the following assertion most certainly applied: "No ethnic group can afford not to measure its accomplishments against those of others. In search of a legitimate place in the nation, each group must guard its gains and insist on all credit due" (Williams

1989, 435). During protest marches and in its press releases, the council consistently made positive reference to Mexican national heroes such as Vicente Guerrero, José María Morelos, and Emiliano Zapata to draw a direct connection between these men, the Indian-peasant movements they led, and the council's contemporary struggle. The council always asserted a common cause with the Mexican people, flew the Mexican flag at all of its events, and appealed to the national constitution as the supreme law of the land. Council members regularly participated in local and national electoral contests and were often in dialogue with government representatives. Furthermore, the council's directors reminded us, the blood shed to make Mexico a nation was *Indian* blood, and this nationalist sacrifice necessarily bestowed legitimacy on late twentieth-century Indian demands for recognition by and inclusion in the nation-state.

In struggling against the prevailing discourse of nationalism, every indigenous movement insists on a substitute nationalist narrative: either one that explicitly includes its members in the dominant settler nation or one that explicitly excludes them as a distinct nation. In Mexico, indigenous peoples have overwhelmingly chosen the first option. Anthropologists writing in *Nation-States and Indians in Latin America* (Urban and Sherzer 1991) were among the first social scientists to articulate the importance of

The Mexican flag was always prominently displayed at council meetings and events. The man with the microphone on the far right is Pedro de Jesús Alejandro, a founder of the council.

the larger nation-state context for studies of indigenous peoples in Latin America. Research and publication since then have shifted their focus from indigenous communities and local culture almost exclusively to regional, national, and transnational political movements for indigenous rights. This shift followed the widespread emergence of indigenous movements throughout Latin America in the 1990s that, like the council, called for a new kind of formal government recognition of indigenous cultural difference (see, for example, Hale 1994; Assies, van der Haar, and Hoekema 1998; Ramos 1998; Brysk 2000; Van Cott 2000, 2003; Warren 2001; Sieder 2002; Maybury-Lewis 2002; Pallares 2002).

In his study of the conflict between the Miskitu and the Sandinista government of Nicaragua, Charles Hale (1994) advances the conceptual work on Indians in nation-states by adapting Brackette Williams's typology (1989) of the class/ethnic groups within any given nation-state to the Latin American context. Hale (1994, 213) suggests that there were "four class/ethnic groups whose boundaries and relations are constituted by the political interactions nation building entails"—criollos and elite mestizos, subordinate mestizos, ethnics, and protonationalists. Ethnics include Indians who do not completely assimilate as mestizos, but who also do not assert radical cultural difference as an oppositional position. As a result, writes Hale (1994, 214), they "languish in the middle ground" because they are different but powerless, whereas the protonationalist group includes strongly self-identified Indians who approach politics "from a space culturally defined as outside and in opposition to the nation." Hale's own case of the Miskitu in Nicaragua obviously fits in this category, as do the movements for Hawaiian sovereignty articulated by, for example, Dennis Pu'uhonua "Bumpy" Kanahele and David "Keanu" Sai in the United States.[8] These are movements where the demand for indigenous self-determination is tied to a clearly demarcated territory that is physically separated from the dominant nation-state.

The history of Indian struggles in Mexico, a history inherited by the council, has been one of *inclusion in* the national story (Mallon 1995; Guardino 1996; Mattiace 2003; Sánchez 1999; Díaz Polanco 1998). Because it asserted an Indian difference firmly situated inside and as part of the larger nation, the council's cultural/political position more closely approximated the politics of the early civil rights movement in the United States than it did the politics of an indigenous "protonationalism." But

---

8. See http://www.hawaii-nation.org/ (accessed 5 May 2003) and http://www.hawaiian kingdom.org/ (accessed 5 May 2003).

because it was also self-consciously indigenous and based its politics on this identity, it did not belong in the category of "ethnics" either. Although it may have questioned the legitimacy of a particular regime in power, the council did not question the legitimacy either of the dominant nation-state or of its claims to the larger territory. Moreover, in the name of nationalism and a common citizenship, the council worked closely even with a regime it challenged in Guerrero, and it did so in the name of nationalism and a common citizenship. The group's nationalism was closely connected to its project for the national integration of indigenous peoples into positions of power at the local and national level. It was also a product of the difficulty of clearly determining the boundaries of an autonomous indigenous territory in central Mexico (and much of the rest of the country).

The council exemplifies the complexity that arises when indigenous peoples share the language of nationalist, homogeneous populism that the dominant nation-state uses. In the San Andrés Accords signed by the federal government and the Zapatistas in 1996, for example, indigenous culture and identity are explicitly *national:* "It is necessary to elevate to constitutional status the right of all Mexicans to a pluricultural education that recognizes, disseminates, and promotes the history, customs, traditions and, in general, the culture of indigenous peoples, the root of our national identity" (*Acuerdos sobre derechos* 1997, 17). And, two years before the accords, a declaration signed by thirteen indigenous organizations (including the council) from the states of Guerrero, Chiapas, Michoacán, Sonora, Veracruz, and Oaxaca placed indigenous autonomy squarely within the nation:

> Our great political project of autonomy is national. In the first place, it is national because it does not deny nor reject the unity that all of us Mexicans have built throughout our history. We are looking to find a political solution for all within the framework of the integrity of the great Mexican nation. But we believe the political, social, and economic regime that a small group has imposed weakens our unity, because it excludes the majority, devalues our roots, marginalizes the dispossessed, and divides the people. Our autonomy proposes that we establish forms of communal, municipal, and regional self-government, autonomous regions, within the framework of national unity. Therefore, our autonomy is not a separatist proposal, something Indian peoples consider a sterile idea. *With autonomy, we want to feel and be real Mexicans, part of one living fatherland that is ours.* ("La autonomía como nueva relación" 1994; emphasis added)

Multiculturalism, Nationalism, and Late Capitalism

This framing of Mexican nationalism and Indianness as complementary took place within the larger context of the newly acknowledged multicultural—or pluricultural (to use the term preferred in Mexico)—nation. The reform of Article 4 of the Mexican Constitution in 1992 followed similar reforms in Argentina (1985), Nicaragua (1986), Costa Rica (1986), and Brazil (1988) that officially recognized the "pluricultural composition" of these countries. In the mid-1980s, the Mexican anthropologist Guillermo Bonfil Batalla contributed significantly to this political shift when he wrote *México profundo*, which redefined the nation in Indian terms and came to be considered a manifesto of the indigenous movement in Mexico. Bonfil Batalla (1996) argued that Mesoamerican "civilization" lives on in the country's many indigenous communities, but also survives often unnoticed as the "matrix" of what is truly Mexican about Mexico—for all Mexicans: this is the "México profundo," the deep Mexico. He acknowledged that Mexicans were differentiated by geography, by urban/rural sectors, and by class and status but they were nevertheless united by something deeper, something truly more profound, more *real*, than the *imaginary* (mestizo and Spanish) Mexico that had dominated the country for the last 500 years. As a result of this cultural domination, Mexico's economic development had turned out to be extremely unequal, and those "who found themselves obliged to choose a life and a job within the development plans of the imaginary Mexico are the first and the most deeply excluded and the ones who must support the requirements of the economic contraction" (Bonfil Batalla 1996, 155). The middle classes, in the meantime, "have wanted to be more cosmopolitan than Mexican" and now they "rage against a country they wanted for their own as an inexhaustible supplier of satisfactions" (156). The solution to this crisis, he argued, "the only option," was a cultural turn. The country had to "draw from the México profundo the historical will to formulate and undertake our own civilizational project" (158).

> When all is said and done, what we are speaking about is civilization. It is at the level of civilization that one measures the transcendence of the problems and recognizes the capacities and potentials of a people. It is there, in the civilizational project, that the fundamental information is to be found for designing the nation we want and are able to build in each historical period. From this perspective, what broke down was the civilizational model of the imaginary Mexico,

a model that had been accepted as the only one possible.... We must recognize the México profundo, once and for all, because without it there is no worthwhile solution. (158)

This recognition would best take place, Bonfil Batalla argued, in a multicultural nation where cultural diversity would be "a central goal of the project" (166). This is the goal taken up by the indigenous movement and the Mexican government (at least officially, if not in practice).

The appeal of Bonfil Batalla's argument for a revaluation of goals in a time of crisis makes a great deal of sense. Claudio Lomnitz-Adler (2001, 264) notes that this appeal also "undoubtedly stems from the ascertainable fact that large sections of Mexico's population are and have historically been shut out of the national public sphere." The problem with Bonfil Batalla's argument is the way he constructs this civilization in local terms ("the renovation and development of local cultures" [Bonfil Batalla 1996, 171]), as a turn inward, away from the structures of global capital.[9] Lomnitz-Adler (2001, 264) writes that "because it cannot extract Mexico from the world capitalist system, the 'deep Mexico' image tends to re-create or revitalize the sort of authoritarian nationalism that was characteristic of the period of growth under import substitution." The connection between multiculturalism and nationalism is explicit in México profundo, the subsequent reform of Article 4, and in the indigenous movement itself. But this new kind of nationalism—this new focus on the many cultures within nations—is also closely connected to the neoliberal moment in which it emerged.

Multiculturalism is not only about the resurgence and revitalization of cultural groups. It is also about "groups struggling to achieve moral solidarity, a precious good in an era of profound transformation and instability" (Cruz 1996, 31). As capital has become more and more globalized with fewer and fewer commitments to stay in any one place, cultural commitments to places have only intensified. Culturalism, argues Jon Cruz (1996, 31), "becomes one of the few weapons of the weak, but within an

---

9. Bonfil Batalla's argument that culture/civilization is the site of real conflict is similar to the one famously advanced by Samuel Huntington in his 1993 article in *Foreign Affairs*, "The Clash of Civilizations?" Here, too, the global economy's role in structuring conflict and inequality is eclipsed by the alleged centrality of deep cultural/civilizational divisions with long histories of antagonism. (Several recent studies debunk Huntington's bad history—see, for example, William Dalrymple's essay in the *New York Review of Books* [2004].) Bonfil Batalla only briefly mentions the long history of class/ethnic heterogeneity of Mexico's Indian peoples that complicates notions of a unitary civilizational project. See, for example, Lockhart 1992; Mallon 1995; Rus 1994; Hu-Dehart 1981.

economically abandoned and fragmented civil society." Identity, after all, suggests possession, something unique that we own and that cannot be taken from us. Such distinctions "register as major psychic as well as social victories. The indulgence in identity politics afforded by multiculturalism can make us feel more whole, more like subjects than objects" (34). But is this feeling not a result, Cruz asks, of the shrinking of the social whole? Multiculturalism, he answers, is thus a "political-demographic fix . . . a patching of fissures that have opened on the social surfaces over the last quarter century" (34). It is a fix reflected, too, in a fashionable cultural analysis that "seeks a presumed epistemological safety in the ahistoricism of the temporal, the turn to the *local,* and the *cultural fragment*" (25).

This is not to say that our cultural commitments are inherently reactionary or self-delusional or that Cruz is suggesting that the long histories of oppression and repression of stigmatized groups do not or should not matter. They most definitely matter. But what we have called "multiculturalism" is not innocent of power: as a notion and as a policy, it emerges within the particular historical conjunction of a rapidly expanding world economy combined with a rapidly shrinking government, particularly in Mexico. We ought to be mindful of this and of how the government's own shift from a discourse of culturally homogeneous to multicultural nationalism both reflects and *supports* these larger historical and material changes. In other words, "invoking the right to 'cultural difference' in this manner . . . not only protects the *economic* interests of the ruling class but does so in a way that is apparently innocent politically and even disinterestedly plebeian—the basis of the 'new' populism" (Brass 2000, 321).[10]

Because of the legacy of indigenismo, with its ambivalence toward the place of Indians in the nation, multiculturalism in Mexico readily became less about multiplicity and more about Bonfil Batalla's matrix, the México profundo that unified all Mexicans ("to feel and be real Mexicans," as the 1994 indigenous declaration asserts). Prominent *indigenistas* such as Alfonso Caso openly asserted the deep Indianness of all Mexicans even as they pursued the assimilation of Indians to mestizo culture. Mexico's is a distinctly populist kind of multiculturalism. A focus on populism reminds us of the importance of the state and, more specifically, of its class

---

10. Rosalva Aída Hernández Castillo, Sarela Paz, and María Teresa Sierra (2004, 21) echo Brass's assertion in their analysis of multicultural policy under the Fox presidency that ended decades of PRI control: "We observe the consolidation of an official multiculturalism that has managed to politically articulate difference as part of the social order, which forces us to dispute visions that see in difference something positive and oppositional without considering that [difference] is being developed within the framework of a neoliberal hegemony."

interest.[11] An ethnic politics based on populist imagery fits easily within neoliberal nationalism; it is not a threat to the larger system of power because it is constructed as "apolitical," a unifying discourse based on shared culture. It is the Indian—the poor Indian located in a small community carrying on a local tradition—that serves as the representation for *lo mexicano,* what is truly Mexican. The government invokes this Indian, and the council invoked it, too. Here the council and the state spoke the same language and operated within the same nationalist paradigm, thus minimizing or eliminating the threat "from below." This is true especially when the image of the populist Indian was and is used to exclude cosmopolitan Indians—those who live and move outside of the local—and "to put them in their place." As a result, the declaration of pluriculturalism in Article 4 and the ratification of ILO Convention 169 can be readily juxtaposed with the North American Free Trade Agreement and the privatization of the countryside. These are not mutually exclusive things; their coincidence is not surprising once we appreciate the function of populism and the agrarian myth, that is, once we appreciate that populism is not anticapitalist. It is, however, anti-industrial, anticosmopolitan, anti-imperialist, and pro-tradition, and all of these elements are present in indigenous movement discourse.

My argument here complements a new body of work that looks back with suspicion on how and why indigenous identity politics in Latin America flourished along with neoliberal economic reforms that reduced the government's support for the poor. Through the 1990s and into the twenty-first century, many researchers celebrated what we understood to be an "undisputed" fact: "The Latin American indigenous movement has provoked a most radical questioning of the models of nation-state, democracy, and development."[12] Witnessing or participating in the political mobilization around "indigenous identity," we seldom stopped to ask what it meant to "organize and defend Indians as Indians" (Yashar 1998, 27). Much less did we ask which Indians we were to organize and defend, or, more important, "who gets to decide which [indigenous] interests need

---

11. The state's class interest was seriously threatened in the 1988 presidential election by a coalition of leftist groups that came very close to toppling the ruling party from power. It is widely assumed that the challenger, Cuahtemoc Cárdenas, actually won the election, which was rigged to favor the PRI. The Salinas administration had to confront a legitimation crisis while simultaneously implementing intensive and extensive economic changes.

12. Taken from a review on the back cover of Maybury-Lewis 2002. The back cover of Postero and Zamosc 2004b includes a similar assessment: "Indigenous movements have become major social and political actors in Latin America, posing radical challenges to the extant model of the nation-state and notions of democracy and development."

to be defended and which defeated?" (Jackson 2002, 103). In particular, awed by the power and reach of indigenous movement discourses and determined to shift the focus of study from Indians as victims to indigenous peoples as agents of change, we tended to ignore the role of the state and its agents in the construction of indigenous identities and interests.[13]

In 2002, however, having investigated development projects in Guatemala, Charles Hale strongly suggested that multiculturalism in a neoliberal era could actually "menace." Like Brass (2000), Hale (2002, 498) argued that neoliberalism was not just an economic policy, but also a cultural project whose goal was "to harness and redirect the abundant political energy of cultural rights activism" by directing resources to "acceptable," relatively apolitical Indian groups who did not challenge the economic and political status quo. Along these lines, Lynn Horton's work (2006) in Panama among the Kunas uncovered a "top-down configuration of state multiculturalism" that focused on the folkloric. Within this configuration, Kuna insistence on essentialized difference allowed for the containment of ethnic/class claims on the nation-state. This political marginalization of Indians in an era of cultural advocacy was further explored by Carmen Martínez Novo (2006) in her study of indigenous migrant workers in northern Mexico, where she found that "indigenous culture/ethnicity" was used by nation-state agents and mestizo elites to justify and perpetuate the economic exploitation of these workers. "Much of what was identified and promoted as 'indigenous culture' by government-appointed and other advocates," she observed (Martínez Novo 2006, 6), "was either a stereotypical construction of 'Indianness' that had little to do with the actual experiences of Mixtec migrants or a manifestation of poverty that was naturalized as culture." We are reminded that Latin American states have long defined Indians as culturally deficient, a practice that continues in only slightly modified form under neoliberal multiculturalism, but with similar negative consequences (Briones et al. 2007).

These more recent studies are closely connected to work that scrutinizes the construction of Indian identity during a period when new subjects came forward to speak for and about indigenous peoples. Who was authorized to do this? On what basis was their authenticity as Indian representatives

---

13. The discursive shift from "Indians" to "indigenous peoples" was part of the transnational movement for the rights of indigenous peoples that culminated in 2007 with the adoption of the United Nations Declaration on the Rights of Indigenous Peoples by the UN General Assembly. "Indian" continues to be used in the Americas, but it does not have the force of human rights law that "indigenous peoples" has come to acquire over the last thirty years or so.

established or questioned? Several issues emerge from this discussion of indigenous authority and authenticity, one of the most pronounced being the way ethnicity and class intersect. Being poor is equated with being Indian and vice versa (Postero and Zamosc 2004a, 12); individuals or groups who fall outside of this equation are likely to be dismissed as inauthentic, but not always—another salient issue to be considered here is the importance of demographics and nationalist narratives and the place of Indians in those narratives. In Guatemala, for example, where Mayas are a majority and where prominent Maya elites have made visible their distinct history, an urban indigenous intellectual is not as much of an oxymoron as it is in Mexico, with its smaller indigenous population and the dominant ideology of cultural *mestizaje*. Even in Guatemala, however, the issue of space/time, which is similar to but analytically distinct from the issue of class/ethnicity, impacts claims to authenticity. That is, there is a dualism constructed between community and tradition, on the one hand, and between cosmopolitan and modern, on the other, with the first set of terms now privileged over the second. In this hierarchy of authenticity and authority, local community members are valued over urban intellectuals, who are considered impure regardless of their commitment to the indigenous cause. The role of the government is always present in questions of authority; its agents typically privilege and promote one kind of indigenous authority over another, though this can change over time, so that those in favor at one point, for example, urban intellectuals, can later be out of favor (Jackson 2002; García and Lucero 2004). All of these issues—class, nationalism, space/time, government promotion, and privileging—are present in the case study of the Guerrero Council, which demonstrates that "even when activism is phrased in terms of being a people (as opposed to class, religion, or political affiliation), the definition of belonging—the terms of inclusion and exclusion developed by these communities in their practice of self-identification—is variable and often situational" (Warren and Jackson 2002, 11). Who defines indigenous, in what context, and how government agents and popular movements deploy this definition in political spaces are central concerns of my project.

A Brief Profile of the Situation on the Ground

Guerrero has a rich history of political conflict. As early as the 1920s, radical agrarian movements began a tradition of electoral politics and engagement with the state and federal governments that the Guerrero Council inherited as one more of the many energetic expressions of popular mobilization in twentieth-century Guerrero (Bartra 1996). The Workers' Party of Acapulco (Partido Obrero de Acapulco) extended along the coast in the 1920s representing urban and rural workers; the League of Agrarian Communities (Liga de Comunidades Agrarias) and the Communist Party of Mexico (Partido Comunista Mexicano, or PCM, of which 90 percent of the state's teachers were members at one point) flourished in the 1930s.[14] The Regional Union of Copra Producers (Unión Regional de Productores de Copra) emerged in the 1950s, followed in the 1960s by the Guerrero Civic Association (Asociación Cívica Guerrerense) and the People's Self-Defense Council (Consejo de Autodefensa del Pueblo), which became the National Revolutionary Civic Association (Asociación Cívica Nacional Revolucionaria) under the teacher-turned–guerrilla fighter Genaro Vásquez from San Luis Acatlán—a birthplace of the Guerrero Council. The Party of the Poor (Partido de los Pobres)—led from 1964 to 1975 by another teacher, Lucio Cabañas, until he was killed by the Mexican army—became one of the largest peasant guerrilla armies in Mexico. From all these earlier groups to the unions of peasant producer organizations of the 1980s, Guerrero peasants and students and teachers consistently made demands on the government for real democracy and economic justice. This agitation, as Armando Bartra (1996) so eloquently documents, has typically resulted in bloody repression by the state and elites and has often resulted in government co-optation of popular leadership and popular movement goals.[15] These are the risks of politics *a la mexicana* and the risks the Guerrero Council took in the 1990s as it championed the cause of all those movements that had come before.

Guerrero is divided into eighty-one municipalities in seven official regions, each represented in a separate building in the sprawling new state capitol located just outside of downtown Chilpancingo. Whereas indigenous

---

14. A communist was interim governor in Guerrero for three days in 1941.

15. Hundreds of "disappeared" remain unaccounted for by the state and federal governments after Mexico's "dirty war" of the 1970s, when the military waged a brutal campaign against peasant guerrillas and their alleged sympathizers in Guerrero (see Montemayor 1997). By 1932, the National Revolutionary Party (Partido Nacional Revolucionario, or PNR)—precursor to the PRI—controlled the governorship (and thus the municipalities) of the state and would remain in power until the Party of the Democratic Revolution (PRD) won the governorship and a majority of municipal seats in 2005. The new PRD governor, however, appears to have accommodated himself well to Guerrero's violent authoritarian political culture. A June 2008 national poll taken by the Gabinete de Comunicación Estratégica found that Guerrero's governor, Zeferino Torreblanca Galindo, was among the three least trustworthy governors in Mexico and ranked last among all governors in leadership skills (Castillo Díaz 2008).

people constitute from 6.5 percent to 80 percent of the total population in the regions of the Montaña, Centro, Norte, and the Costa Chica, the other regions of Guerrero are almost entirely mestizo, with indigenous people, most of them migrant workers in the agriculture and tourist industries, accounting for less than 2 percent of the total population.[16] This regional and apparently also ethnic division belies a past and present of interregional and interethnic mobilization that includes all of the movements and political parties listed above.

There are no monographs in English about twentieth-century Guerrero, which is surprising given the prominence of the state in national politics in the nineteenth century (Guardino 1996). This prominence has continued in the national indigenous leadership, in which the Guerrero Council has been visible and vocal. Director Martha Sánchez Néstor, for example, was a spokesperson for the National Indigenous Women's Coordinating Committee of Mexico (Coordinadora Nacional de Mujeres Indígenas de México) as well as the executive director of the ANIPA in 2003–5. Another council director, Marcelino Díaz de Jesús, was a federal congressman from 1997 to 2000 and continues to represent Mexican indigenous peoples at the United Nations. His cousin, Pedro de Jesús Alejandro, was an indigenous delegate from Mexico to a variety of international forums and worked in the federal Congress with Marcelino; in 2001, he was chosen to head the Guerrero offices of the federal government's National Indigenous Institute (Instituto Nacional Indigenista, or INI, now the National Commission for the Development of Indigenous Peoples [Comisión Nacional para el Desarrollo de los Pueblos Indígenas, or CDI, also known as "Conadepi"]). Another indigenous activist and anthropologist from Guerrero, Marcos Matías Alonso, was chosen in 2000 to be director general of the National Indigenous Institute in Mexico City.[17] Guerrero's proximity to

---

16. See http://www.guerrero.gob.mx/?P=municipios/ (accessed 20 August 2008). Export agriculture has been prioritized in the Tierra Caliente (sesame and melons) and Costa Grande (copra, coffee, timber) regions of Guerrero since the 1950s, while Acapulco has been a major tourist destination since the same period. There has been no comparable development whatsoever in the indigenous regions of the state, which are extremely mountainous (with peaks higher than 12,000 feet) and have little access to irrigation despite the presence of major rivers throughout.

17. Not coincidentally, all four individuals mentioned here—Sánchez Néstor, Díaz de Jesús, de Jesús Alejandro, and Alonso—are Nahua, even though Sánchez Néstor identifies as Amuzga, having grown up in Xochistlahuaca, a predominantly Amuzgo region (but with a Nahua name). The Nahuas of Guerrero continue a centuries-long tradition of Mexica/Nahua dominance of the Tlapaneco, Mixteco, and Amuzgo peoples, which dates back to the Mexica conquest and settlement of the region beginning in the 1440s (Carrasco Zuñiga 1994). In an interview on 5 February 2000, non-Nahua Indians told me this ethnic hierarchy was the result of the Nahuas' being "more conquered" (*más conquistados*), losing their

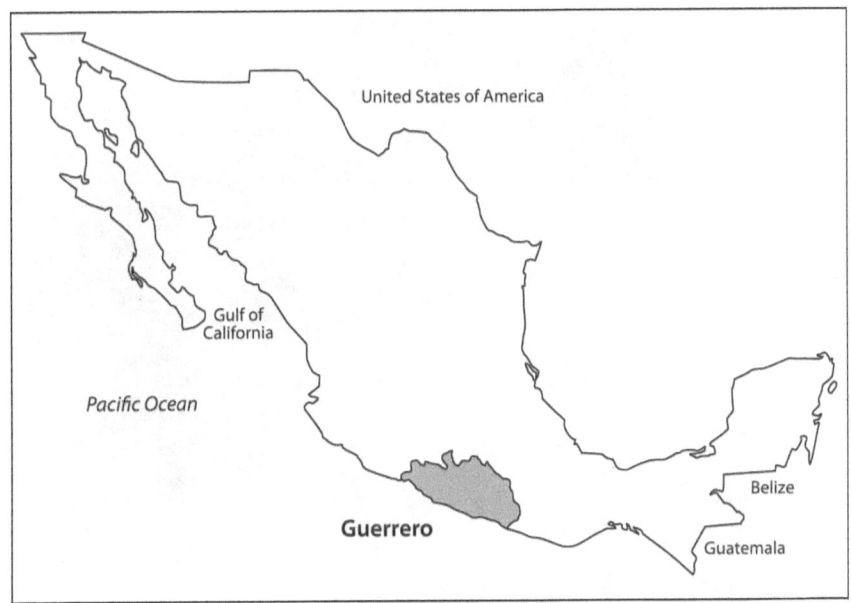

Mexico, with Guerrero highlighted. Map: Pamela Nishikawa.

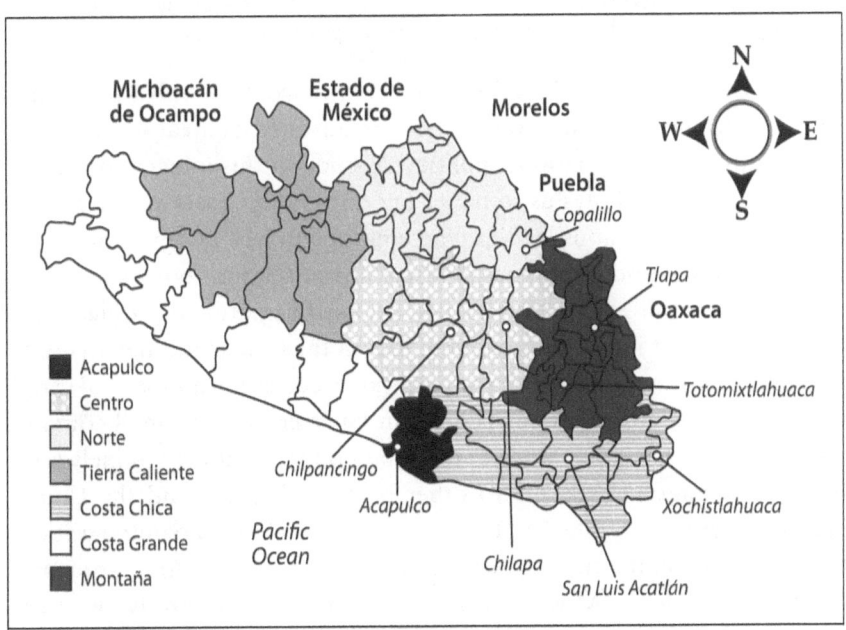

Official regions of Guerrero, with locations of key places discussed in the book. Map: Pamela Nishikawa.

Martha Sánchez Néstor, one of a handful of women leaders of the council, registers participants at one of its regional meetings to discuss indigenous rights.

Mexico City, the country's political and cultural center—only three hours by car—has allowed indigenous activists to advance their cause while also making an impact on national politics. A study of this indigenous movement in Guerrero allows us to better understand the goals and strategies of prominent indigenous leaders who continue to have a significant presence in national and international discussions of indigenous issues.

The indigenous leadership in Guerrero used its national profile to improve the lives of indigenous communities in the state. Although many of the council's former directors have a university education and several travel a good deal, most indigenous peoples in Guerrero live in small communities and are quite poor. Some of the state's poorer regions routinely send indigenous migrant workers to other parts of Mexico and the United States. Other regions, like San Luis Acatlán, have almost no outmigration, though most communities experience some mixture of outmigration and permanent residency. Most indigenous communities collectively own their

---

identity, and "imposing" everything foreign. As evidence, they pointed to Nahuatl, which has incorporated many more Spanish words than have other indigenous languages in the state.

land under the agrarian reform regime called "bienes comunales," although some hold land under *ejido* title, which is more closely regulated by the government. These communities are places with long histories in Guerrero, many of them with claims, and many others with formal titles, to their land dating back to colonial times. They are defined as indigenous by this long history, by their language, and by their reliance on agriculture as their primary means of subsistence.

Agriculture with its yearly cycles predominates in all indigenous communities and is the basis for the continuation of sacred ceremonies devoted to natural forces. Corn is the main crop; each family's basic survival depends on the success or failure of the year's corn crop. The family is the primary unit of labor, with children helping out at crucial times of the year. In places where the soil is good and water is more plentiful, families grow additional crops such as beans, sweet potatoes, other vegetables, and even fruits. Most communities, however, have little, if any, fertile land; typically, they farm nearly exhausted soil, often at extreme inclines and high altitudes, and depend entirely on rainfall to irrigate their crops. This puts most indigenous communities in a chronically precarious position year after year, and forces them to depend on migration and government support (Martínez Rescalvo and Obregón Tellez 1991). The repeated crises faced by these communities are local expressions of a larger, ongoing crisis in the Mexican countryside, made worse by new competition with heavily subsidized U.S. farmers, thanks to the implementation of NAFTA.

That outmigration from Guerrero's indigenous regions has persisted for decades in and of itself complicates the folkloric notion of economic and cultural isolation. Of Guerrero's twenty-two municipalities with an indigenous population of 30 percent or more, seventeen are in the category of "expulsion" or "high expulsion"; their emigrants are predominantly Nahua and Mixteco, whose destinations include Acapulco, where they work in the tourist industry, and Tierra Caliente, Sinaloa, Baja California, or Jalisco, where they work in export agriculture (*Migrar o morir* 2005, 25). In the Montaña region, all nineteen municipalities have high levels of outmigration and "absolutely all are inserted into the migration business that distinguishes the region" (25). According to the Mexican government, the predominantly indigenous Centro, Costa Chica, and Montaña regions are all "zones of expulsion" (SEDESOL 2007).[18] There are

---

18. The SEDESOL program for agricultural day laborers attended to the housing and food needs of 234 municipalities that sent and received migrants, 101 of which were indigenous municipalities as defined by the National Commission for the Development of Indigenous Peoples (CDI). In 2007, 93,504 persons were attended to in Guerrero, which was ranked

more and more communities where the only people in residence are the community authorities, seniors who cannot migrate, or families who already have someone in the United States—only 5 to 10 percent of a community's total population may actually remain behind (*Migrar o morir* 2005, 25). Typically, families migrate together with young children, who work the fields to contribute to the family's wages and thus lose the chance to receive any formal education. In 2007, more than one-third of migrant workers receiving assistance from the federal government were under 14 years of age (SEDESOL 2007).[19] Although some indigenous individuals do enter the migrant stream to the United States, most migrate internally as families, preferred by local labor contractors and large farmers for their "hard work," an expression of the desperate conditions in their home communities. Thus a cucumber farmer in the Tierra Caliente region comments on his preference for indigenous laborers, echoing what U.S. farmers often say about Mexican migrant farmworkers, who are increasingly indigenous themselves:

> When we're harvesting we need extra workers day and night, weekends and holidays, and the local [mestizo] workers won't do this. They won't work weekends, they don't want to work overtime, and when there are rodeos in neighboring towns they leave me with the work. In contrast, with the indigenous this doesn't happen. We have them staying close to the fields, they're more obedient and work well, they don't protest, they work for less money, they're less argumentative and they resist the high temperatures well. That's why we prefer people from the Montaña. (Bustamante Álvarez, López, and Terrazas Mata 2000, 171)[20]

---

third after Oaxaca (95,599)—also predominantly indigenous—and Sinaloa (118,907), where most of Guerrero's migrants work. States with large populations of indigenous peoples—Oaxaca, Guerrero, Chiapas, Hidalgo, Veracruz, Puebla, Michoacán, Yucatán—are also states that have such high levels of emigration they are experiencing net losses in population (INEGI 2000).

19. See *Migrar o morir* 2005 for an excellent report on the work and living conditions of migrant worker families in the fields of Sinaloa.

20. The supposed lack of a work ethic among mestizos is likely a reaction to the unequal relations of production in the Tierra Caliente region, where big business sets the terms and peasant holders often resist these terms by withholding labor (Bustamante Álvarez, López, and Terrazas Mata 2000, 90). Mestizos from Tierra Caliente are also effectively forced off their land when they lease it to Del Monte and other agricultural corporations for the current standard of five years. Without access to their land, these *ejidatarios* migrate en masse to the United States (91). Agribusiness and farmworkers—indigenous and mestizo—are strongly linked across Mexico and into the United States in one contiguous and extremely stratified labor market.

When indigenous migrants return to their home communities to work their own plots for a few months,

> they return with other customs, other forms, and break with everything that is customary in the region, in the community. If they come back from the United States, it's even worse; they come with a completely different mentality. This is a serious problem when it comes to the family and society. . . . Now there is more incorporation of Spanish. When they leave, they don't feel good speaking [their native language] and so they lose it, and when they return, Spanish becomes the family's language. They are losing the meaning of their language. ("Entrevista" 1999)

The extreme instability of indigenous communities and regions that expel such high numbers of their members to other regions and states in Mexico and to the United States puts the lie to folkloric poverty. It provides strong evidence that economic and social forces "on the ground" are changing ideas about Indians even as the older ideas continue to be politically useful.[21]

My Place There

My research methods allowed me to place the Guerrero Council and its politics both in the context of Guerrero's indigenous communities and their histories and in relation to state and national Indian policy. Along with extensive fieldwork in Guerrero, in the state capital, and in indigenous towns, as well as in Mexico City, I interviewed officials in the state government and Indian affairs agency, the National Indigenous Institute (INI). I collected documentary data from the archives of the Guerrero Council, the INI in Mexico City, and the National Agrarian Archives, also in Mexico City. After conducting this research over twelve months between

---

21. According to the newspaper *El Imparcial* (Hermosillo, Sonora), the indigenous La Mixteca region of Oaxaca is "the largest exporter of labor to the American Union [United States]." See http://www.imparcialenlinea.com/?mod=leer&id=51287&sec=capitulo&titulo=La Mixteca, mayor exportadora de mano de obra hacia los EU/ (accessed 18 August 2008). Many of these migrants end up in western Washington state, where about a quarter of farmworkers are indigenous from Oaxaca and Central America. See http://seattletimes.nwsource.com/html/localnews/2008117324_apwaindigenousfarmworkers.html/ (accessed 18 August 2008).

1998 and 2000, I returned to Guerrero in 2005 to talk with former council members about the final years of their group.

My fieldwork was regional, not community-based; frequent trips between Mexico City and Guerrero allowed me to repeatedly shift my perspective from contemporary, rural, provincial, and Indian to historical, urban, national, and official, although these categories blur and merge. After visiting the Indian communities of Guerrero's Montaña region for a few weeks and attending local meetings of groups that participated in the council, I would travel to Mexico City to interview government officials and to read through archival documents about indigenous communities in the 1930s and 1940s before returning again to Guerrero.

In part because of my language limitations, the voices of indigenous community members do not predominate in *Folkloric Poverty*. Although fluent in Spanish, I do not speak Nahuatl, Tlapaneco, Mixteco, or Amuzgo. I had to rely on bilingual speakers, whether to translate for me or to switch from their native language to Spanish for my benefit. More important, however, the focus of my study is the multiethnic leadership of the council based in Chilpancingo, the state capital, rather than any particular indigenous community or language group. My trips to the countryside were almost always as the guest of one of these leaders; only twice did I venture out on my own, though again, as an invited guest of someone I had met in Chilpancingo. My home in Guerrero was the apartment Martha Sánchez Néstor shared with her brother Daniel and their three cousins in Chilpancingo. My conversations with Martha, with Daniel, who is a lawyer, and with other university-educated directors in the council's offices shaped my understanding of indigenous peoples in Mexico.[22] I spoke with

---

22. Pedro, for example, is trained as an engineer, while Marcelino is an accountant. Other council directors have degrees in sociology, chemistry, horticulture, and education. Martha and Daniel are in their late thirties and are from the Amuzgo municipality of Xochistlahuaca, which shares a border with the state of Oaxaca to the southeast. They are decidedly multicultural: the children of a Nahua mother and a Tlapaneco father, they grew up in the Amuzgo cultural center. Martha left home to attend high school in Chilpancingo and cleaned homes to earn money. As she was finishing high school, she answered an employment ad for a secretary in the office of the Guerrero Council. Before this, she had never even considered the indigenous movement but she learned about the issues on the job and worked her way into a leadership position. Though lacking the higher education of many of her mostly male peers, Martha is a sharp, vivacious, and politically savvy woman who is well respected for her passion and her dedication to indigenous peoples. Daniel studied law at the University of Guerrero in Chilpancingo and has practiced agrarian law for several years, mostly helping to settle conflicts over land between individuals and communities. He has also served as a political advisor to a municipal president and head of the legal affairs department at Conadepi (CDI) in Chilpancingo. He has two daughters and commutes regularly from Xochistlahuaca to work in the state capital.

community members when they visited Chilpancingo and when I visited their towns. I spent time in the Nahua regions of the Alto Balsas and Chilapa; in the Mixteco town of Rancho Nuevo de la Democracia; the Tlapaneco municipalities of Acatepec and San Luis Acatlán (which is also Mixteco and Nahua); the Nahua/Tlapaneco region of Tlapa; and the Amuzgo municipal seat of Xochistlahuaca. In all these places, I was able to speak with individuals and attend local meetings about local issues. I have used the information I obtained not to trace out the localities in any detail, but to deepen my understanding of the council's larger goals and strategies.

Because I was both a live-in guest of Martha and Daniel and a regular visitor to the council's offices, the interviews I conducted in Chilpancingo typically took place in relaxed settings as conversations without a tape recorder. Nor did I use a tape recorder for most of my interviews in the communities I visited. Instead, I took notes either during these conversations or shortly thereafter. In Chilpancingo and in my travels throughout the state, I spoke at length with eleven of the council's fourteen directors and with community members and leaders, in addition to attending eight different regional meetings (held both in Spanish and in indigenous languages) about a variety of issues. I also interviewed mestizo academics who had participated in the Guerrero Council but were no longer closely connected to the group, as well as human rights activists in Mexico City, Chilpancingo, and Tlapa.

I took a different approach to my investigation of the National Indigenous Institute (INI), setting up formal appointments with INI officials and conducting structured interviews during my allotted time, typically an hour. After speaking with them about their respective departments and their role within the larger institution, I would ask for their opinions of (1) the history and contemporary relevance of national Indian policy (indigenismo) and (2) the indigenous movement's demands for self-determination and autonomy. In total, I spoke with fifteen former or then-current INI officials—most in Mexico City, but also in Guerrero and Oaxaca—from the national director general to the directors of the INI's outposts in Chilapa and Tlapa, Guerrero. At the INI's archives in Mexico City, I researched the institute's official newsletter, *Acción Indigenista* (1953–70), and unpublished sources documenting the INI's work in Guerrero, beginning in 1954.

My archival work at the council's offices in Chilpancingo consisted of sorting through long-neglected piles of documents dating back to 1990. Because the group had never systematically collected these documents and had moved its offices at least twice in the previous decade, my gleaning of these papers revealed only a partial record of the group's history. I supplemented this documentary evidence with interviews of those directors who had been in the council from the beginning, and of mestizo supporters who helped form the council in 1991. But many details have been lost. For example, most of the council's documents date from 1991 to 1995, when it experienced its greatest growth as an organization. After 1995, there are fewer documents, though these repeat themes and ideas and proposals first developed in the early years of the movement.

Organization of the Book

Chapter 1 begins by asking how and why the Guerrero Council was able to form in 1991 out of several different peasant ethnic groups. The answer to this question is found in the crisis of the federal government's declining support for the peasantry over half a century, and in the opportunity presented to peasants of a new "indigenous" identity in the "500 Years" movement, which opposed official celebrations of Columbus's arrival in the Americas. The chapter shows how much the state and its various agents facilitated the development of an indigenous identity that indigenous peasant groups appropriated to demand new kinds of rights.

Chapter 2 examines the ideological basis for national Indian policy, indigenismo, through an analysis of the first anthropological study of Guerrero's Montaña region (out of which the council formed), which was written in 1955 but never published. Indigenismo was the revolutionary nationalist ideology and praxis that guided the Mexican government's Indian policy in the twentieth century. In its heyday in the 1950s, indigenismo was internationally recognized and respected. Indigenistas—the anthropologists charged with implementing Indian policy at the National Indigenous Institute—were much concerned with the definition of a populist subject, the Mexican Indian, because who and what "the Indian" was determined what actions were to be taken on the subject's behalf. They were committed to a modern nation-state project of homogeneous integration that defined "authentic" Indians as physically and culturally distant from Mexican society, mired in poverty, community-bound, and in dire need of economic integration with national markets; in short, as poor peasants. The indigenistas insisted on this definition despite their own good evidence that it was mostly false; it has persisted in both national policy and the indigenous movement.

Chapter 3 provides the national political context for an indigenous movement in the 1990s, with a focus on the troubled revision of the national constitution to include new rights for indigenous peoples. It then examines at length the council's political strategies, presenting the voices and experiences of local community members that detail the context of extreme neglect and abuse within which the council worked. It discusses how the Guerrero Council embraced a particular kind of Indian populism when engaging the state and federal governments. It was a strategy strongly embraced by the council's leaders, despite its inherent limitations. Populist appeals appeared to legitimate the council's claims on the government. But these claims also legitimated the government's capricious power. The construction of an identity between the nation-state and citizens is precisely the work of national populism. Populism in turn provides the ideological framework within which citizens consent to the hegemony of the government in power, which simultaneously coerces them to ally with its projects.

Chapter 4 places the council's work in the context of national development policy in the 1990s. President Salinas de Gortari's "Solidarity" program was the inheritor of indigenismo and its "authentic Indian." The integrationist and modernizing imperatives discussed in chapter 2 did not go away by the 1990s, but they were now joined by language that openly favored a new, participatory relationship between indigenous peoples and the state. The proliferation of this discourse gave the council a legitimacy that it would not otherwise have had, though at a price: the "participation of indigenous peoples" was defined in a way that legitimated only a particular kind of indigenousness—one necessarily tied to the local, peasant community. This populist definition of the Indian suited the federal government's need for legitimation during rapid and profound economic restructuring. As Rosalva Aída Hernández Castillo (2001, 299) notes, "During the transition from a mestizo Mexico to a multicultural Mexico, the state again assigned itself the right to legitimate certain indigenous identities and to deny others." The council's use of populist imagery meant that, inevitably, the group also accepted this discourse and the limits it placed on indigenous politics.

The book's conclusion presents an update on the council and on the Mexican indigenous movement after 2000 more generally. Indigenous peoples, it asserts, have exhausted the opportunities provided them in the 1990s and are at an impasse in Mexico; the movement appears to be entering a second phase, complicated and enriched by the emergence of more indigenous women leaders, government officials, and political party operators with competing agendas for the present and future. As before, however, the political and economic context within which indigenous peoples struggle will continue to limit the possibilities for real change in those places most in need of change. This is the fundamental challenge the new leaders face as they map out a strategy for the twenty-first century.

ONE

THE ANTI-QUINCENTENARY CAMPAIGN IN GUERRERO, MEXICO: INDIGENOUS IDENTITY AND THE DISMANTLING OF THE MYTH OF THE REVOLUTION

The 1992 quincentenary marking the arrival of Christopher Columbus in the Americas was a process of discovery, not so much for Europeans this time, but for the Indian peoples who mobilized to oppose celebrations of the officially titled "Encounter Between Two Worlds." A continental campaign of opposition to the quincentenary began in 1989 in South America and soon spread to Central and North America under the banner of "500 Years of Indigenous and Popular Resistance." In Mexico, the Mexican Council 500 Years of Resistance (Consejo Mexicano 500 Años de Resistencia) formed in 1990 to enlist state and regional indigenous, peasant, urban popular, labor, student, and academic groups to oppose the celebrations and participate in a cross-cultural dialogue about social justice in the Americas. In other countries, different groups participated at different levels, with either self-identified peasant or indigenous or urban popular groups having more influence in a particular national campaign. Although general opposition to neoliberalism was a key element in the "500 Years" campaign in Mexico, it was the audacity of the planned European and mestizo elite *celebrations* of Columbus there that provided a focus for the movement and privileged the historical and contemporary experience of indigenous peoples. In Guerrero, the campaign was taken up overwhelmingly by indigenous *campesinos* and constituted a key moment in the construction of a pan-indigenous identity among the varied groups of Indian peoples in the state. Five hundred years after Columbus, the indigenous peoples of Guerrero discovered not only that they were all "indigenous," but also that with this identity came a new kind of political power.

This chapter tells the story of the "500 Years" movement in Guerrero: how it emerged and who participated in its development. The central government claimed to be the inheritor of a peasant revolutionary legacy, inspired by leaders like Emiliano Zapata to defend the campesino right to the land—but it was mostly concerned with the need for rapid industrialization and it supported agribusiness magnates, not small-plot peasant farmers. The *idea* of the state as truly revolutionary, however, was real enough in its effects (facilitating land reform and providing crop subsidies, for example) that it could maintain the loyalty of peasants throughout most of the twentieth century. Officially recognizing the rights of a class of people—campesinos—the central government nurtured the revolutionary idea, even if, in practice, these rights were often ignored. With the severe economic and agricultural crises of the 1970s and 1980s, however, the government lost much of its regulatory strength and resorted to high levels of repression in the countryside, putting its revolutionary claims in serious doubt. The elitist, capitalist nature of the state—notwithstanding its professed social commitments to everyone—became still more obvious when the Mexican government announced the end of agrarian reform and implemented the structural adjustment measures mandated by the World Bank and the International Monetary Fund in the late 1970s in order to secure larger foreign loans. For many peasants and Indians, the revolutionary myth began to unravel.

It is out of this ideological and economic unraveling that the Guerrero Council 500 Years of Indigenous and Popular Resistance comes together in 1991, for the first time uniting the four ethnicities in Guerrero as "indigenous peoples," along with a few urban popular groups like journalists and academics. The "500 Years" movement allows us to examine how a pan-indigenous identity is constructed out of the interaction between the government, mestizo academics, and peasant ethnic groups. It reminds us of the way in which identity is always dependent on a specific historical conjuncture for its realization—and dependent especially, in the case of "indigenous peoples," on the neoliberal state itself. In the last quarter century or so, the government of Mexico—like that of many other countries—has initiated wide-ranging economic reforms to reduce its reach, leaving those most vulnerable to the market even more exposed. During this same period, it has adopted an expanded human rights discourse to include indigenous peoples as a protected category of personhood, a category that indigenous peasant groups in Guerrero were quick to inhabit.

When the Guerrero Council formed (on 14 September, the anniversary of the Congress of Anáhuac convened in 1813 in Chilpancingo by the Independence leader José María Morelos y Pavón), twenty-four different groups participated, most of them indigenous peasant groups that had varying histories of mobilization for resources and, to a lesser degree, for rights. It is important to emphasize here that the council is fundamentally a peasant organization with peasant concerns—this identity is as strong as an "indigenous" one (if not stronger in many communities).[1] The "popular" groups consisted of a local from the state teachers' union, a group of academics from the University of Guerrero, and members of the local journalists' union. Most of the participating groups, however, had their origins in two different movements that involved indigenous peasant issues; it was these groups that remained in the council after the urban popular groups fell away. The older movement involved regional associations of peasant producer organizations of different ethnicities that had first appeared as part of a national development program in the early 1980s. By 1991, these associations had almost ten years of experience coordinating the warehousing and marketing of crops and participating in rural stores selling basic goods at wholesale prices—all activities aimed at liberating communities from the monopoly on these services traditionally held by rural elites in league with local officials.

The other movement was more recent and involved only the Nahuas of the Balsas River region just to the north and east of Chilpancingo. This

---

1. In my narrative, "peasants" are those who live or claim residence in officially titled ejido communities or agrarian communities (mostly Indian and mostly in the southern part of the country), farming for subsistence but also working as laborers for others. Many peasants do not have their own plots to farm, and many also migrate to cities or to the United States to work while retaining a place in their home community, something that is increasingly true thanks to the change in agrarian law permitting plots to lay fallow for an indeterminate time without ejidatarios losing their claim to them (see Kearney 1996 on the "categorical ambiguity" of the peasant today). The identity of the peasant (campesino) in Mexico is a social and political category derived from the interaction of landless laborers (*peones*) with the postrevolutionary state's agrarian reform (see Boyer 2003 on the creation of this identity in Michoacán). President Cárdenas (1934–40) further institutionalized campesinos with the creation of the National Peasant Federation (Confederación Nacional Campesina, or CNC) in 1938, which almost exclusively channeled peasant demands and resources for several decades, though not without challenges to its power (Flores Lúa, Paré, and Sarmiento Silva 1988, 12–13, 32–34). This chapter tells how this institutional or corporate entity disintegrated over time into a multiplicity of independent peasant organizations with varying degrees of subordination to the nation-state.

region had begun to mobilize in late 1990, when communities there discovered the federal government was secretly planning to build a dam on the Balsas that would inundate their homes and fields. The imminence of this project focused the actions of members from twenty-two villages, who united their efforts in an unprecedented regional organization that lobbied state and federal governments and eventually appealed to the international community to help stop the dam's construction. Unlike the peasant producer organizations, the Nahuas of the Balsas region self-consciously came to frame their movement as a fight for their cultural and territorial rights. When organizers from the Mexican Council 500 Years of Resistance looked to Guerrero to form a state council, it was no surprise that these two movements—one older and distinctly peasant based, the other younger and, though also peasant based, using a new discourse of indigenous rights—would constitute the foundation of the new movement.

What is less obvious is why groups and regions that had never worked together before and certainly never as "indigenous peoples" would do so now, at the beginning of the 1990s. Why at this time? Why would groups long identified by their peasant status choose to claim their indigenous identity as a new kind of status? What were the larger social and political forces bringing these groups together? Which individuals, working at a local level, acted as catalysts to help create an "indigenous movement"? To answer these questions, we need to examine the history of the government's relationship with the peasantry. The significant change in this relationship that comes in the 1970s and 1980s and that leads eventually to the formation of "indigenousness" has to be understood within the larger context of a revolutionary promise betrayed.

Indians and the Liberal Nation-State: Defending Community

The close relationship today between neoliberalism and the emergence of a pan-indigenous identity is part of a long history in which Indians have adopted national ideologies to defend their own interests. Indigenous peasant communities were active participants in the nineteenth-century conflicts between liberal federalists and conservative centralists, and were often found fighting on both sides depending on which particular faction was perceived to guarantee best the autonomy of indigenous communities. As Eric Van Young (1993) suggests for the earlier independence struggle, indigenous participation in national elite conflicts was motivated, above all, by this desire for relative political autonomy from nonindigenous authorities, an autonomy the communities had managed to preserve to a great extent during the colonial period. In Guerrero, many indigenous communities supported the federalism of liberal leaders such as Juan Álvarez against the centralism of conservatives who were intent on superseding local community political structures, though many communities opposed liberal attempts to secularize community government—an opposition still based on the logic of autonomy (Flores Félix 1998a, 60; Guardino 1996). Peter Guardino (1996, 163) notes five related themes running through peasant discourse in the mid-1800s: control of local government; citizenship and its boundaries (contesting centralist income restrictions on citizenship status); an explicit commitment to federalism (asserting the right to name local authorities); an opposition to the monarchy; and an opposition to Spain.

By 1850 (and even earlier), liberal state and federal governments were passing laws that affected indigenous communal lands, abolishing the legal and political status of the indigenous community and therefore its right to possess property. Time and again, indigenous communities responded to attempts to privatize communal land with violence, resisting the division of their land into private plots for many years. But they also responded by using the very tools and terms liberalism provided, referring to liberal land legislation itself to defend their communities (Mallon 1995, 123). Indeed, it is litigiousness and legalism, more than violence, that characterized their resistance over the centuries (see, for example, Gibson 1964 and Lockhart 1992 for evidence of this during the colonial period); this remains true today. With the goal always of maintaining intact their community's territory and autonomy—the basis for their survival—indigenous representatives learned the limits of their rights under the law and pushed hard against them.

In the midst of nineteenth-century threats to their integrity, communities bought and sold land under a legal provision for joint ownership (*condueñazgo*); as joint owners, they successfully defended their private property in court against claims by individuals or other communities (Escobar Ohmstede 1993, 184). Communities also designated particular individuals who purchased privatized plots carved out of communal lands as "private landowners"—a practice that complicated the restitution of former communal lands after the Revolution (Escobar Ohmstede and Gordillo 1998, 47). For example, Pueblo Hidalgo, an indigenous community in San Luis Acatlán that has played an important role in the Guerrero Council, petitioned the federal government in the early 1940s to have its "communal" lands surveyed and boundaries drawn. When federal engineers arrived, however, they discovered that, though managed and farmed communally, all of the town's land consisted of private holdings purchased in 1895. Town representatives presented the government with twenty-five land titles and the agreement of all the title holders to cede their titles to the town in order to constitute a communal title. In this case, as in many others, an indigenous community inserted itself within the prevailing national discourse to protect itself from outside encroachment, pragmatically using this discourse to its advantage (*Bienes Comunales* n.d.).[2]

The Myth of the Mexican Revolution

From its beginning in 1910, the Mexican Revolution was never an ideologically united force for change. Rival factions represented by elite landowners, middle-class professionals, and peasant community leaders all fought for control of the central government and for the benefit of their particular constituencies (Knight 1986; O'Malley 1986). With the successive assassinations of prominent leaders by the early 1920s (Madero, Zapata, Carranza, Villa), however, the power of the federal government began to consolidate under the leadership of General Álvaro Obregón and other middle- and upper-class revolutionary commanders from northwestern Mexico. Obregón and his allies were able to hold onto the central government in the 1920s in large part because they realized they could not ignore Mexico's overwhelmingly peasant population, as Venustiano Carranza had by returning to landowners the properties seized by peasant armies (O'Malley 1986, 75). The armies of Emiliano Zapata and Francisco "Pancho" Villa had been strong and organized enough to force bourgeois revolutionaries to accept the inclusion of radical agrarian reform provisions in the 1917 constitution, and remained a significant threat even after their deaths. The importance of at least appearing to support the campesino demand for rural reforms was clear. But it was equally clear that the new Mexican government could not afford to alienate its

---

2. The irony is that, in the twentieth century, government officials did not immediately recognize Pueblo Hidalgo's private property titles as proof of communal land ownership. Instead, the required standard of proof was the same in the 1940s as it had been since the colonial period—a "titulo primordial" documenting the royal grant of land to a village. The confirmation of Pueblo Hidalgo's communal land was finally completed in 1966, fifteen years after the town had presented the government with an 1804 document demonstrating its colonial existence. The frustration expressed by community representatives in their correspondence over the years with government agrarian agencies was exceeded only by their determination to see the process to its end.

supporters among the bourgeoisie at home and in Washington, D.C. (O'Malley 1986, 116).

Out of this predicament was born the myth that the Mexican government was revolutionary, popular, nationalist, and committed to social justice. Government-sanctioned histories of the Revolution obscured the serious ideological and class conflicts between revolutionaries as different as Zapata and Carranza or Obregón and asserted that a united revolutionary front of homogeneous heroes had overthrown the venal and decadent regime of Porfirio Díaz (1884–1911) (O'Malley 1986, 127). The class interests of those who had managed to survive assassination to form a new government were thus also obscured, especially as the myth of the Revolution took hold in popular consciousness and the government began to enact some of the reform measures in the Constitution. By 1946, the dominant party was named the Institutional Revolutionary Party (PRI), and its close connections to national power made it the de facto national party in Mexico for decades. The identity of the nation-state and the Revolution was now complete.

Agrarian Reform and a Revolutionary Peasantry

An important foundation for real reform in the countryside was the ejido, a new legal entity created by the postrevolutionary state. The ejido consisted of farmlands and village properties in a community (e.g., the ejido of Xalitla) parceled out to individuals under usufruct titles granted by the federal government. Ejido land, typically of poor quality, was expropriated by the government from hacienda lands that peasant families had long rented from absentee landlords. Although many indigenous communities held title to *bienes comunales*—communal lands defined as in the possession of an Indian community "since time immemorial," and parceled out to families according to local custom—the ejido represented by far the most common form of peasant land tenure; indigenous and mestizo peasant communities alike petitioned the government for ejido parcels. The importance of the promise of these lands for campesinos cannot be overstated—it is what made the Mexican government "revolutionary."

Under President Lázaro Cárdenas (1934–40), agrarian reform became a tangible reality for tens of thousands of peasants for the first time. Cárdenas was concerned with modernization and productivity, but he understood that improving the Mexican countryside was a key part of the progress he envisioned for the nation. There was a particular urgency associated with rural reform in the early 1930s because the Depression hurt the agricultural export sector: domestic production of corn and beans fell almost 30 percent; two-thirds of the income from export crops had to go toward the importation of food (Bartra 1985, 58). The virtual halt to land redistribution under President Plutarco Elías Calles (1924–28), combined with the loss of peasant employment opportunities in the agricultural export sector and exacerbated by the forced return of 300,000 Mexican laborers from the United States, meant the countryside was in turmoil. Peasants seized lands from haciendas at an alarming rate, prompting Cárdenas to act speedily and extensively (Bartra 1985, 61).

In easing this unrest, Cárdenas had two related goals in mind: the elimination of the latifundio and the creation of a large, free labor force no longer subject to the extraeconomic controls of the hacienda. Both goals were important elements of expanded capitalist development (Morett Sánchez 2003, 64). During Cárdenas's presidency, the ejido was understood "not as a temporary way station on the road to agrarian capitalism nor as a mere political palliative, but as the key institution which would regenerate the countryside, liberate the campesino from exploitation and, given appropriate backup, promote the development of the nation" (Knight 1991, 258). With the prohibition against selling individual parcels, the ejido served as an obstacle to the reconstitution of the hacienda even as it also "perpetuated the domination of ejidatarios by the State" (Morett Sánchez 2003, 68). The expanded power of the central government was reflected in numbers: ejidos had held 15 percent of cultivated land in 1930, whereas they held 47 percent in 1940; the ejido population doubled from 668,000 to 1.6 million during the same decade (Knight 1991, 258). The federal government also created the National Peasant Federation (Confederación Nacional Campesina, or CNC) in 1938 and encouraged peasants to organize under its official auspices. There was a huge growth in rural schools under Cárdenas, with teachers encouraged to support peasant demands for land, to supply practical help, and to organize communities (Vaughan 1997).

But both agrarian reform and activist ("socialist") education policies waned by the late 1930s as budgets became tighter and the right-wing opposition grew stronger (Knight 1991, 272). An ambitious Cardenista plan to integrate rural teacher training with a program of peasant agronomy in the Regional Peasant Schools (Escuelas Regionales Campesinas) was completely abandoned at the end of Cárdenas's term. Many right-wing organizations, such as the National Sinarquist Union (Union Nacional Sinarquista) and the National Action Party (Partido Acción Nacional, or

PAN), had already appeared by the late 1930s and were strongly against the Revolution or anything else that resembled "socialism." With Manuel Ávila Camacho as the new president (1940–46), land redistribution slowed to one-third the rate during the Cárdenas administration. What land was distributed was of inferior quality, and the government now took longer to complete land claims (Knight 1991, 312). Meanwhile, small property owners benefited the most from government investments in irrigation and public credit, as the result of a "profound ideological shift" away from the 1930s (313).[3] Ejido members, faced with credit shortages, became even more dependent on patrons like the CNC, now firmly tied into the official state apparatus but weakened by the competing demands from its different constituents: ejidatarios, landless wage laborers, and commercial owners (Smith 1991, 341). Already the ejido was no longer the centerpiece of social and economic change, but "a productive adjunct of the booming urban, industrial economy, and the ejidatarios the most docile clients of the official party" (Knight 1991, 313). Most government agricultural investment and subsidies went to northern farms and ranches, not to peasant-dominated southern and central states. Morett Sánchez (2003, 92) notes that, by 1940, the Agrarian Code had significantly increased the limits of private property: up to 100 hectares (about 250 acres) of irrigated land; 200 hectares (about 500 acres) of rain-fed land; 150 hectares (about 375 acres) dedicated to cotton or henequen; and 300 hectares (about 750 acres) for plantations of coffee, cacao, bananas, and other fruits. None of this land could be taken for ejidos. Armando Bartra (1985, 66) notes the irony of Cárdenas's reforms in the countryside: "The miracle of domesticating the conflictive rural world of the two first postrevolutionary decades is the work of Cardenismo. Not only because the drastic land redistribution of the thirties considerably eased rural tensions, but also because the legitimacy acquired by the State, and the monopoly on peasant organization attained by the CNC, allowed post-Cárdenas governments to implement, without much friction, an agrarian counterreform that before Cárdenas would have been impossible."

But despite the increasing regulatory power of the state, something significant had happened when the federal government supported agrarian reform and recognized the peasantry as an economic and political actor.

---

3. Jesús Carlos Morett Sánchez (2003, 67) argues that Cárdenas created the modern small property, which the ejido made possible. "By diminishing [peasant] pressure on land, subsequent governments concentrated on promoting small property. In other words, it is precisely the Cárdenas agrarian reform that makes possible or initiates the subsequent period that privileges private property" (71).

The institutionalization of land redistribution not only made the government the ultimate arbiter (and landowner) in rural areas, it also obligated it to recognize the peasants' right to the land, legalizing, Bartra (1985, 27) notes, a kind of rural class struggle "that questioned nothing less than the sacred principle of capitalist private property." The paradox is that national agrarianism institutionalized the peasant movement even as it called into being the negation of the economic order privileged by the state. If the myth of the revolutionary government worked to mask the fundamental class interests behind national policies, it nevertheless also continued to nourish a peasant movement with an awareness of its own legitimacy and special rights.

The government first organized indigenous peoples as "indigenous" during the Cárdenas administration, in an attempt to keep ethnic movements separate from peasant movements—just as the government had created the National Peasant Federation as a movement separate from the official labor union (Mejía Piñeros and Sarmiento Silva 1991, 39; Flores Lúa, Paré, and Sarmiento Silva 1988, 12). In 1948, the administration of President Miguel Alemán Valdés (1946–52) created the National Indigenous Institute (INI) as part of the continent-wide establishment of national offices for Indian affairs proposed in 1940 at the first Inter-American Indigenist Congress in Pátzcuaro, Mexico. Chronically underfunded from the start, the INI was nevertheless the only national agency that maintained regular contact with Indian people *as* Indian people and that attempted to understand Indian culture on its own terms despite a continuing policy of integration. This was the important work that would have repercussions decades later: national Indian policy recognized a national "indigenous" subject formed out of the kaleidoscope of ethnic and community identities that make up Mexico's Indian population. This recognition served to elaborate particular national regulatory policies without consulting indigenous communities. But it also attracted many anthropologists who were concerned about improving indigenous lives, who lived in indigenous communities, and who learned to be critical of official policies. Such academic government agents, hired to carry out a government program limited in scope but who took seriously the government's promise of social justice, would play a crucial role in the development of an indigenous movement in Guerrero.

There were a few indigenous organizations active in the 1950s and 1960s that claimed to be national in scope but were in fact formed by indigenous government workers and professionals sponsored by the Ministry of Public Education's Indigenous Affairs Office (Mejía Piñeros and

Sarmiento Silva 1991, 43). Their principal demands were educational and cultural: for new schools, more scholarships for indigenous students, and state subsidies for their organizations—all of which would continue to be demands in the 1990s. In 1968, the Mexican Association of Indigenous Professionals and Intellectuals (Asociación Mexicana de Profesionistas e Intelectuales Indígenas) formed and began to criticize national Indian policy; indigenous professionals or "acculturated Indians," the organization asserted, should elaborate and implement this policy (44). This, too, continues to be a demand of the indigenous movement today, met in part by the appointment of a Nahua anthropologist as INI director general in 2001. There are certain continuities, then, between the demands of earlier indigenous organizations and their more contemporary expressions by the new indigenous movement since 1990. What is different about the movement in Guerrero examined here and about the contemporary indigenous movement more generally is the mass participation by peasant communities as ethnic communities. Whereas indigenous professionals continue to have prominent positions in national organizations, at a regional and local level indigenous peasants have crossed the ideological gap that tried to keep these two subject categories separate. As they assert the unity of "peasant" and "indigenous," they use long-established and officially recognized identities to make demands on the state. How indigenous peasants arrived at this point is the subject of the following section.

Underdeveloping the Peasantry

For about twenty years, from 1940 to the late 1950s, Mexican agriculture had managed to grow faster than the national population, exporting enough agricultural products to pay for as much as 50 percent of imported industrial technology (Bartra 1985, 94). Food imports were low during this period, as were food prices, which kept the cost of living down in urban areas. But this prosperity had come at the expense of peasant farmers in the center and south, whom the government largely ignored in favor of an emphasis on federal aid for private farmers in the north and northwest (Hewitt de Alcantara 1976, 16). These northern farmers benefited, above all, from government irrigation districts that provided heavily subsidized water to their high-yielding (but also input- and capital-intensive) export crops. The private sector had increased its control over capital since 1940, with private agricultural credit providing 69 percent of the national total in 1964 (55). Meanwhile, federal agricultural credit was targeted toward capital improvements on private farms and channeled in part through private credit unions and banks, putting large landowners in the best position to take advantage of the new technology associated with the green revolution (57). Yet because imports exceeded exports by 419 million dollars and the government began to increase its foreign debt already in 1958, this policy did not result in stabilizing Mexico's balance of payments (Morett Sánchez 2003, 150). By 1960, "the lack of participation of nonirrigated agriculture in government-sponsored programmes of modernization thus left 83 per cent of all farmers of Mexico at a subsistence or below subsistence level . . . an almost unbelievable figure for a nation which fought a long and bloody revolution to redress the poverty of the countryside, went through a major agrarian reform, and was the early home of pioneering agricultural science" (Hewitt de Alcantara 1976, 130).

When agricultural production and export prices fell in the late 1960s and early 1970s, and Mexico became a net importer of grains, the situation for peasants took a turn for the worse. Not only was soil fertility on peasant farms exhausted by this time, but the peasant agricultural products destined for the domestic market now had to compete against the massive importation of corn, wheat, rice, and other food crops (Bartra 1985, 97). The number of landless peasants had increased over the years, as the rural population almost doubled from 1940 to 1970 without a parallel increase in available arable lands (Hewitt de Alcantara 1976, 130). Employment for these peasants on large farms decreased over the years with the mechanization of export agriculture—and decreased still more when the export sector contracted. Moreover, the average annual real income for agricultural workers had dropped from 700 pesos in 1960 to 500 pesos in 1969 (133). This was the crisis the peasantry faced.

In a situation similar to the early 1930s, conflicts in rural areas over land, prices, and wages began to increase in 1970. By 1973, they had spread all over the country. Peasant communities, often with the support of students, systematically invaded hacienda lands—and were systematically removed by the army; scores of peasants were jailed or assassinated (Bartra 1985, 106–30; Canabal 1984). Two of the most important outcomes of the crisis and the subsequent unrest were the formation of many independent peasant organizations and the diminished ability of the National Peasant Federation (CNC) to manipulate its members. President Luis Echeverría Álvarez (1970–76) responded to the chaos in the countryside by attempting to organize ejidos into collectives, strengthen federal agricultural agencies, redistribute more land, and bring together three large peasant organizations that had proclaimed their independence from the federal government. Echeverría also drastically expanded the scope of the INI by ordering the establishment of fifty-eight new regional offices and sponsored the First National Congress of Indigenous Peoples in 1975, during which indigenous communities expressed their shared identity as indigenous peasants, for whom the questions of land and culture were central. They also proclaimed the right to self-determination in their traditional government and organization, a right they asserted did not imply their isolation but rather their conscious incorporation into the nation (Sarmiento Silva and Mejía Piñeros 1991, 162).[4] Instead of better controlling peasants and Indians, Echeverría's policies—which failed to improve conditions in the countryside—encouraged peasant groups to expand their alliances with each other across communities and regions. The indigenous groups participating in the 1975 congress formed the National Council of Indigenous Peoples (Consejo Nacional de Pueblos Indígenas, or CNPI) and began to pressure the federal government for changes in indigenous policy, beginning with the demand for the inclusion of the CNPI in a new indigenous affairs agency that would replace the INI.[5]

The populist governmental policies under Echeverría were similar to those under Cárdenas forty years earlier and were undertaken in the same climate of rural crisis and peasant unrest. What was different in the 1970s was the power and organization of large producers, an elite the federal government had helped to create through its modernization policies. With the new administration of President José López Portillo (1976–82), the government reaffirmed its close relationship with large landowners. The new secretary of agrarian reform, for example, was a northern landowner himself and a former representative of John Deere in Mexico. In 1979, he announced that land redistribution would end by 1982, and he placed a priority on the security of private property (Fox 1992, 62). Expropriated land was indemnified and "repression was endorsed as the proper response

---

4. An official declaration of the 1975 congress reads: "We proclaim the right to self-determination in our traditional government and organization, to maintain the communal property and use of the land, our language for communicating among ourselves, our ethics and the artistic expressions we nurture."

5. The agency that would replace the INI was to be called the "National Commission for the Social and Economic Development of Indigenous Peoples" (Comisión Nacional para el Desarrollo Social y Económico de los Pueblos Indígenas)—very close to its name today. The National Council of Indigenous Peoples (CNPI) was to have a central role in this new agency. The government's response to this proposal was the creation of the National Program for Depressed Areas and Marginal Groups (Coordinación General del Plan Nacional de Zonas Deprimidas y Grupos Marginados, or COPLAMAR, discussed below), directly connected to the president's office (Sarmiento Silva 1985, 208).

to further land invasions" (Foley 1991, 48). Whereas Echeverría had emphasized social justice in the countryside (protecting peasants from corrupt caciques and intermediaries), López Portillo focused on expanding business relationships between ejido and more prosperous farmers in order to improve output. The federal government's role in the countryside changed from ultimate arbiter between peasants and landowners on land redistribution to chief creditor for those ejidos with medium to high productive potential. As Michael Foley (1991, 49) put it, "The shift was momentous." The emphasis was now on production, not redistribution, and the government initiated a new program to coordinate peasant communities that would end up facilitating a new kind of indigenous peasant organization, one that crossed community and ethnic boundaries. After years of conflict and repression, the government had lost some of its power to manipulate the hopes of poor peasants and its pretension to populist legitimacy was "definitively" questioned (Bartra 1985, 130).

Working with the State . . . a New Kind of Movement

The López Portillo administration initiated the National Plan for Depressed Zones and Marginal Groups (Coordinación General del Plan Nacional de Zonas Deprimidas y Grupos Marginados, or COPLAMAR), coordinated by the INI and, in the administration's early years, targeting indigenous groups. Its larger purpose was to control peasant discontent and keep independent peasant organization within certain limits, while steering clear of any conflict with the agrarian oligarchy (Fox 1992, 155). Unprepared to meet indigenous demands to make the INI more representative of indigenous peoples, López Portillo offered another welfare program instead.[6] As part of it, on the theory that only genuine community participation would guarantee the final destination and price of the food, a rural consumer food subsidy program (CONASUPO–COPLAMAR) resulted in the organization of hundreds of indigenous villages into regional networks

---

6. Gonzalo Aguirre Beltrán, the preeminent anthropologist who had been INI director general since the Echeverría administration, resigned in anger, denouncing COPLAMAR as the abandonment of the "integrationist spirit" of indigenismo. In an attempt to ease the conflict at the Institute, Aguirre Beltrán's successor in the INI announced a new policy of "participatory indigenismo," which would impact the CONASUPO–COPLAMAR program — though this policy would end with the next president, Miguel de la Madrid Hurtado (1982–88 [Sarmiento Silva 1985, 209–10]). President Salinas de Gortari revived participation in 1989, with important consequences, discussed in chapter 4.

for the first time (Fox 1992, 157).[7] In an earlier version, the individual entrepreneurs who ran the rural stores that sold government-subsidized food products had often diverted the products to other stores or had sold them at market value, often three to four times the official prices. The goal of CONASUPO–COPLAMAR was to sell basic foods at below the local market price, thereby weakening patron-client ties with rural bosses (caciques), who typically provided expensive informal credit to peasants to buy food in the months before harvest. By designing a structure for community participation, planners deliberately created "a political force for oversight that would counter the temptation for abuse at the operational level" (Fox 1992, 159). They carefully selected sites for warehouses, often choosing areas where grassroots peasant organizations had recently appeared, with the clear intention of consolidating regional democratizing movements (160).

The political motivation of CONASUPO–COPLAMAR planners mattered greatly in the development of the program. Many of these planners were products of the post-1968 student movement in Mexico City who had entered government with a social justice agenda and had maintained friendships with radical activists working outside government institutions (Fox 1992, 163). An INI anthropologist I interviewed on 15 June 2000 spoke wistfully of his participation in CONASUPO–COPLAMAR as a time of real commitment to indigenous peoples. He had gone to eastern Michoacán to help community members organize a CONASUPO store selling twenty-one staple goods. "I called community assemblies to explain the program, telling members that they had to build and administer everything themselves and that they had to provide the land for the store and warehouse. I told them, look, I'll bring so much to sell, there will be vehicles to transport it, and the warehouses will be community property. What do you think?" Having just graduated from college, he now had to confront the violence of local merchants angry at being displaced in their lucrative role as middlemen. "And then they expelled me from the program because I was promoting control by the people. They called me and others 'communists.'" Many young activists would share his fate when the central government realized how the program was evolving in the countryside.

---

7. The National Company of Popular Subsistence (Compañía Nacional de Subsistencias Populares, or CONASUPO) began operating in the early 1960s to provide government subsidized food to rural areas and urban neighborhoods. The National Program for Depressed Areas and Marginal Groups (COPLAMAR) added an additional level of community organizing that was not present in CONASUPO stores alone. In 1991, the government began selling off CONASUPO stores as part of the larger privatization of government companies.

This outcome is not surprising, given that CONASUPO–COPLAMAR planners were particularly open to recruiting leftist activists, including some former political prisoners, as promoters who would organize the initial community assemblies to choose members for the Village Food Committee. This committee managed the village store and sent representatives every month to meetings of the Community Food Council (Consejo Comunitario de Abasto, or CCA), which oversaw the warehouse supplying the region's villages. Jonathan Fox points out that socially committed anthropologists had designed these community participation structures to coincide with existing indigenous traditions, with the result that the program was most effective in areas where "indigenous traditions of cooperative labor and community decision making by consensus continued to evolve" (Fox 1992, 178). Not only did this federal program encourage peasant politicization, but it also specifically encouraged the politicization of *indigenous* peasant communities within a regional space. Not surprisingly, CONASUPO–COPLAMAR almost immediately encountered resistance from regional elites and their allies in the federal government. Purges of promoters and pressure on national policy makers to depoliticize the program limited its scope; by 1982, the new administration of President de la Madrid completely shifted responsibility for administering COPLAMAR from the federal government to the states. Nevertheless, as with earlier government actions, the CONASUPO–COPLAMAR experience set in motion community mobilization that would not end with a particular president's term. Instead, it would lay part of the foundation for a new kind of politicized indigenous peasant movement in Guerrero.[8]

One of the most important groups to form the Guerrero Council in 1991 was an association of Nahua communities from the Chilapa region, about an hour's drive to the east of the state capital. According to its own written history, this association began in 1980 as the region's Community Food Council—"the focus that brought peasants together" (Meza Castillo 1995, 4). The monthly meetings of village representatives to discuss problems regarding warehouse supplies sparked thinking about other regional

---

8. The National Coordinating Committee of the Plan of Ayala (Coordinadora Nacional Plan de Ayala, or CNPA) was also a precursor to the politicization of an indigenous peasant movement in Guerrero. Formed in 1979 as an association of peasant groups, many of which were indigenous, the CNPA openly challenged the anti–agrarian reform policies of the López Portillo administration. While the government was switching from land reform to production programs, the CNPA's rallying cry was "Today we fight for the land and for power!" The CNPA made explicit the necessary connection between land and culture for indigenous peoples that, in the 1990s, the Zapatistas and other indigenous peasant groups like the Guerrero Council would continue to emphasize. See Bartra 1985; Canabal Cristiani 1984; Flores Lúa, Paré, and Sarmiento Silva 1988; Mejía Piñeros and Sarmiento Silva 1991.

necessities that included production and marketing issues. Up until this time, government credit agencies were virtually nonexistent and peasants were at the mercy of intermediaries and private creditors, who monopolized the sale of fertilizer and primary products (such as the palm fiber used to make hats). The village and regional committees of the CONASUPO–COPLAMAR program, along with the warehouse, stores, and vehicles the program provided, "were the bases on which the peasant organization developed. . . . From the problems associated with supply, a habit of meeting and of discussion was generated among the producers in different communities" (Meza Castillo 1995, 7, 11). Thirteen village stores opened in 1980. By 1984 (after the end of COPLAMAR), there were thirty-four stores; in 1985, there were forty-eight; and in 1995, the region had a total of ninety stores, all opened by the communities themselves. The corn and bean supply for the population improved during these years, and the low prices the stores offered reduced the total cost of living. As the organization gained experience and began to take more control of the warehouse (though always working with managers hired by the central government), members decided to buy and sell fertilizer collectively, which helped keep prices down throughout the region.

The Alliance of Autonomous Peasant Communities of the State of Guerrero (Alianza de Comunidades Campesinas Autónomas del Estado de Guerrero) formed in 1985 and began coordinating the Community Food Council (CCA), which in 1987 established its own Direct Purchasing Program to complement the warehouse program. To raise the necessary capital for the new program, the CCA created community funds based in each village store, and a general fund that held all the money from the fifty-six participating communities. The food council raised money through raffles, bazaars, and the sale of pork—and then went in search of suppliers in Mexico City's huge central wholesale market. With low operating costs (they were able to use warehouse vehicles during the first year), the CCA was actually able to make a profit even as it sold products at lower prices than those offered by the government or private businesses (Meza Castillo 1995, 27). Meanwhile, both the regional warehouse and the warehouse program in Guerrero more generally were suffering from a lack of supplies and funding, due in large part to the federal government's devolution of control of the program to the states, which had little money to keep it viable (30). In April 1990, the Community Food Council based in Chilapa created a legal organization registered with the government and gave it a Nahuatl name: "Zanzekan Tinemi," or "Together, We Continue."

Also organizing themselves through the Community Food Council structure, fifty-eight Mixteco and Tlapaneco communities had formed a registered association in 1988.[9] The Alliance of Autonomous Peasant Communities of the State of Guerrero coordinated the food council in San Luis Acatlán, as it had in Chilapa. Like the Guerrero Council later, the CCA worked toward "obtaining better production and marketing conditions on the basis of a close working relationship [*una relación de concertación*] with the State, arguing that the appropriation of the productive process (which in this case would be the process and the warehouse network) was a basic condition for the construction of the autonomy of the peasantry with respect to the State" (Consejo Guerrerense 2001, 4). The CCA in San Luis Acatlán gradually lost all government support and, by 1991, was using its own resources to operate its own warehouse network (5).

These associations in Chilapa and San Luis Acatlán formed a core group of the Guerrero Council. In ten years, indigenous peasant associations begun under the auspices of the federal government had evolved to exceed their original scope, becoming in the process more organized and more autonomous as the government withdrew from its supporting role. Thanks to the legacy of unrest during the 1970s and the government's abdication of its central mediating role in the countryside, indigenous peasants had achieved an unprecedented degree of independence from direct governmental regulation. Their economic autonomy was the consequence of the neoliberal model of national withdrawal from social services. The central government's renunciation of its revolutionary populist role—in practice if not in its rhetoric—also provided the political space for the resurgence of campesino self-determination in Guerrero.

Building an Ethnic Coalition Against a Dam

In August 1990, the other core group in the Guerrero Council was only just beginning to doubt the truth of the central government's revolutionary rhetoric. It was during this month that the Federal Electricity Commission (Comisión Federal de Electricidad, or CFE) hired anthropologists to carry out socioeconomic studies of the Upper Balsas region, north and

---

9. A union of coffee-growing communities, the Light of Montaña Union of Ejidos and Communities (Luz de la Montaña Union de Ejidos y Comunidades, or LuzMont), had already formed in 1985 in this region to provide production and marketing support; many of the communities involved in this organization were also involved in the San Luis Acatlán Community Food Council.

east of Chilpancingo. The purpose of the studies was to fulfill a World Bank requirement for the funding of a dam the Mexican government had been planning to build on the Balsas River since 1959 (Díaz de Jesús 1992, 13).[10] Looking over the maps of the project, one of the anthropologists noticed that not only his own hometown but twenty-one other towns as well were located within the dam's "reservoir area"—and no one had been notified of this by the federal government (Hindley 1999, 210). All these towns shared a Nahua identity and had maintained indigenous traditions of community governance, but there was no formal regional economic or political organization that united them as the Community Food Councils had the communities in Chilapa and San Luis Acatlán (211).

The anthropologist immediately set out to inform town leaders, bypassing the mestizo municipal authorities, who were most likely to cooperate with the federal government; the town leaders then helped spread the news around the region (Hindley 1999, 212). He also enlisted the assistance of other indigenous professionals from the region—accountants, an engineering student, and other anthropologists who lived and worked in Mexico City and returned home on weekends, several of whom would go on to become prominent leaders in the Guerrero Council—to find out more about the CFE's plan for the Balsas and about the construction of other large-scale dams in Mexico. As a result, the towns came together for their first joint assemblies in the fall of 1990 to discuss their plan of action and the structure of community participation. Invited and present at the second assembly in October 1990, along with community members and leaders, were academics from Mexico City and from the University of Guerrero. Also present—and uninvited—were two municipal presidents, both members of the PRI. Marcelino Díaz de Jesús (1992, 21) relates how the assembly managed to exclude these men simply by asserting the shared cultural identity of its participants: "Finally we left them out of the Constituent Assembly because, wisely, we changed the language in which we communicated: from Spanish that kept us exposed before the government agents we switched to Nahuatl, which is understood exclusively by the Nahuas of the region. This is how, in front of these municipal presidents, the Council of Nahua Communities of the Upper Balsas [Consejo de Pueblos Nahuas del Alto Balsas, or CPNAB] was born. Without their being able to stop it."

Opposition political parties were involved from the beginning of the

10. See also Flores Félix n.d. for a chronicle of the Alto Balsas mobilization against the Balsas River dam.

anti-dam movement. The Revolutionary Labor Party (PRT) governed the Alto Balsas municipality of Copalillo; the municipal president, Sabino Estrada Guadalupe, was Nahua and had an economics degree from the National Autonomous University of Mexico (Universidad Nacional Autónoma de México, or UNAM). In the community of Xalitla, a group of college students that included Díaz de Jesús and his cousin Pedro de Jesús Alejandro worked within the Party of the Democratic Revolution (Partido Revolucionario Democrático, or PRD); it was this group that proposed changing the name of the movement from the nonethnic "Regional Committee of the Balsas Riverside Towns" to the distinctly ethnic "Council of Nahua Communities of the Upper Balsas," as the group came to be officially called (Díaz de Jesús and de Jesús Alejandro 1997, 161). Members of both the PRT and the PRD would enter the Guerrero Council as important leaders who remained active in party politics through the 1990s and beyond.[11]

Early in the campaign against the dam, the Nahua council had mestizo allies—academics and journalists, mostly—who helped to frame the group's message. A key moment was the discovery by an INI anthropologist working in Chilpancingo that Mexico had ratified International Labor Organization (ILO) Convention 169 on Indigenous and Tribal Peoples in September 1990. Remarkably, he told me on 4 May 2000, the INI did not

11. Pedro de Jesús Alejandro was attending the Polytechnic University and Marcelino Díaz de Jesús the UNAM, both in Mexico City. They had been active in student organizations on campus and in the National Coordinating Committee of the Urban Popular Movement (Coordinadora Nacional del Movimiento Urbano Popular), where they met a member of the National Council of Indigenous People (CNPI) who invited them to participate in the March for the Dignity of Indigenous Peoples held annually in Mexico City on 12 October. "From that moment, year after year, we participated in this march, to demand the rights and dignity of Indian peoples. So that when the fight against the dam began we humbly brought our modest experience acquired in the social movements of Mexico City. Our Indian identity really flowered and we perceived the importance of giving the struggle a more appropriate direction, less socialist [partidario] and more indigenous" (Díaz de Jesús and de Jesús Alejandro 1997, 160). Sabino Estrada Guadalupe (1955–96) was about ten years older than Pedro and Marcelino and from a generation of young indigenous men who were the first to attend university in relatively large numbers. Like many of these men, Sabino lived in the Indigenous Student House (Casa del Estudiante Indígena) in Mexico City while he attended the UNAM. It was dormitory and Marxist-Leninist study group rolled into one, where poor Indian students from all over Mexico gathered (Alonso 1997, 23). Two other Revolutionary Labor Party (PRT) municipal presidents in Copalillo also stayed at the house, as did Marcos Matías Alonso, who became the first indigenous director general of the INI in 2001. Alonso (1997, 24) writes that "for several of us, the Casa del Estudiante was our real school, where we came to know and participate in peasant, worker, and popular struggles.... These were times of great student mobilization." After getting his degree, Estrada Guadalupe went to work for the INI in Chiapas and then ran for and won the municipal presidency of Copalillo.

then know about this convention, the first international instrument to define and outline the rights of indigenous peoples living within independent states. Convention 169 replaced the older assimilationist Convention 157 with a new definition of indigenous self-determination. The INI anthropologist found out about it "purely as a fluke" and presented it to CPNAB, which adopted it as its rallying cry: "Our struggle was given another meaning when its foundation became a demand for the indigenous rights protected by Convention 169 of the ILO" (Díaz de Jesús and de Jesús Alejandro 1999, 161).

The Mexican government had ratified Convention 169 and established the country's first national human rights commission in response to the growing continental movement against the quincentenary and to polish Mexico's domestic and international image, especially given the widespread allegations of massive fraud in the 1988 elections that kept the PRI in power at the federal level. Moreover, the new president, Carlos Salinas de Gortari (1988–94), keenly desired to sign a free trade agreement with the United States and open Mexico's economy to the world. Thus the ratification initially had little to do with the indigenous peoples of Mexico, whom the government had not consulted (Hindley 1996). But the convention acquired a new meaning once an indigenous peasant movement appropriated it as its own. When members of the Council of Nahua Communities of the Upper Balsas marched on the state government building in November 1990, they brought with them a letter for the governor, a copy of Convention 169, and a copy of the CPNAB's letter to the ILO requesting its intervention on the Nahuas' behalf (Hindley 1999, 216). Indigenous culture had become a tool of political resistance: "In front of the state government building we finally spoke in our Nahuatl language, which had been repressed so many times, but this time without shame—because education in Mexico is designed in such a way to make us feel inferior when we speak our Indian languages—discovering that the use of our Mexican Nahuatl language gave us greater unity and the respect of the non-Indian organizations that supported us" (Díaz de Jesús 1992, 22).[12] The Nahua council's own history tells us this about the raising of

---

12. Aline Hémond (2002, 136) reports that recent archaeological work in the Alto Balsas suggests the region has shared a cultural identity since the preclassic period (ca. 1800 B.C. to A.D. 250), a history that the Council of Nahua Communities of the Upper Balsas (CPNAB) explicitly referenced in its use of Olmec imagery. See Good Eshelman 1988 for an anthropological study of the internationally renowned painters of the region whose material success based on sales to tourists since the 1960s helped support the movement against the Balsas River dam. Migrants living in the United States—in Los Angeles particularly—also sent funds regularly to the region and publicized the CPNAB's goals abroad (Flores Félix

a new consciousness: "In this initial stage, the towns of the Alto Balsas realized that there are other indigenous peoples in Guerrero, that is, the Mixtecos, Tlapanecos, and Amuzgos could be in solidarity with the CPNAB. This is how it [CPNAB] approaches the indigenous regions of Guerrero in search of contacts and connections with these regions and their leaders. During these months the CPNAB's work coincides with a new national movement led by the Mexican Council 500 Years of Indigenous, Black, and Popular Resistance" (Consejo Guerrerense 2001, 22).

By early 1991, several mestizo academics from Mexico City and Chilpancingo working on the national "500 Years" campaign had begun to make contact with different indigenous groups in Guerrero. Anthropologists for the most part, these were men and women who as students in the 1970s had helped organize peasant groups around the country. Renato and Judith were a married couple living in Chilpancingo; he was a historian at the University of Guerrero and she worked in government rural assistance programs. They both had a long history of involvement with indigenous peasant communities—her father was a Jaramillista in Morelos—and continue this work today. Both also had a long history of working with the federal government: Judith was a promoter in the COPLAMAR program and Renato worked off and on in the INI as a researcher (he was also a friend and colleague of the INI anthropologist in Chilpancingo who brought Convention 169 to the CPNAB's attention). By 1990, the couple were in contact with several indigenous groups in Guerrero. Judith knew several Amuzgos from the Costa Chica region through her interest in marketing the textiles made by women artisans. Renato knew Tlapanecos from his oral history work on the Luz de la Montaña organization; he also knew the Nahua anthropologists working in the Alto Balsas against the dam, as well as Sabino Estrada Guadalupe. Both Renato and Judith were in close contact with Martín Equihua, a mestizo who had helped coordinate the CCAs in Chilapa. As they told me on 5 April 2000, "We had a strategic position from which to call all these different groups together," and in May 1991 they took several community leaders from Guerrero to a meeting of the Mexican Council in Morelos, where they made contact with other indigenous groups from around the country. Renato and Equihua together put the word out to the various indigenous organizations and set up the first meetings of the Guerrero Council, including

---

n.d., 23). This savvy mix of the "ancient" and the modern, the local and the extralocal, characterizes most indigenous political mobilization and contradicts notions of isolated Indian peasants stuck in closed communities, an idea discussed at length in chapter 2.

the Constituent Assembly of September 1991; they were also responsible for drafting the council's proposed organizational structure and political position. Joaquín Flores Félix, a Mexico City–based anthropologist who was researching Guerrero's indigenous communities and who had worked with unions and peasant groups in the 1970s and with indigenous movements since the mid-1980s, would also help form the Guerrero Council through his contacts with indigenous peasant groups. In an interview on 12 June 2000, he affirmed that "academics served as links between indigenous groups throughout the country." In 1989, Flores Félix had participated with other academics and NGOs, along with many indigenous communities, at a meeting in Oaxaca to begin the "500 Years" campaign in Mexico.

The concept of specific indigenous rights had been discussed at the United Nations (in the Working Group on Indigenous Populations, or WGIP) since 1982; the "500 Years" campaign would incorporate a discourse of rights in its platform. Margarito Ruiz Hernández, an indigenous organizer from Chiapas who worked in the Mexican Council, writes that the Mexican Academy of Human Rights also "played a relevant role in the formation of indigenous leaders who had a perspective of the knowledge and defense of their rights" (Ruiz Hernández 1999, 24). Beginning in 1987, the academy implemented a training program for indigenous leaders from Mexico and Central America focusing on international and indigenous law. It was here that Ruiz first heard about the defense of indigenous rights based on international legal instruments and began to form alliances with other indigenous leaders in the region. This building of alliances and the new emphasis on human rights would be important for the indigenous movement later in the 1990s.

Much of the construction of a new kind of pan-indigenous identity, then, took place in the interactions between Indian communities and Indian and mestizo intellectuals, in the context of a weak national peasant movement and with a new focus on international human rights. The state's considerable withdrawal of its recognition of the "peasant sector" meant that the possibilities for *peasant* mediation with the central government were weak (Zermeño 1997, 197). Julio Moguel (1992, 42) noted that the peasant movement was "disaggregated, dispersed and [did not] always have defined program proposals. It [had] enormous difficulties converting its proposals for unity into solid projects with the capacity to put pressure on and negotiate with the State."[13] The central government's

---

13. Ironically, the emergence of the oppositional Party of the Democratic Revolution (PRD) contributed to this sectoral weakness with groups such as the National Union of Autonomous Regional Peasant Organizations (Union Nacional de Organizaciones Regionales

loss of revolutionary legitimacy had also weakened its ability to regulate the subjects it had helped to create. Finally, the new national political party led by Cuauhtémoc Cárdenas that became the Party of the Democratic Revolution (PRD) had injected new life into popular groups and encouraged the political organization of the countryside in opposition to the ruling PRI—especially in Guerrero. By 1991, it was clear to indigenous peasants that the government was not interested in them as peasants anymore, if it ever really had been. The first major indication of this lack of interest had come in the 1970s, when the government declared the end of land redistribution. And then, "throughout the 1980s the peasant movement had suffered serious reversals as a result of the change in government agrarian policy. Several organizations that had cemented their membership on the basis of making demands for improved production support . . . lost this membership as they became inefficient" (Consejo Guerrerense 2001, 24).

The "500 Years" movement, on the other hand, offered peasants a new and politically more visible identity as "indigenous peoples" who apparently had a powerful right to self-determination. Given this historical conjuncture, the emergence of the anti-quincentenary campaign was a political opportunity that indigenous peasants were quick to embrace. Pedro and Marcelino (Díaz de Jesús and de Jesús Alejandro 1999, 163) wrote about identity formation among the Alto Balsas Nahuas:

> One of the most important effects of the resistance struggle against the dam was the construction of our regional collective identity as Nahuas from the Alto Balsas. Before this experience, the indigenous Nahuas felt they were "Copalillenses" from [the town of] Copalillo or "Huitzuqueños" from Huitzuco, among other restricted identities. The decisions about the fate of the Nahua people of the Alto Balsas did not come from a single decision, but from different decisions made in seven different municipal seats and not one of these said a single word in favor of [the Nahuas'] survival. These were years of faithfulness toward the system. The people were faithful and submissive toward the state party. Nevertheless, or maybe because of it, the resistance movement emerged when the people had more information about the government [dam] project.

Campesinas Autónomas, or UNORCA)—the national umbrella group that included the Alliance of Autonomous Peasant Organizations of Guerrero (Alianza de Organizaciones Campesinas Autónomas de Guerrero) splitting into party factions, which only exacerbated the lack of access to government funding.

About the formation of the Guerrero Council, Pedro added: "We realized that some people were beginning to look to participate in this national and continental movement... but it was evident that there was an absence of an essentially indigenous organization from Guerrero that participated at the national level" (Consejo Guerrerense 2001, 28). This was an entirely new kind of national coalition that focused on indigenous peoples: "Taking into account that at the local level, in the state of Guerrero, the indigenous movement had hardly any strength, the response to the call to reject the celebrations of the quincentenary was impressive" (29). "Florencio," a coffee grower who had worked for many years on the San Luis Acatlán warehouse committee and was active in the Guerrero Council as a director, told me it was his participation in a 1992 march on Mexico City to protest the quincentenary that "educated" him politically. We talked on 9 February 2000 about Florencio's formation as an indigenous peasant while he flipped through the well-worn copy of the International Labor Organization Convention 169 on Indigenous and Tribal Peoples he always carried with him in his travels to Guerrero's indigenous communities. "I don't want power," he told me. "I have all the work I need in my town, but I will organize the people, too, so that self-determination can be put into practice."[14] This new language of indigenous difference and rights is echoed by Pedro and Marcelino (Díaz de Jesús and de Jesús Alejandro 1999, 164):

> Little by little the people in the resistance movement discovered that identifying themselves as indigenous Nahuas had various advantages. They differentiated themselves from the municipal seats, controlled

---

14. Florencio is a powerfully built man in his forties and is an important leader in the Community Police (Policía Comunitaria) of the San Luis Acatlán region that Tlapaneco and Mixteco communities began in 1995 in response to widespread violence the state police did nothing to stop. Coming from a small community, he completed primary school away from his family and worked on a ranch to support himself. "I worked before and after school and slept only from 11 P.M. to 3 A.M.," he told me on 9 February 2000. "The ranch owners didn't even feed me regularly so I had to steal tortillas, dry ones, and dip them in water so they wouldn't hear me eating them at night. Dry tortillas thunder when you eat them!" At age 14, Florencio went to work in Mexico City, where he was not treated much better and where he spent nights shivering under newspapers. He ended up in the army for a year and was a police officer for four years. Meanwhile, back in San Luis Acatlán, the army had increased patrols of the area, violating people's rights, and fifty-three children had died of measles. "While I was living in Mexico City, I had met someone from the World Food Program, so it made sense that my town chose me to go back to the City to denounce the situation to the United Nations office," he said. It was in 1991 that he met Pedro and Marcelino, whom Florencio mischievously derided as "intellectuals." He told me he considers himself a campesino, not an intellectual (though he liberally quoted not only from Convention 169 but also from the Mexican anarchist and revolutionary Ricardo Flores Magón).

by politicians and authorities indifferent or even opposed to the interests of the Nahuas and at the beck and call of the state government. The other issue we came to perceive for the first time was that being indigenous was not harmful, but profitable since, as indigenous, we could appeal to other international laws that gave us more prerogatives than the Constitution itself gave to the rest of Mexicans.

There is a good deal of pragmatism in this description, which is strongly reminiscent of nineteenth-century indigenous uses of prevailing legal and political discourse, and which challenges claims to an "essential" indigenousness behind the indigenous movement. Indeed, indigenous identity in Guerrero comes as much from outside as from within ethnic communities, and it is in the alchemy of this mixing that a pan-indigenous identity forms. Moreover, this identity depends on an intimate relationship with the government, which helps call "indigenous peoples" into being. This close relationship between the national government and Indians in indigenismo is the subject of chapter 2.

TWO

INDIGENISTA DREAMS OF THE MEXICAN INDIAN

The success of the plans [for integration] depends, to a high degree, on the attitude of aboriginal groups and their active and direct participation. A requirement of this participation [is] the substantial modification of the current feudal structure that maintains servile obligations for peasants and . . . the destruction of mechanisms of forced segregation and noncommunication that impede the integration of these groups to the national society.

—GONZALO AGUIRRE BELTRÁN, *Acción Indigenista*, APRIL 1965

This chapter tells the story of the first anthropological study of indigenous peoples commissioned by the National Indigenous Institute (INI) in Guerrero. The study and the anthropologist who carried it out illustrate the postrevolutionary state's relationship to indigenous people, as expressed in the revolutionary nationalist ideology and praxis that were the basis for the Mexican government's Indian policy in the twentieth century—indigenismo. Two contradictory impulses guided indigenismo: the desire for an ethnically, racially, and culturally homogeneous Mexico, on the one hand, and the desire for a Mexico that respected and promoted the diversity of its indigenous peoples as integral parts of the Mexican nation, on the other. Indigenistas, the anthropologists charged with implementing INI policy, could embody at once a firm loyalty to the modern, nationalist project and a radical critique of the status quo, in large part because both impulses found a home in the myth of "la Revolución."

For a national government concerned with modernization, the Revolution meant urbanized industrialization, not agrarian reform and rural development. For peasants, it meant a privileged place in nationalist discourse and government policy. Indigenistas could embrace both interpretations. They found themselves representing parts of the country and entire peoples, especially in the center and southern states, that the central government largely ignored, but they came to them with a modernizing agenda. In developing these areas, the INI agents were to concentrate on small economic projects and local infrastructure for indigenous communities. The emphasis was always on economic development; questions of politics and power affecting indigenous peoples were officially ignored.

As discussed below, however, indigenistas never really ignored politics and power. Indigenista policy was framed around the definition of the Mexican Indian as a populist subject—the actions to be taken on the Indian's behalf were justified and authorized by who and what that Indian was. The Mexican anthropologists who represented the central government in much of the countryside were committed to the modern nation-state project of homogeneous integration. This project defined Indians in terms of what I call "folkloric poverty," as physically and culturally distant from Mexican society and as desperately in need of economic integration with national markets. It paralleled the larger postwar development project that "necessarily involved the creation of an institutional field from which discourses are produced, recorded, stabilized, modified, and put into circulation" (Escobar 1995, 46). In this system, the "less developed" people contrasted easily with the "developed," who made themselves responsible for uplifting those dragged down by isolation, tradition, and general backwardness. Like peasants—which most Mexican Indians were—the Indian "became a prototypic Other" (Kearney 1996, 52). In Mexico, this definition was fundamentally racist: it necessarily ranked the Indian below the mestizo, which placed the reform and assimilation of the Indians largely beyond question. It exemplifies the integral role of racial ranking in modernization, especially in the context of the nation-state, itself a construct that belies a heterogeneous reality.

It is important to acknowledge here that, as mestizos with a revolutionary nationalist ideology of mestizaje (racial/cultural mixing), INI anthropologists also went beyond the simplistic and reductionist definition of the Indian noted above. If the mestizo was the proud embodiment of two great cultures (and the revolutionary mestizo was), then it was hard to denigrate the Indian. As a result, indigenistas could genuinely respect indigenous cultures. Nevertheless, this respect was expressed always within the larger mestizo nationalist project of cultural and political integration, that is, as part of making "real Mexicans" out of isolated Indians. Aguirre

Beltrán, in the epigraph above, emphasizes this isolation as the ground for an integrationist project—under the direction, of course, of the INI.[1]

In Guerrero

At the end of the rainy season in 1954, Alfonso Fabila prepared to set out from Chilpancingo with César Tejeda, an anthropology student assigned to be his research assistant. From the state capital, the two would make their way, on foot and on horseback, through the Montaña region of Guerrero. They would spend four months walking 2,000 kilometers (about 1,200 miles), interviewing community leaders and residents, taking many notes and photos, and producing the first anthropological study of the region. The goal was to write a report—commissioned by Alfonso Caso himself, the director general of the INI—that would serve as the basis for the first Indigenous Coordination Center (Centro Coordinador Indigenista, or CCI) in Guerrero. There were only four CCIs in Mexico at the time (in Chiapas, Chihuahua, Oaxaca, and Veracruz), and the INI wanted to spread the economic and social programs pioneered there to other indigenous areas of the country. Each center would serve as an agency coordinating the federal government's development of a particular region, introducing small agricultural projects such as fruit orchards and community vegetable gardens, building roads and drinking water systems, and providing basic health and veterinary care as well as bilingual education for individual communities. The plan was an integrated development for indigenous regions based on the detailed knowledge of the cultural, economic, and social conditions of the peoples to be developed. Fabila's report was to provide this knowledge.

The Montaña region located in northeastern Guerrero and bordering Oaxaca is home to almost half of Guerrero's indigenous population and still one of the poorest regions in the country. As its name suggests, it is mountainous with almost no flat land, making agriculture particularly difficult. The infertility of much of its land is an important factor in the poverty of its inhabitants, though it is by no means the only factor, as Fabila notes well in his report. In 1998, illiteracy rates in indigenous communities of the Montaña reached 68 percent, whereas the state average

---

1. Aguirre Beltrán's mention of "participation" in 1965 is ahead of its time. It reemerges briefly as official policy in the late 1970s but does not become a key element of national Indian policy until the advent of official multiculturalism under the Salinas administration, a development discussed in detail in chapter 4.

Illiteracy rates, especially among indigenous women, are extremely high in Guerrero—though this is no obstacle to their participation in council events.

for the same year was 24 percent. Of indigenous homes surveyed, 77 percent lacked piped drinking water, more than double the state average; 97 percent of indigenous homes were unconnected to a sewage system; and 77 percent did not have electricity, compared to only 12 percent of homes statewide.[2] Half a century after Fabila trekked through the Montaña, living conditions for indigenous peoples have changed little.

Fabila's report details the poverty, the systems of land tenure, the condition of the land, intercommunity relations, agricultural production, market and interethnic relations, cultural expressions, the state of health and education, and even the political situation in the region. It is a report remarkable for its author's frankness, empathy, and abiding hope that the dismal conditions he encountered could be remedied by a government that took seriously the problems of the countryside in general, and of indigenous peoples in particular. Fabila's own dream of the Indian is most

---

2. Statistics on the Montaña region and Guerrero are taken from the INI's magazine in Guerrero, *Xinachtli,* October–November 1998, 8. As of the 2000 Census, indigenous adults in Guerrero had an average of 3 years of formal education (men had 3.6 years and women only 2.5 years on average), the lowest in the country. Nationally, the average was 7.3 years, with men (indigenous and nonindigenous) living in Mexico City having the most formal education, 9.9 years on average. See http://www.inegi.gob.mx/ (accessed 18 August 2008).

remarkable, however, because it reveals the persistence of indigenismo's revolutionary vision of integration, even during a time when the government had embraced altogether different revolutionary ideals, ones that had little to do with rural development. Fabila reveals the inherent contradictions within postrevolutionary Mexico, which boasted a social revolution in the countryside while maintaining a dependent, capitalist status quo that privileged urbanization and industrialization. Fabila's report represents revolutionary, nationalist indigenismo in some of its most radical manifestations, where it tries to approach indigenous people on their own terms and to appreciate indigenous cultures as an important part of Mexican culture. But indigenismo would consistently come up against the larger imperative to homogenize and modernize Mexico by making Mexicans out of Indians. These contradictory positions shared a common image of the Indian that has continued to dominate political discussions to this day.

The Mestizo and the Indian: Who Is (Inside) Mexico?

Mexico is without doubt, in a very real sense, an indigenous country, not only because 10 percent of its population is, but because the presence of the indigenous—and of indigenousness—is apparent in many aspects of our life. Now, I believe that because we are indigenous we can defend ourselves from the penetration of stronger and more technically advanced nations than ourselves. That is to say, what Mexico has that is indigenous has made it possible to conserve its features, its idiosyncrasy, its own way of being.
—ALFONSO CASO, *Acción Indigenista*, JULY 1959

The idea of indigenismo in Mexico—an idea that includes an appreciation of and concern for indigenous people and their traditional cultures, while simultaneously and contradictorily believing that the survival of the indigenous depends on their assimilation to European culture—has its origins in the early colonial period with the work of Spanish friars such as Bernardino de Sahagún and Vasco de Quiroga. Its modern form took shape with the advent of the 1910–20 revolution, during which indigenismo became a revolutionary, nationalist ideology closely tied to the emerging postrevolutionary state.[3] The 1916 publication of Manuel Gamio's *Forjando patria* (Forging the Fatherland) was the first articulation of this modern, statist

---

3. Modern indigenismo did not lose its religious roots, however. Thus, in the July 1960 issue of *Acción Indigenista*, Alfonso Caso wrote that, to be an indigenista, "knowledge is not enough, in effect, but it is necessary to have an apostolic vocation to carry to the indigenous population the benefits already enjoyed by the other members of the Mexican community."

indigenismo, and it has served as a starting point for indigenistas ever since. Gamio was concerned above all with the problem of defining a single "Mexicanness," given the ethnic heterogeneity of the country. The solution to the problem, for him, was the construction of a racial and cultural unity based on mestizaje—the foundation of a new nation-state.

The preoccupation with mestizaje, or racial/cultural mixing, was strong in the nineteenth century among Latin American intellectuals concerned with defining their own national cultures and what it meant to be American (Martínez-Echazábal 1998; de la Cadena 2001). In Mexico, mestizaje—in this case, the mixing of Indian and European—took on a unique meaning. Indians and Europeans had long mixed; indeed, mestizos and even an Indian, Benito Pablo Juárez, had become celebrated presidents, President Porfirio Díaz being only the most prominent mestizo in the 1800s. Here the "culturalization of racialized discourse" (Martínez-Echazábal 1998) offered members of the nationalist elite such as Gamio and José Vasconselos a means to reject the fixed, biologized European notion of race in favor of a historically contingent and malleable notion of culture—while nevertheless implicitly and sometimes explicitly retaining a strong sense of race in their writings.[4] The importance of embracing culture over race was not to reject race, but to make social improvement possible through education, for example, which, it was assumed, could positively influence a group's cultural condition. The emphasis was on the *goodness* of mixture as part of the total social improvement of Mexico and the Americas.

Writing in 1909, Andrés Molina Enríquez equated the racial idea of the mestizo with the concept of a class that was revolutionary and liberal, one that was destined to overthrow both conservative landowning criollos and the "new" capitalist criollos allied with English and U.S. interests. Molina Enríquez appreciated Indian resilience and adaptation and believed Indians had a future—through absorption into the mestizo. Only the mestizo would be capable of achieving the (racial/cultural) unity that was indispensable for the formation of a nation-state. Indians were not capable of this because of their isolation and lack of culture; criollos were conscious only of their group and its exclusive interests, much of which were

---

4. Michael Omi and Howard Winant (1994) discuss a similar maneuver in the United States, where the notion of fixed biological races gave way to a culturalist ethnicity paradigm during the first decades of the twentieth century in U.S. social science, which was similarly preoccupied with the assimilation and integration of "ethnic minorities." A center for this new thinking was the University of Chicago, where Manuel Gamio was in residence for a few years in the 1920s.

Education is the way forward toward cultural change and mestizaje for Indians in Mexico. Note the "non-Indian" clothes of the teacher and his students on this CCI–Tlapa mural.

strongly tied to foreign interests (Villoro 1996, 216). For Molina Enríquez, however, the mestizos presented "a unity of customs and desires," a "community of feelings, acts, and ideas" that made them "a great family" (Villoro 1996, 217). Entirely a chimera, the mestizos, elaborated by Molina Enríquez and later universalized by José Vasconselos as the "raza cósmica," became part of the myth of the Revolution. The chimera would undergo some changes later in the writings of Manuel Gamio, Alfonso Caso, and other indigenistas, who emphasized the greatness of Mexico's Indian past and claimed it as the nation's legacy while nevertheless insisting on the need to change the present-day Indian way of life.

The shift from race to culture in Mexican nationalist discourse was aimed at Indians, whose assimilation to a mestizo ideal would complete the cultural homogenization needed for national unity. Mixing was by no means the equivalent of cultural heterogeneity or a celebration of difference. On the contrary, it was always assumed that mestizaje would be the result of the formation of real, essential Mexicans who combined the strengths of both Indians and Europeans. Ultimately, mestizaje and indigenismo were both about modernization and progress, which necessarily meant the rejection of a rural, religious Indian identity in favor of a new urban, Europeanized one.[5] The movement from countryside to town or city was explained as a cultural move, with Indians leaving behind their native garb and language to dress in the clothes of the mestizo and speak Spanish. Thus, in an article from the August 1953 issue of *Acción Indigenista*, Alfonso Caso, the INI's first director, wrote that the difference between indigenous communities and other communities in the country was not "of race, but of certain elements of social and cultural life that have remained stagnant, without progressing as the other peoples of the country have progressed." Caso went on to explain: "What we want to say is that if an individual leaves his community and learns Spanish and goes to work for example in a factory, or to live in a city, and acquires the customs and habits of the inhabitants of this city, he is no longer an indigenous, but forms part of the great mass of the Mexican population." Praising the greatness of "our indigenous ancestors," he pointed out that "thousands of Mexicans who have indigenous blood" were professionals and professors and that the line between mestizo and Indian was not very clear.

Mexican philosopher Luis Villoro (1996) discusses the modern mestizo ambivalence toward Indians that is present in Mexican mestizaje and indigenismo. There is, on the one hand, an insistence on the radical isolation of indigenous communities in Mexico that serves to justify not only the work but the very existence of an agency like the INI. As another Mexican philosopher, Antonio Caso, wrote in *Sociología* (1939), "The archaeological race continues to live outside of general civilization; the language and the religion, the collective soul of the conquerors, is neither expressed nor understood by the Indians; criollos and mestizos segregated from the rest of the demographic group have not been able and have not known how to form a people with the indigenous" (in Villoro 1996, 232). Aguirre Beltrán echoed this almost thirty years later when he clarified indigenismo's uniquely mestizo origins: "The Indian, as such, cannot propose an indigenista policy because the scope of his world is reduced to the parochial, homogeneous, and preclassical community that has only a vague sense and notion of nationality" (Aguirre Beltrán 1976, 25). Aguirre Beltrán further asserted that "indigenista policy is not what the Indian formulates for his own community, but the manner in which the national

---

5. Lourdes Martínez-Echazábal (1998, 23) suggests the same homogenizing process was at work in the construction of the mulatto in Latin America: "When reading mulatto fictions in conjunction with the various projects of nation building and state fashioning in Latin America, what surfaces ... is not the recognition and proclamation of ethnic difference or of a heterogeneous identity but the Eurocentric glorification of a cultural sameness, of similarity in identity."

group contemplates the treatment it should give to the groups named indigenous, according to national values and interests" (24). Here the "national" is emphatically not "indigenous." Thus the historian Miguel Othón de Mendizábal wrote that "the ideology of today's indigenous does not differ essentially from pre-Hispanic, and occasionally prehistoric, ideas" (in Villoro 1996, 232).

The idea of indigenous isolation was behind the INI's furious pace of road construction in the 1950s—"Roads of Penetration," proclaimed *Acción Indigenista* in 1954—and its emphasis on the promotion of national civic ceremonies in indigenous communities. It was, the newsletter had declared in September 1953, "indispensable that [the indigenous] feel they belong not to the small, isolated community, to their municipality or to their state, but to the great community that is the Mexican Fatherland and that is symbolized by its flag."[6] In this same issue, the caption under a photo of indigenous boys holding the national flag (which has the word *indigenista* printed under the eagle) reads, "In order to integrate the indigenous of Chiapas into the body of the Mexican nationality the worship of the fatherland is given great importance during the course of study with ceremonies in which our national symbol is emphasized." The penetration of Indian isolation by the INI's anthropologists was thus a patriotic duty furthering the consolidation of a national culture. Implied here was a process of modernization and mestizaje, in which "Indian" communities would become "Mexican"—with the understanding that to remain an Indian was to remain a foreigner in Mexico.

On the other hand, indigenistas such as Manuel Gamio asserted that the opposite was true, that the Indian was the *essence* of mestizo authenticity and belonging, an essence we can also see in Alfonso Caso's quotation at the beginning of this section. Gamio wrote that the purest source of Americanness, "the most vigorous connection that binds the men of this continent to the ground on which they live is the indigenous who inspires us from Alaska to Patagonia" (Villoro 1996, 235). Moreover, "the indigenous culture is the true basis of nationality in almost all the American countries" (254). Gamio looked to the future and suggested that the old Indian cultures would accommodate themselves to modern times and, in "a transcendental consortium with Occidental civilization," would give the peoples of the continent, and especially the "Indo-Iberians, a new physiognomy of the most genuine Americanness" (256). A July 1959 interview

6. According to *Acción Indigenista* in November 1960, from 1953 to 1960, the INI had built 1,200 kilometers (about 750 miles) of roads in indigenous regions.

with Alfonso Caso in *Acción Indigenista* expressed the apparent ambivalent position of the Indian in Mexico:

> *Interviewer:* Could we say that despite the fact that the Indian is Mexican, and in a certain sense the most Mexican that we have in Mexico, our indigenous communities are groups of foreigners in their own land?
>
> *Caso:* That is how they seem, in many ways. Of course, as you say very well, the Indians cannot be more Mexican. They came much earlier than all those others who have come. But these groups have remained at the margins of the social, economic, and political life of Mexico.

Luis Villoro (1996, 234), writing from the mestizo perspective, sums up the oscillation between indigenous difference and sameness within mestizaje:

> Certainly, the indigenous continues to be seen as something separate and split off our life and culture . . . but to this is added a contrary characteristic of the indigenous. The indigenous is, at the same time, something belonging to oneself, that is within ourselves and constitutes our self as much biologically as spiritually. In Gamio, this idea comes to express itself with deep insistency. The indigenous culture, which we had seen totally separate from ourselves, appears at the same time as the indispensable root of our own specificity before the cultures of other countries.

Developing Isolation

The suggestion here is that Indians and Indian communities are not so isolated from the nation after all, an idea that complicated the work INI had set out for itself. Although Alfonso Caso was careful to point out the "marginalization" of Indian communities in Mexico—thereby reinforcing the idea that there was a clear constituency for the INI's integrationist work—other observations in *Acción Indigenista* asserted something altogether different. In 1955, for example, the Mexican delegation at the meeting of the International Labor Conference expressed the official indigenista position on the issue of the identification of indigenous people. It was easy, said the delegation, to know who was indigenous when communities lived on reservations, isolated from the economic and cultural life of the nation and part of a reduced people. It was more difficult, the newsletter would note in April 1957, to label "indigenous" those who "in the majority of occasions do not live isolated from the mestizo or national population, but, on the contrary, there exists between both population groups a symbiosis that allows them to live side by side." This was the case in Mexico. As the newsletter went on to report, thanks to the INI's work in an indigenous region (Chiapas), the Mexican delegation had discovered the form and mechanism of interaction "that over the course of four centuries of contact, indigenous and mestizo communities had constructed to integrate a common life." There had long been, in other words, strong economic and cultural links between mestizo towns and surrounding indigenous communities. Indeed, it was this mestizo-indigenous region that became the focus of the INI's development discourse, although, in practice, indigenistas would continue to work only in discrete indigenous communities. The oscillation between indigenous closeness to and distance from the nation was an important element not only of mestizo identity but also of indigenista policy and practice as these were elaborated by mestizo anthropologists.

There are similarities here with development policy in other parts of the world. Thus James Ferguson (1990, 56) notes how the development discourse characterizes Lesotho's economy as an aboriginal one "virtually untouched" by the modern world. Isolation—physical and psychological—is the great problem to be solved by development agencies charged not only with building a network of roads to transform "traditional" subsistence agriculture into commercial production for export, but also with changing "traditional" attitudes and values to bring them into harmony with modernity (58). The emphasis on Lesotho's economic and psychological isolation persists in this discourse even though the people of Lesotho have been marketing crops and livestock since the 1840s, and even though Lesotho currently imports a great deal of food, the introduction of roads having made imported goods cheaper than those grown locally (57).

Ferguson writes about development policy in the late 1970s, but, as early as 1958, according to a February 1958 article from *Acción Indigenista*, the INI had outlined a similar approach to Mexico's Indian communities, describing, for example, the characteristics of the "Mexican indigenous economy." Among these were the low levels of production due to poor land and rudimentary agricultural technology; subsistence consumption and a minimal level of economic necessity, which meant indigenous communities did not buy things, limiting the possibility of economic stimulation; almost no paid work; and the predominance of the "cultural factor," a traditional conservatism that was resistant to change and dominated by a magico-religious worldview. But the most important characteristic of the indigenous economy was that, far from being isolated, it actually formed part of a regional economic system in which a mestizo center dominated surrounding communities economically and politically. As a result, the article points out, the needs of the center distorted the economy of the communities, just as developed countries distorted the economies of underdeveloped countries:

> In this way, the indigenous community is obligated to satisfy, in the first place, the needs of urban supply, providing the governing center with foodstuffs . . . and, in the second place, the indigenous community provides, to a large extent, the manual labor for the satisfaction of the needs of the urban center's economic activity; thus, the male indigenous population provides the peon carriers that are used in these centers; and the female indigenous population provides the great majority of domestic servants that satisfy the domestic demands of the urban centers. On the other hand, the indigenous community also has to satisfy the commercial demands of the metropolis; and this is how the governing centers realize the stockpiling of products that are objects of demand in the national market . . . and whose prices in this market are so high that their acquisition in indigenous zones is cost-efficient, in spite of the high price of transportation. Such products are, for example, coffee, tobacco, eggs, butter, and so forth. . . . The governing center also fulfills the task of satisfying the needs of indigenous consumption [selling goods of poor quality at inflated prices] and thereby contributing in this form not only to the impoverishment of the Indian, but also to the deformation of his aesthetic tastes.

Although this description of indigenous communities well integrated into regional and national economies clearly contradicts the idea of indigenous isolation (Fabila also contradicts this idea—and himself—in his report on the Montaña), the article nevertheless concludes that such a situation is somehow anomalous and anachronistic. Thus the ideology of the local center is characterized by feudal relations, "fanaticism, racial discrimination, in a word, caste division"—which is to say, the local centers are remnants of the colonial past and "very distinct from the [principles and fundamental laws] that prevail in the capitalist system."

Here again is the contradictory expression of the closeness and strangeness of the Indian in Mexico. The conclusion that the regional indigenous-mestizo economy is foreign both to Mexico and to capitalism directly contradicts the evidence presented in the February 1958 article that these regions provided the nation with its basic foodstuffs. In 1950, for example, the Montaña region grew almost half of all of Guerrero's corn, most of which left the region as an export crop (Muñoz 1963, 68). Fabila noted in his 1954 report that indigenous producers sold up to 50 percent of their crops and received very little in return from the government, despite "the indigenous contribution to the nation's economy for decades, if not centuries" (Fabila and Tejeda 1955, 1:193). Moreover, indigenous communities not only provided a significant amount of labor to the regional center, belying the assertion that there was almost no paid work among indigenous peoples, but they were also important consumers of mestizo goods. Maurilio Muñoz, an anthropologist who studied the Montaña region in the early 1960s, wrote that the indigenous peoples there "unquestionably" kept the local economy alive and that mestizo merchants acted only as intermediaries, though "political predominance and commercial activity are strongly intertwined" (Muñoz 1963, 104). Then, as now, mestizos sold high-priced items manufactured in other regions of the country

The Chilapa market continues to be an important regional center of trade between mestizo merchants and indigenous farmers.

(shoes, clothes, fabrics, dry goods in general, plastic goods, cigarettes, etc.), whereas indigenous people sold crops, other plants, and food from their farms (onions, sweet potatoes, tomatoes, plums, flowers, chilies, tamales, salt, cheese, eggs, etc.)—all at very low prices. Large, weekly markets in mestizo towns such as Chilapa and Tlapa continue to be the sites of this important commercial exchange.

The insistence, despite evidence to the contrary, that the "indigenous economy," like the "indigenous community" and "the Indian" in general, exists as a discrete entity separated from the national economy and the nation-state is revealing. As noted above, this insistence arises from a modernizing, integrationist indigenista agenda that requires a proper traditional and unintegrated subject to justify its existence. At a deeper level, however, it reveals the instability of a modern self-conception that relies on clear distinctions where there are none. Thus, even though some indigenistas quietly asserted that the economic and cultural lines between indigenous and mestizo, tradition and modernity, subsistence consumption and capitalism were blurred at best, indigenista discourse insisted on drawing a clear distinction between the terms in each pair. As Ferguson (1990, 69) observes with regard to Lesotho, "For an analysis to meet the needs of 'development' institutions . . . it must make Lesotho out to be an enormously promising candidate for the only sort of intervention a 'development' agency is capable of launching: the apolitical, technical 'development' intervention."

The INI's apolitical, technical discourse constructed indigenous communities as the perfect candidates for the agency's development work, and it did this for decidedly political ends. Beyond the concern for its own existence, the INI acted as an agent of a federal government keen on consolidating its influence in Mexico's disparate regions. Ferguson (1990, xv) calls this expansion of bureaucratic national power through the use of depoliticized development discourse and practice the "anti-politics machine." This characterization of "development" helps to explain the INI's consistent failure to make significant, positive changes in indigenous communities over the years of its existence, even as it continued to propose more projects and build more centers.[7] Noticeably absent from the INI's agenda is any discussion of the relationship between political power and indigenous poverty and status. The emphasis is always on economic and cultural differences as causes of indigenous poverty, and it is these factors the

---

7. As reported in *Acción Indigenista*, October 1966, the INI's budget was calculated to come to only 6 centavos spent each day for each indigenous person the institute attended to in the country.

INI set out to change, *not* the inherently unequal relationships of power between mestizo centers and surrounding indigenous communities that reflected the larger inequalities of power at the national level.

Mexico: Modern, Not Indigenous

The tension within Mexican indigenismo and mestizaje between indigenous sameness and strangeness came to be expressed in contrary desires: on the one hand, the desire to preserve what was original and typical about "the Indian"; on the other, the desire to bring the Indian closer to "us" and to allow Indians to progress so that they would abandon their harmful separation.[8] The paradox here is only apparently resolved through the adoption of a *gradual*, ostensibly gentle progress toward "civilization." As a part of this progress, mestizo anthropologists learned indigenous languages and studied indigenous communal structures—always from an objective, scientific perspective—to understand how best to insert "national" culture into the indigenous community. A foundational text of indigenismo (Aguirre Beltrán and Pozas 1991, 24) asserted, "The development of the heterogeneous indigenous communities, behind in the progressive evolution of the country, is achieved today by exercising multilateral actions on the community and using, in order to carry them out effectively, the guiding elements extracted from the very heart of the community, so that they are trained in the methods and techniques whose introduction it is hoped will favorably modify local conditions."

Villoro (1996, 243) aptly expressed the sentiment behind such a program: "We will choose for [the Indian], but he must at each moment ratify the choice we have made." A French writer affirmed the colonialist spirit of such a sentiment when he stated proudly in the May 1964 issue of *Acción Indigenista* that Mexico's Indian policy was remarkably similar to that pursued by the French in Africa. France had nurtured the same intention to bring native peoples into the national community for 100 years and had called forth men who knew the African well to carry out this program: "European efforts have been considerable and have certainly

---

8. It was nevertheless also acknowledged that closer communication with "the nation" and modernity could actually have disastrous effects. The roads INI worked so hard to build, for example, brought not only medicine and education: "If our world arrives at the remote indigenous world, it subjugates it and sucks it dry," declared *Acción Indigenista* in December 1960. "Clearly and simply, it commits robbery while it also shatters the emotional stability of its beings. People foreign to them . . . can make them think that isolated they live better, attributing everything bad to outside forces difficult to overcome."

borne fruit, like the formation of intellectual elites, from among whom today's independent states recruit their leaders and diplomats."[9]

But the assimilationist idea of "bringing the Indian into the nation" also needs to be understood within a uniquely Mexican/indigenista nationalist context that considered Mexico's racial situation more advanced than what was current in the United States in the 1950s and 1960s. A barely veiled comment by Alfonso Caso on this superiority in his July 1959 *Acción Indigenista* interview is notable for its equation of indigenous separation with the maintenance of indigenous inferiority: "Countries that have taken the indigenous [person] for a minor have protected him, segregated him from the national community and have managed to convert him into a permanent incompetent. Our policy and our proposal are completely contrary [to this]. . . . We do not want our indigenous [person] to continue being one for all time; on the contrary, we want for him at a certain point to incorporate himself into the life of the country and be a Mexican." The contrast between this last statement and the one in which Caso calls himself indigenous ("Mexico is without doubt, in a very real sense, an indigenous country") is striking, all the more so because both were made during the same 1959 interview. In almost the same breath, indigenous identity and the *overcoming* of indigenous identity become the foundation of a Mexican nationalism set up in opposition to what Caso characterizes as the "very advanced peoples" north of the border. The contrast epitomizes the instability within indigenista and mestizo identity discussed above and highlights the nationalism inherent to this identity. Caso deliberately ignores the unique political history of Indian reservations in the United States—which are the hard-fought legacies of larger Indian territories jealously protected by Indian tribes themselves—to cast them as areas of forced segregation. When Caso gave this interview, the U.S. government was winding down tribal termination, but the integrationist policy remained official through the 1960s (Cornell 1988, 124). In that same decade, the civil rights movement in the United States dedicated to the integration of African Americans into mainstream white society was gaining increasing prominence.

Caso's comments came at a time in the United States when involuntary (in the case of Indians) and voluntary integration was taking place among the most marginalized groups as never before in the twentieth century.

---

9. It is certainly true that Mexico, through its educational system, similarly assisted the creation of an indigenous intellectual elite that has emerged as an important part of the national movement for autonomy and self-determination. See Gutiérrez 1999.

But the INI director was determined to make the contrast between Mexico and the United States particularly stark. He even made it a point in this interview to mention the importance of the "one-drop rule" without mentioning the United States: "There are countries in which race is considered the most important and permanent thing in the world; there are those, even, that think only one drop of blood converts into black the person who has it, no matter how white their skin may be." In contrast, Mexico was a "wonder" because only in Mexico could people change their race through culture. The INI, Mexican life, and, most important, "even in its most obvious aspects," the Revolution made possible this transformation: "so that even the simple fact of giving an indigenous [man] a horse, a rifle, and an ideal, and letting him go into the hills makes it possible that when this man returns he is no longer indigenous."

President Cárdenas created the Autonomous Department for Indigenous Affairs in 1934 to promote research and to help mobilize communities for democratic governance and against regional caciques (Peña 2002; Dawson 2004). The department came up with ideas such as an ethnolinguistic project in Michoacán that taught literacy and encouraged literary production among Tarascans. But this ethnic empowerment did not last long. In 1940, President Manuel Ávila Camacho (1940–46) dismantled the department because it was "dangerous for the new policy of national unity," necessary in the context of World War II (Peña 2002, 50). The INI's creation in 1948 was part of an emphasis on capitalist industrialization, political centralization, and cultural homogeneity that was the backdrop for Fabila's adventure in Guerrero.

Centralization, Modernization

Alfonso Fabila was born in 1897 in the state of México. The son of campesinos, Fabila had attended a rural school with mostly Otomí children (though apparently he was not an Indian himself). He graduated from UNAM and entered government service early on, working in the Ministry of Education's peasant schools and its rural cultural missions as a literacy teacher.[10] Manuel Gamio himself hired Fabila as his assistant in the Valle del Mezquital in Hidalgo. As inspector of rural cultural missions for the Ministry of Education, Fabila traveled throughout the country visiting

---

10. Biographical information on Alfonso Fabila is taken from *Acción Indigenista,* July 1960.

indigenous and peasant communities until Alfonso Caso appointed him to be an INI researcher in 1954. His revolutionary credentials, in the agrarian reform tradition, were impeccable. Walking through the Montaña region, Fabila writes about the "disagreeable feeling of finding oneself in a strange and absurd country, where little is known of our latest social revolution, and where not only is there poverty and ignorance, but colonial and even pre-Hispanic remnants that fill one with anguish" (Fabila and Tejeda 1955, 1:ix). Fabila's sense of the injustices in the region inspired him to appeal in the strongest and most utopian terms for its development and the development of the country: "Once we strive with seriousness in the task, these things will change to the point where this place will become a paradise with the resources it still has, its climate, and its marvelous panoramas. To work with the Indians of this forgotten region is more than just, and cannot be postponed; it is a yearning to contribute to the integration and the greatness of a new Mexico" (Fabila and Tejeda 1955, 1:xi).

Fabila writes repeatedly about the "attitude of frank resentment and bitterness" he encountered among indigenous peoples (Fabila often uses the old colonial term *naturales* to refer to Indians) toward the white and mestizo population—and the prejudiced attitudes of mestizos and whites toward Indians: "They believe the natives are lazy, dumb, and unrepentant, and they belittle them, exploit and humiliate them, with everything ending up in vulgar, negative situations" (Fabila and Tejeda 1955, 1:ix). If the relations were bad between indigenous and nonindigenous people, they were no less conflictive among indigenous communities themselves. Fabila encountered enough of this intercommunity violence that he often had to travel far out of his way in order to avoid it, almost always caused by disputes over land, which communities begged government officials to adjudicate, to little avail. The constant and copious communication between communities and state and federal government agencies about these conflicts contradicts Fabila's assertion that the indigenous peoples of the region were ignorant of the Revolution. They often knew—or at least the community scribe or teacher often knew—even the articles of agrarian law to which they could appeal for justice from the government.

The problem, Fabila writes, was the physical isolation of many areas that allowed *cacicazgos* (small fiefdoms under boss rule) to flourish "completely out of control"—that is, out of national political control. Although never stated explicitly, an important goal of the INI was to centralize power in the national government by assimilating local and regional systems of power into the federal web.[11] National cultural, economic, and political integration were part of the same assimilationist program.[12] For an INI anthropologist like Salomón Nahmad Sitton, local elite political and economic control has always been the enemy. "Those local powers appropriate all the production of the small localities," Nahmad Sitton told me on 21 January 2000.

> If you look, for example, at Tlapa, at hat production, everything is concentrated in Tlapa or in Chilapa, and from there it enters the national and international market. But these local elites control the market. And they pay miserable wages to the people. And moreover they controlled corn — it's a region with a corn deficit — and they brought corn and sold it very high to indigenous people, and bought hats. And the indigenous also didn't have a voice, nor the vote in local elections. The PRI would come — and still comes — and fills the ballot boxes and says that the indigenous had all voted. Like [it does in] Oaxaca, Guerrero, Puebla. The local and federal representatives are the sons of these elites. And the indigenous are subjugated by them and these elites dominate the state government.

11. Ángel Palerm (in Aguirre Beltrán 1976, 15) wrote that "the real problem... which is the central question of indigenista strategy, consists in attaining the integration of the regional system into the national one." For him, this was a Marxist-informed strategy conceived in terms of the inevitable integration of these caste-based regions into a modern, national class-based system: "The process is of a dialectical nature, so that during its progress the regional system dissolves and the Indian and the mestizo are simultaneously liberated from their old ties of dependency and domination. This liberation, of course, must be understood as a passage from caste or quasi-caste relations to relations of social class."

12. "In my opinion," comments anthropologist Juan Luis Sariego Rodríguez (2000, 5) of the National School of Anthropology and History (Escuela Nacional de Antropología e Historia, or ENAH), "the... profound commitment to indigenous cultural integration into national society... impeded an understanding, in its own terms, of the internal indigenous logic, to the point that a false homogeneity of the country's ethnic diversity was established." Danièle Dehouve (2001, 22) reminds us that the anthropological consensus on the indigenous "closed, corporate community" as one that was relatively isolated and culturally and economically homogeneous and self-sufficient emerged within the context of the Cold War. The "supposed stability of the postwar world was an ideological representation" of this period that anthropologists reflected in their theory of the Mesoamerican indigenous community. With the fall of the Berlin Wall, Dehouve suggests, the old anthropological theory began to fall, too. The research of Xóchitl Leyva Solano and Gabriel Ascencio Franco (1996, 103) among the indigenous colonists in the Lacandon jungle is a case in point: "The challenge is to go beyond the folkloric register of the fact, to attempt a holistic interpretation of social reality that demonstrates how the phenomenon of identity is a *permanent* process, unfinished, a constant search for definition." This line of inquiry has been followed since by other researchers (Schryer 1990; Lomnitz-Adler 1992; Rus 1994; Field 1994; Mallon 1995; Rubin 1997; Hernández Castillo 2001).

Given the economic subordination of indigenous communities and the INI's mandate to improve their situation, the conflict between the INI and local powers seemed inevitable—but there were complicating factors, as Nahmad Sitton pointed out: "The INI wanted to confront this [situation], but not totally, because the INI also formed part of the PRI. . . . what we anthropologists wanted to do, was to break this system. To change the economic and political conditions of the regions, so that indigenous people would participate in the national project."

The INI was part of a continuing desire to centralize federal power over microregional elites, who would then be pulled in toward the center. "But this didn't work," Nahmad Sitton explained, "because these [regions] became part of the center. These caciques had their houses in Mexico City and were the governors of the states. The networks integrated nationally within the PRI. The INI was impotent." "If we had been good ethnologists," Nahmad Sitton (1999) wrote in an unpublished paper, "we would have done an ethnography of the indigenista agency and we would have known better its real project: to denounce local caciques, but not as part of the organization of the system. In the hallways, we heard people comment on who would be the new presidential candidate, master Caso would dine with Corona del Rosal, president of the PRI, who was one of the caciques in the region of the Valle del Mezquital." In fact, power did become centralized, according to Nahmad Sitton, just not in the way that idealistic anthropologists had hoped it would. Instead of diminishing the power of the rural fiefdoms that subordinated indigenous communities, the federal government working through the dominant political party accepted much of this local control in exchange for party support (Lomnitz-Adler 1992; Pansters 1997; Rubin 1997).[13]

13. After speaking with "Librado," an INI analyst based at the Indigenous Coordination Center (CCI) in Tlacoapa on 4 April 2000, I understood how little the INI has changed basic conditions in the countryside. In order to get projects approved for a community, the INI has to speak with the local municipal representative (*comisario*) and the headmen (*principales*) but it is the local cacique who provides the list of those who will get government assistance. "The cacique controls people," Librado told me. "If someone is sick, for example, then he lends them money to buy medicine, or he gets them medicine in exchange for their labor. But in all cases the people are at his mercy." Moreover, when a cacique does not like someone at the CCI, he will approach the CCI delegate and the state government to have the person sent elsewhere. "The INI goes into a community but we can't get to everyone so we have to decide who will get help, who won't, based on two main criteria: are they 100 percent indigenous and are they the poorest? Even then, the cacique has his own list of followers and sometimes his list does not match ours and the cacique gets upset. Some comisarios are under the thumbs of the cacique and some aren't. This is how a civil war can erupt in a community." Without the desperate poverty of many rural areas and the support of the

The ultimate end for indigenistas was also the end of the Indian: industrialization. Indeed, the INI was actively involved in the late 1940s relocating indigenous populations from their traditional lands in order to make way for hydroelectric projects in Veracruz and Oaxaca (Gutiérrez 1999, 103; *Acción Indigenista,* February 1954).[14] And, as noted in chapter 1, the Cárdenas reforms in the countryside that had privileged land redistribution and the creation of new ejidos in the 1930s were significantly slowed already by the early 1940s. World War II had disrupted international trade and provided Mexican entrepreneurs with new business opportunities the Mexican government was eager to promote through official protectionist policies, subsidies, and increased foreign investment (Hewitt de Alcantara 1976, 8). Federal spending on "social development" in areas such as public health and education decreased while physical infrastructure projects received increasing government investment (9). And, after 1940, the budgets of the Agrarian Department, the National Ejido Credit Bank, rural schools, and clinics were "severely limited" (12). The INI's fixation with distinguishing the indigenous/traditional from the national/modern and the Mexican government's privileging of industrial and urban areas were part of a more general postwar development discourse dominated by modernization theorists such as Neil Smelser and Walter Rostow and by Latin American economists working on the Economic Commission for Latin America (So 1990; Escobar 1995, 81). It was within this larger development landscape dominated by modernization discourse that indigenistas like Fabila worked to improve indigenous lives.

Inside and Outside the Nation

Although Fabila devoted most of his study to the economic relations of the Montaña region, his account makes clear that there was an intimate

---

state government, caciques would not have the power they continue to hold. The meager resources the INI provides—Librado commented on his own poor salary—scarcely affect this inequality but they present enough of a threat to the hegemony of local power holders to create conflicts, which inevitably end, however, with a return to the status quo ante. Little changes that is not connected to the larger system of power. As Miguel Ángel Gutiérrez Ávila (1999, 69) notes in his history of "despots and caciques" in the *municipio* of Xochistlahuaca, "Because of the specific characteristics of the history of the Guerreran political system, any local or regional power is possible only as a result of the support of the state government."

14. According to *Acción Indigenista,* April 1958, the National Indigenous Institute established an Indigenous Coordination Center in the Veracruz-Oaxaca region specifically for this relocation work—"to convince the peasants to abandon their towns, transfer the population and restructure the affected towns in zones of reaccommodation."

relationship among the economic, political, and ethnic. All of these revealed the indigenous peoples of the region to be thoroughly assimilated to national and international market relations, even as they retained their own local structures of governance. It is this larger panorama of power that modernizing development discourse carefully ignores. Moreover, Fabila is not reluctant to criticize state and national governments. Regarding land conflicts, for example, Fabila notes how local leaders and caciques thrive in the midst of an intercommunity violence they do nothing to stop, and how they maintain their own prestige before villagers and state authorities by exacting revenge in the name of their followers. Fabila blames this situation on agrarian officials, municipal authorities, caciques, local leaders, "and we do not know who else, because, as we said, at the bottom of all these questions lie outside interests" (Fabila and Tejeda 1955, 1:6). The outside interests Fabila mentions included monopolists based in Puebla who controlled the national and international trade in straw hats made by indigenous people, and the state government based in Chilpancingo, which unilaterally appointed local municipal officials. He does not implicate the national government directly, but he is clear about the negative effects of government neglect on the lives of people in the Montaña. Without specifying exactly who is to blame, Fabila nevertheless incisively describes the ways in which local, state, and national governments worked against the interests of indigenous people.

Race was an important element in this governance. Although municipal authorities were almost exclusively mestizo and white, indigenous communities retained some autonomous control of village affairs. Fabila writes that indigenous peoples appeared to be accustomed to this racial hierarchy of power, in large part because of their widespread illiteracy and because the state capital imposed municipal authorities on them. It is likely that, faced with a hostile political environment, indigenous communities withdrew into themselves and relied on village government to order their daily lives. To outsiders, this looked like acquiescence. But, as Jan Rus (1994) has written about highland Maya communities in Chiapas, a withdrawal from the mestizo-white power structure—to the extent that this was possible given the ongoing economic exploitation of indigenous labor—signified a strengthening of local village control over daily affairs. Local village politics, structured by a complex system of political/religious offices and a council of principals or elders, was very much alive and well in the mid-1950s and not at all on the verge of collapse. Fabila writes that in the small villages where most indigenous people lived, he hardly ever met any mestizos, and that here the authorities were "of the traditional type," in which the council of principals had the last word on all village matters.

Fabila believed this kind of self-government was good for indigenous peoples. In some majority-indigenous municipalities in the Montaña, a council of principals continued to govern, whereas in others, political parties had made their appearance, and indigenous community members complained about their influence. They told Fabila that, if they had been able to designate the municipal authorities, they would have chosen individuals who were better suited for their communities, but that, with the party system, they were subjected to impositions from places that did not understand the problems people faced. Fabila even names the Institutional Revolutionary Party (PRI)—the national ruling party—as one of these meddlesome political parties and cites examples:

> According to the political officials, authorities in the municipal seats are elected by a majority of votes, but, in reality, they are designated by higher-ups. The political party that controls the great majority of municipalities is the PRI. In the municipality of Ahuacuotzingo, there is still the tradition of [governance by] the Principals; they are upset that the [municipal] authorities are members of a political party (the PRI), instead of being designated by them, but they are not openly opposed [to this]. In the municipality of Xochihuehuetlan, the municipal council is also composed of PRI members; there, the Principals still have a lot of power and their opinions influence the decisions of the municipal president. In Atlixtac, there was a municipal council made up of members of the same party, but it seems they committed various excesses and were replaced by a municipal council composed of PAN [National Action Party, a conservative, Catholic party] members, directed by the Catholic priest of the place. He is now the one who directs politics there. (Fabila and Tejeda 1955, 2:420)

"Thinking over the validity of this complaint [by indigenous people]," Fabila writes, "we thought that the manner by which indigenous communities govern themselves is the one that best suits their own interests" (2:421). The duplication of authorities, constitutional and indigenous, was common in the region (e.g., municipal councils and a council of principals in one municipality) and prompted Fabila to note that indigenous authorities "frequently were more effective" than their legally recognized counterparts (1:ix).

This is bold support for indigenous autonomy made during a time when the national government was consolidating its hold on popular sectors, especially through the national labor union and the National Peasant Federation. The National Peasant Federation (CNC) fully backed government policies, even when they obviously favored large-scale businesses at the campesinos' expense. In 1953, the secretary-general of CNC "expressed his support for the project in disarming style. 'Given this example of unquestionable and positive activity, peasants affiliated to the CNC have only to fulfill once again their patriotic duty'" (Smith 1991, 351). And in the Chiapas highlands, the INI was routinely meddling in local indigenous affairs by using its selective support for literate scribe-principals "to advance projects whose benefits were not primarily for Indians" (Rus 1994, 291).

Fabila found further evidence of the contrasting performance of official and indigenous institutions in the working of the legal systems of the region. Whereas "justice for the poor, the ignorant, and the defenseless is a dead letter in the hands of corrupt authorities" (Fabila and Tejeda 1955, 1:xi), in the small villages Fabila was told the principals decided what should be done with prisoners and how to deal with crime in general; he heard no complaints by community members about this form of justice. These local village leaders judged minor offenses and those directly affecting indigenous families according to customary, not written, law and sent the adjudication of more serious crimes to municipal judges located in the municipal seat. If these judges could not resolve an issue, it was sent up to the district seat (which oversaw several municipalities), where the Court of First Instance reviewed the case. The public prosecutors employed to take on these cases had rarely completed their legal training and often took bribes to shorten or eliminate jail time for the accused. Fabila notes that "frequently, the public prosecutors work together with the state police to exploit the ignorance of the indigenous. In the city of Tlapa, there is a lawyer with the Department of Indigenous Affairs who told us that he has to protect indigenous individuals on a daily basis from the injustices inflicted on them by the public prosecutor and the chief of police. The indigenous are always asking him to defend them from unjust fines and other extortions. The problem is very serious" (2:433). Thus people were happy with their own system of justice, but as soon as the public prosecutor intervened, "things changed": Fabila encountered widespread complaints about corrupt prosecutors. Well-informed persons told him "that the Revolution has not come to the region, so far as justice and other aspects of modern culture and the benefits of economic well-being are concerned" (2:434).

Fabila's advocacy of a certain amount of indigenous self-determination is nevertheless tempered by his belief in the ultimate goodness of the Revolution and the national unity it would bring. An important foundation for this unity in the countryside was the ejido, though in the Montaña region, as in many indigenous regions of the country, Indian communities held title to lands called "bienes comunales," which were historically and explicitly Indian. For Fabila, the existence of two different land tenure systems, one in which individuals registered with the federal government and the other in which they did not, presented an obstacle to national unity. As Gonzalo Aguirre Beltrán and Ricardo Pozas (1991, 89) write, in the case of the ejido, the Revolution "reserved eminent domain over these lands for the nation and only gave the ejido usufruct rights . . . affirming that the rights [ejidatarios] had over agricultural lands were irrevocable and inalienable and thus they could not in any case nor in any form, cede, transfer, rent, mortgage or sell them." Under the system of bienes comunales, on the other hand, the indigenous community and not the nation is the legal owner. This is an important distinction since the possession of bienes comunales signifies community territorial and cultural rights not recognized under the ejido system.

Aguirre Beltrán and Pozas (1991, 93) write at length about the "benefits" of acculturation brought by the ejido, the primary one being the high level of individuation and secularization of the old indigenous communities, "destroying definitively the sacred and communal characteristics that had persisted in them." The ejido made the indigenous community "permeable" to cultural change because its establishment, maintenance, and expansion required constant contact with government representatives: "This [contact] induces, in those groups that choose this social structure, an attitude favorable to cultural change and a notable indifference toward community and sacred norms, which facilitate the integration of Indian people" (96). For his part, Fabila suggests that, to eliminate the ethnic differences between indigenous people and mestizos (by making mestizos out of Indians), the INI should push for the "ejidotization" of indigenous communal lands. He likes the bienes comunales system only because "it automatically disappears when the indigenous reach a level of culture similar to the national [mestizo]; it is not therefore a problem for the country's institutions because it can be a useful instrument for the improvement of the situation of indigenous [people]" (Fabila and Tejeda 1955, 1:95).

After Fabila

The INI established an Indigenous Coordination Center (CCI) in the Montaña region in 1965 after it sent two more anthropologists there in 1963 to "complete" Fabila's 500-page report, which was never published as an INI monograph. As Nahmad Sitton explained to me on 21 January 2000, the decision to locate a CCI in the Montaña at that time came because the secretary of the presidency under President Gustavo Díaz Ordaz (1964–70) and General Cárdenas himself were interested in developing the region. The secretary was from Chilapa and presumably had a personal stake in the region's development; Cárdenas was head of the Balsas River Commission and keen on developing the entire Balsas basin, which included parts of Oaxaca and Puebla as well as the Montaña. The INI was to attend to the "social part" of this project. In contrast to many other regions in the country, Nahmad Sitton said, here the INI was the first government agency on the scene. Other than newer census figures for the region, the "completed" report would add little to Fabila's. More important, however, was what it omitted: all of Fabila's frank support for indigenous political self-determination and most of his critique of local power relations. When understood within the larger institutional and political context, the trimmed final version of Fabila's work in the Montaña comes as no surprise. It is a reminder of what the government would tolerate within the definition of "development" for rural areas and indigenous peoples.

We need also to make a distinction between this final, official version of the Montaña report and the intent of its primary author, Maurilio Muñoz (a young Salomón Nahmad Sitton was assigned to Muñoz as his assistant). Muñoz was an Otomí (Ñañhu) from the state of Hidalgo, Nahmad Sitton said, and had been a rural teacher, as had his father before him. He was monolingual as a child, speaking no Spanish until General Cárdenas invited Maurilio's father to send his son to an indigenous school.[15] From there, he went on to finish courses in anthropology without actually obtaining his degree. Cárdenas then recommended Muñoz to Alfonso Caso, suggesting he hire him at the INI — Nahmad Sitton said that Caso and Cárdenas were "very good friends" — at a time when "generally the high functionaries in the INI were not indigenous, or are not [still]." Working with Muñoz, Nahmad Sitton was able to understand a little more how indigenous intellectuals thought; and he observed how Muñoz questioned "the way functionaries looked at indigenous people, and how these functionaries looked at him." Muñoz had the hope that more indigenous people would be trained, as he had been, to assume a

15. According to locals in Hidalgo, Muñoz was only thirteen when President Cárdenas came to the state to inaugurate a bridge on the Tula River in 1935. "He sold Cárdenas a newspaper, and the president, impressed by the enterprising youth, promised him a scholarship to study for a career as a rural teacher" (Dawson 2004, 159).

more relevant role in Mexican society. His work in the Montaña (he was named the first director of the Tlapa Indigenous Coordination Center) was toward this end and it helps to illustrate the distinction between the INI as institution and the indigenistas who worked in indigenous communities. In an unpublished paper, Nahmad Sitton (1999) related that

> the coexistence of the communities in the Tlapa region made us see the profoundly miserable conditions of the indigenous and the exploitation of their craft work. The unjust resale of corn and the conditions of malnutrition and hunger that oppressed the population especially children and women. Maurilio and I visited all the communities in the municipalities, he was untiring walking and jogging along the paths, we spoke with authorities and leaders, with school teachers. We took a sampling of houses in order to understand the living conditions of domestic family units and we edited the report hoping that our proposed projects would become reality.

Muñoz visited the INI's head offices in Mexico City with the report in hand but "returned disappointed and upset . . . nothing was decided" (Nahmad Sitton 1999). He found the offices divided between those knowledgeable about rural problems but without decision-making power, and a bureaucratic elite that "paralyzed" the institution.

> Maurilio had to invite [a bureaucrat] to breakfast in an elegant restaurant in order to obtain the funds for the work. Upon the arrival of "the master Caso," the bureaucratic courtesans waited in the doorway of the institution and upon his leaving the circle accompanied him to his car. The ritual was daily and important matters waited. Indians were not a part of this environment. Some photographs of them decorated the walls, however. We worked for two years and never saw a budget; both the reality of the countryside and the reality of the men who were in charge exasperated us. The wheeling and dealing of national, university, and internal politics dominated. One had to define with whom and with which group one was attached: with the utopians and leftists, or with the refined administrators. (Nahmad Sitton 1999)

Arriving at the head offices to lobby for a project or to follow through on matters that were sometimes grave given local conditions, a staff member from an Indigenous Coordination Center (CCI) typically found that

A mural on the outside of the Indigenous Coordination Center (CCI) in Tlapa portrays the INI's immunization campaign.

those who had administrative power and to whom the member had to relate the facts of rural life constituted a real barrier. The urban industrial bias of the state and its projects clearly informed the INI, too, despite the institute's overwhelmingly rural constituency. Writing in the April 1965 issue of *Acción Indigenista*, Gonzalo Aguirre Beltrán considered this bias a serious obstacle to the institutional changes necessary for the "equitable redistribution of power and the equitable redistribution of the status or social position of the indigenous in the national structure."

Conclusion

By the time Alfonso Fabila entered the Montaña region and *La política indigenista en México* was published in 1954—just when the work of the INI was beginning—the concerns of indigenistas were no longer the concerns of the national government. Though hallmarks of the presidency of Lázaro Cárdenas (1934–40), Mexico's own "great leap forward" in agrarian reform and its federal attention to rural areas were followed by a significant decline in government concern for peasant and indigenous affairs. Even the establishment of the National Indigenous Institute in 1948 can be seen as part of this general trend, replacing as it did the Autonomous Department of Indigenous Affairs established by Cárdenas in 1934. Whereas the department had operated independently of a larger government agency, the INI was from its start a dependency of the Ministry of Education. Like rural areas and the indigenous peoples who lived there, the INI played a minor part in the government's modernizing agenda. The national political and economic environment in which the INI was established and Fabila conducted his research did not nurture radical visions of an equitable indigenous integration.

That said, the INI anthropologists continued to believe in the possibilities of a different revolution, now more mythical than real. Fabila writes eloquently about how rural teachers especially embodied this national ideal: "Only because of them do we feel the living presence of Mexico and the Revolution; without them, one would feel in a strange and most absurd country. The fatherland lives on because of their daily toil and in the civic acts they carry out on their respective days" (Fabila and Tejeda 1955: 2:502). Fabila seems to have cast himself in much the same role as these teachers, quixotically speaking about a revolutionary Mexico that did not exist. Meanwhile, indigenistas also asserted that Indians were strangers in their own country. There are two different countries here, named by different times: the premodern Mexico (of the Indians) and the becoming-modern Mexico (of the anthropologists). These are expressions of the clear distinction indigenistas drew between tradition and modernity, in which the INI cast itself as crusader for progress and modernization. This was despite everything the institute and its anthropologists knew about the intimate connections joining the two elements of the tradition/modernity dualism, connections that made such a distinction irrelevant, if not unreal. But indigenistas clung tenaciously to the distinction, no matter how dubious and equivocal it was, because it justified what they did and who they were. The push and pull between homogeneity and diversity, sameness and difference, the nation and peoples runs throughout the writings of indigenistas. The strange promise of indigenismo was its ability to articulate this push and pull within Mexican revolutionary nationalism. The ejido is a concrete example. On the one hand, the ejido is an important part of a national policy deliberately aimed at the modernization and deculturation of indigenous communities. On the other, it is the national institution that has most nurtured both a peasant revolutionary consciousness and an indigenous peasant movement fully aware of its legitimacy.

The story told here is out of a different time, a different place, when modernization meant economic and political centralization and cultural homogenization. As a national agency, the INI supported these goals. In the process, indigenistas claimed the authority to speak about and for a certain kind of imagined Indian, which acted as an obstacle to the achievement of nationalist cohesion. This imagined Indian made the INI's work indispensable, at least in the eyes of indigenistas, whose mission was eliminating it. But like the feudal economic relations and the power of local caciques that indigenistas hoped to dismantle, the Indian did not disappear. Instead, it became the emblem of a self-consciously nationalist movement of indigenous peoples that has championed the full integration of Indians at all levels of national life. Today, multiculturalism, not cultural homogeneity, is the integrationist slogan. Emerging forcefully at the moment of neoliberal reform in Mexico (the centrifugal state, the globalized economy), the discourses of multicultural citizenship and indigenous autonomy make sense. They repeat and reinforce the fragmentation of the social—that is, the new modernization—that Mexico and multilateral lenders like the World Bank have deliberately pursued for more than a quarter century. The government-sponsored developmentalism that the INI so proudly represented in the "golden age" discussed here—from the 1950s to the 1970s—is over. Despite the enormously changed political economic context, however, the populist Indian of that earlier period remains vital to both indigenous politics and the idea of indigenousness itself, whose uneasy relationship will be explored in the chapters that follow.

THREE

INDIAN POPULISTS: THE INDIGENOUS MOVEMENT AND THE GUERRERO COUNCIL, 1991–2000

A large part of the contemporary political thinking of Mexico's indigenous peoples is focused on the right to autonomy. Local village demands are now part of a national demand. Our organizations have insisted that the problems we have as Mexican indigenous peoples concern not only villages and communities but also the entire Mexican nation.
—MARCOS MATÍAS ALONSO, PRESIDENT OF ALTEPETL NAHUAS, JULY 1998

What I am calling the "indigenous movement" in Mexico is a loose network of community and regional organizations with disparate ethnic, social, and political backgrounds united by the demand for autonomy that Marcos Matías Alonso discusses above. The movement is nationalist but it rejects old-style integrationist national policies while seeking greater inclusion in national political decision making as Mexican citizens with full rights. The movement's agenda is in fact integrationist and makes extensive use of populist language to appeal to the government and the wider public. As Alonso suggests in the epigraph above, however, there is a distinction that needs to be made (as this chapter will illustrate), namely, between a nationalist-oriented leadership and a more locally oriented constituency or base. Although this distinction is not hard and fast—the leadership has also privileged the local, for instance, and communities are creating regional spaces for themselves—it was the cause of some tension within the council's group of directors, and it complicates both the desire and the need to redefine what it means to be an Indian in Mexico.

The emergence of a national movement is closely tied to a generational shift, as younger men began in the 1970s to act as cultural brokers in towns that had better access to formal educational opportunities. On the evening of 21 November 1999 in Acatlán, Guerrero, Marcos Matías Alonso and José Leonor Sánchez Capistrano, co-founders of Altepetl Nahuas, a local development NGO, told me more about what led to this shift.[1] Both men are now in their early fifties and are part of the first generation of indigenous men to be educated beyond primary school.

> *José Leonor:* The people who were comisarios, principales were 60, 70 years old; they were traditional leaders in communities but could barely read a piece of paper, barely wrote; they *wanted* to write but they couldn't write. So that's where they saw the advantage . . .
> *Marcos:* That's how they called us, that's how we got involved [*como entramos*].
> *José Leonor:* "Here, read this to me" [they'd say] and it was read well.
> *Marcos:* Or "write this letter."
> *José Leonor:* And so the letter was written. They couldn't put together an official document like that. . . .
> *Marcos:* [laughing] No, they didn't know how.
> *José Leonor:* Because they didn't go to school. That's how it opened up [for the younger generation]. Not because it was nice to do [*lo bonito*] but because of the work that was accomplished. Now, this is the experience of one community [Acatlán] but from here you can see the same in all the communities and in the state.
> *Marcos:* The same thing happened with Pedro [de Jesús Alejandro] and the dam. They called them the "old men," told them to get involved because "we need you."
> *José Leonor:* "We want professionals. How are we going to put together documents?"
> *Marcos:* And "how to get involved in politics?"
> *José Leonor:* "To express our wishes [to officials]." This necessity induced the participation of young men, well, more than young men, students.

1. Marcos Matías Alonso had been director of the INI's Indigenous Coordination Center in Chilapa in the early 1990s and was appointed INI director general in 2000, a position he held for less than a year before he was forced to resign (see Nahmad Sitton 2004, 87). By 2008, he was a federal congressman.

Marcos: There is a first generation, the generation of the old men, those who [in the 1970s] were 60 years old. These are the ones we call the "principals" [*principales*], the "old ones" [*ancianos*], the guides of our people. And after them followed the next generation, those who were 40 years old, 45 years old—an intermediate generation. After them came us, the young ones, in our twenties and younger.

Until 1970 or 1972, there was no electricity [in Acatlán] and the school went only to third grade. Those who wanted more education had to walk to Chilapa [the municipal seat, about 5.5 miles away]. But it wasn't a bilingual school there—pure Spanish! [laughing] And you didn't understand anything! Because we just spoke Nahuatl all the time. Only two or three trips a day to Chilapa, in an old car, and if you missed it you had to go the next day. So you have an idea of the isolation we lived in.

The changes came very quickly here. The principales, the ancianos had a lot more power then. They could command with great authority [*tenían más mando, pues*]. They were more respected. There came a moment when the old men called on the younger men—children almost, some 14, 15 years old—to help them and we created a generational alliance. So, they call us. Questions of land titles, of health, of deaths—anything to do with our community governance.

And the curious thing is that these kids, these young adults at a political level they became the guides of the people, and not just in Acatlán, not even just in Guerrero, but I would say in Mexico. Pedro de Jesús—how old is he?—he was a municipal representative [*comisario municipal*] because the older ones told him "You guide the people and the town [*el pueblo*]." This leadership today is no older than fifty today, 40–45 years old, in general.[2]

A similar shift took place among Amuzgos in Xochistlahuaca during the 1970s. A new road from Xochistlahuaca to the larger town of Ometepec made a secondary education possible for Amuzgo children for the

---

2. Comisarios can be elected to supervise ejidos or communal lands or they can be town representatives to the municipal seat; all are recognized in Mexican law. Principales are elected through "customary law," which remains unrecognized in state and federal law, and are considered elders with the power to enforce town customs or laws that maintain community order.

first time. Many of them became bilingual teachers who sought political power in the municipality, some in partnership with the principales and others in opposition to the older generation (Gutiérrez Ávila 1999, 78–79). Surveying the history of popular mobilization in Guerrero, it becomes immediately clear that public education has been of enormous importance in the development of an indigenous leadership since the late 1970s. In 1982, for example, the state delegation of the National Union of Education Workers (Sindicato Nacional de Trabajadores de la Educación, or SNTE) was one of the first in the country to push for democracy within the union, forming the Central Council for the Struggle in Montaña, Guerrero (Consejo Central de Lucha de la Montaña de Guerrero). More recently, the Guerrero State Coordinating Committee of Education Workers (Coordinadora Estatal de Trabajadores de la Educación en Guerrero, or CETEG) has led the teachers' movement in the Montaña (Flores Félix 1998b, 92, 94), itself part of a larger socialist movement highly active in Guerrero's indigenous regions. The predominantly Mixteco municipio of Alcozauca was governed in the early 1980s by the Communist Party of Mexico (PCM) under the leadership of the communist teacher Othón Salazar; it was the first municipal government of a leftist opposition party in Mexico (Flores Félix 1998b, 122).[3] The PCM's presence in Alcozauca, the creation of the Regional Indigenous Council of Montaña (Consejo Regional Indígena de la Montaña), and the creation of a union of ejidos affiliated with the independent national rural workers' union, the Independent Confederation of Agricultural Workers and Peasants (Central Independiente de Obreros Agrícola y Campesinos), for a time gave the Montaña region the nickname "Red Mountain region" (Montaña Roja).[4] But as Marcos and José Leonor discussed, the traditional male authorities—the comisarios and principales, in particular—have long held and continue to hold power in indigenous communities, regardless of their political affiliation. Women remain excluded from these positions of authority and, although this has not kept them from organizing production cooperatives within their communities that have raised their families' standard of living, they must constantly fight the machismo of men not keen on sharing resources or power with women (Alemán Mundo 1997). The issue of sexism among the indigenous leaders, both traditional and newer, was not, however, an issue that was openly discussed in the 1990s, when the focus of the movement was on autonomy.

3. A communist teacher was municipal president of Tlapa in 1941 (Flores Félix 1998a, 123).
4. Times change and remain the same: in 2008, the PRI again governed Alcozauca.

Autonomy Is . . .

Because one's autonomy makes no sense if others do not recognize and support it, if it is not part of a larger system of mutual respect, the recognition of and respect for autonomy requires close and effective connections to the larger structures of power that are most likely to affect the autonomy of peoples and places. When indigenous peoples call for autonomy, then, it is to reach outside of their communities in order to establish a system of mutual respect—through a restructuring of political power—that can protect their communities, not to retreat into isolation (Díaz Polanco 1998, 54).

Although expressed at the United Nations by indigenous peoples from around the world, the demand for autonomy is traditionally and conspicuously Mexican, embraced not only by Mexico's indigenous movement but also by other social movements in the country that, at least since the 1970s, have attempted to work outside government control (Foweraker and Craig 1990; Rubin 1997). The indigenous demands for autonomy and self-determination add a distinct cultural dimension: the right to exercise control over their language, religion, and customs. Indigenous self-determination is also connected to a political space, in terms of both government and territory. In many indigenous towns, community members (almost always men) choose their leaders through open discussion and consensus, not by a majority decision determined by official secret ballot. Local leaders (again, almost always men) are valued for their long-term voluntary service to the community in traditional civil and religious positions called "cargos." They act as important liaisons between their respective towns and the larger municipality (the equivalent of a county in the United States). Because their leadership is not officially recognized, however, it is often ignored by municipalities dominated by mestizos that have the legal right to appoint village governments. The exercise of this right often results in violence, which can last for many years. In contrast, the indigenous movement's insistence on self-determination expressly recognizes the legitimacy and jurisdiction of indigenous local government. It is important to note, however, that both self-determination and autonomy at the level of the community fit comfortably within a Mexican federalist tradition historically defended by indigenous peoples (Guardino 1996; Mallon 1995). By no means do they suggest separation and radical difference from the rest of Mexico. This is made abundantly clear in the 1996 San Andrés Accords: "The exercise of autonomy by indigenous peoples will contribute to the unity and democratization of national life, and will strengthen the sovereignty of the country" (*Acuerdos sobre derechos* 1997, 13).

In its larger sense, indigenous autonomy includes an expanded understanding of territory that goes beyond the community. This is problematic, not only because Indians and mestizos share the same spaces, but also because Mexico's indigenous (and peasant) peoples identify most closely with their home community, their pueblo. Although this identification with the community has not prevented indigenous peoples from forming regional associations united by a common language or cause, nevertheless, it remains the strongest—the primary—identification, before all else. Even in an indigenous movement like the Guerrero Council with a decade of regional, national, and international experience, there was still a strong tendency to privilege one's own pueblo over the larger movement. (Indeed, given the status of the pueblo in Mexico, the organization of "Zapatistas" from many different pueblos and ethnic groups in Chiapas, and under extremely difficult conditions, is a remarkable accomplishment.) The concept of "indigenous territory" applies less to the Mexican context (with the exception of the Yaquis in Sonora) and is vaguely defined in the San Andrés Accords: "All indigenous people are located in a territory that covers the total habitat that indigenous peoples occupy or use in some manner. The territory is the material base of their reproduction as a people and expresses the indissoluble union of man-land-nature" (*Acuerdos sobre derechos* 1997, 14).[5]

Autonomy in Practice: The Council as Client and Broker

[The council is] an organization that is not of the PRI, it's not a part of the government. It is an organization that has a certain amount of autonomy . . . no, not a certain amount, we have complete autonomy, an organization independent of the government.

—"ROBERTO," DIRECTOR OF GUERRERO COUNCIL, JANUARY 2000

This and the sections to follow show how the leaders of the Guerrero Council strongly embraced a particular kind of Indian patriotism when

5. The San Andrés Accords draw primarily on the language in International Labor Organization Convention 169, on Indigenous and Tribal Peoples, which Mexico ratified in 1990. They occupy a central place in the indigenous movement because they are the product of an unprecedented national consultation, during which scores of indigenous and nonindigenous community members, movement leaders, academics, and politicians worked together to fashion a document on indigenous rights and culture that both the Zapatistas and the federal government signed. The federal Congress later made a series of unanticipated amendments to the accords, however, that weakened or rejected sections recognizing the collective rights of indigenous peoples, which was a great disappointment to the council and other indigenous groups (see Mattiace 2003).

they engaged the government, and how they did so despite the inherent limitations of such a strategy. Strictly speaking, the council was a client of and broker for the government despite the group's assertions of autonomy. The council attempted to resolve this contradiction by asserting its identity as the true representative of the nation and by invoking the slogans of Mexican Independence—such as Morelos's "El poder real dimana del pueblo" (Real power comes from the people)—to authorize indigenous autonomy from the state. This presented two real problems, however: (1) the state used the very same populist language and slogans to assert its own legitimacy; and (2) in legitimating its claims on the government, the council was also unwittingly legitimating the capricious power of that government.

This is not surprising, given that the council was an organization of peasants with a close connection to the postrevolutionary Mexican state, which had long nurtured campesino loyalty to an official history of the nation. Thus, in recalling that "when Cárdenas came here . . . he said, 'Down with the rich and up with the poor.' He was with Emiliano Zapata. He and Zapata were for the poor people"—even though they in fact commanded opposing armies in the Revolution—a 92-year-old Zapoteca woman reproduces that pantheon of national heroes constructed by the state through its official history and public rituals (Stephen 1998, 24; O'Malley 1986). Loyalty to this history can have contradictory outcomes, as Lynn Stephen (2002) discovered in her comparison of ejidos in Oaxaca and Chiapas. In Oaxaca, it led to cooperation and compromise with the federal government because ejidatarios there had had positive experiences with land reform agents. In Chiapas, on the other hand, the official history became an inspiration for rebellion *against* the government, which was perceived as an ally of the oppressive mestizos controlling Chiapas. In both cases, however, "the particular rhetoric of the Mexican national revolution has been interiorized by the subordinated classes, even in their radical moments" (Gledhill 1991, 380; see also Benjamin 2000, 164).

Foremost on the council's agenda was the restoration of the original wording of Article 27 of the Constitution, which made ejido lands inalienable; the reform of the article in 1992 allowed for the private ownership and sale of individual plots, something that had always taken place at low prices but that was never legal. Like other indigenous groups, including the Zapatistas, the council romanticized the ejido as a place that protected and nurtured the community—a uniquely Mexican agrarian myth of rural communalism. It is true that, without the land reform that led to the creation of the ejido, mestizo and indigenous peasant communities would not likely have persisted into the twenty-first century; the ejido is understandably the symbol of community resilience. As indigenistas well understood, however, even though the ejido system provided land to the landless, it was also the quintessential tool of political control over the peasantry. Ejidatarios and *comuneros* (those who held land under the regime of bienes comunales, mostly members of indigenous communities) had always had precarious possession of their lands. As Jesús Carlos Morett Sánchez (2003, 212) notes, "This situation was not accidental or due to a bureaucratic system, but *was a deliberate State policy* to keep peasants in fear that they could lose their parcels if they held political positions opposing the government. With this kind of blackmail, peasants remained loyal to the government for fear of losing their parcels. In this way, the immense majority of ejidatarios and comuneros lacked their Certificate of Agrarian Rights, the official document that testified to the legal possession of an ejido parcel." It was a situation that also led to ongoing land conflicts within and between communities over borders that took years to be officially determined but that, even then, were subject to dispute because formal land surveys were rare (Martínez Rescalvo 1991). Rural violence continues to be associated with these conflicts.

This history of the ejido was never mentioned in the council's discourse. More typical was the sentiment expressed by Tlapaneco community council members in a 20 April 1992 letter to President Salinas de Gortari. The original Article 27 "protects and shelters us, the Indigenous, in our land," they wrote. "[You] are going to end the right and the guarantees that we Indigenous have to defend our lands." Tellingly, they closed their letter with the revolutionary slogan that appeared on all official correspondence for decades: "Sufragio Efectivo. No Reelección" (Effective Suffrage. No Reelection [no rigged elections]). As Stephen saw in Oaxaca, campesino loyalty to official history often translated into an expectation that revolutionary slogans be fulfilled, and, as Marilyn Gates writes (in Baños Ramírez 1998, 43), "Many peasants feel entitled to credit and other subsidies, irrespective of the harvest outcome, as part of their rightful due ... promised social justice under the 1917 Constitution and still awaiting payment in full." But it was clear early on that the Mexican state had no intention of fully supporting ejidatarios or comuneros, either through equitable land distribution or through adequate production supports. Land reform from the Cárdenas presidency on was a necessary part of the import substitution phase of Mexican industrialization, when agriculture was important only insofar as it supported the development of domestic industry. Today "the new industrial phase and its corresponding neoliberal model does not contemplate, as a *necessary* condition for its development, the existence of small peasants and still less of peasants ruined by the very dynamic of the previous [development] model" (Morett Sánchez 2003, 113). When peasant groups appealed to the state in the language of populism, as the council did, they affirmed their loyalty by ratifying an official history of postrevolutionary Mexico that has deliberately obscured the enduring systemic injustices to which peasants have always been subject. And there was the rub. How could they frame their demands without reproducing the structures of power (both material and discursive) that made those demands unrealizable?

The 1991 Manifesto: Somos Campesinos, We Are Peasants

Today, the 14 of September 1991, a day when we commemorate a founding moment of the fatherland, the Amuzgos, the Nahuas, the Mixtecos, the Tlapanecos, together with the peasant organizations of the state of Guerrero, are establishing this honorable State Council 500 Years of Resistance. . . . All of our peoples have made their contribution to the nation and created great wealth while you have kept us in poverty and in real misery. Our contribution is evident in the construction of grand cathedrals, in the prosperous cities, in the palatial homes you own, in the offices where you work.

—"CONSEJO ESTATAL GUERRERO" (1991)

The manifesto drawn up by its Constituent Assembly frames the Guerrero Council's fundamental reasons for being and provides a touchstone for evaluating all that comes later. The date the assembly chose to meet, 14 September 1991, is the anniversary of the First Congress of Anahuac convened in Chilpancingo by José María Morelos y Pavón during the War of Independence in 1813, a highly charged nationalist event visibly commemorated in this city's center. The First Congress drew up some of the founding principles for what would become an independent Mexico. From the very beginning, then, the council constructed itself as a group entirely within the nation—indeed, with a more legitimate claim to the nation than others had. The emphasis on a peasant identity accompanied this nationalism and also significantly determined how the group would negotiate with the government. It is important to keep in mind that the council's peasant-based strategy was inherently a populist strategy that necessarily drew on patriotic notions of belonging to the nation. In a context of extreme inequality that no amount of populism could paper over, it was a strategy with real limitations.

Indigenous peasant groups dominated the 1991 assembly. They listed their grievances and made proposals for change that the council would continue to emphasize in the following years. Among them were denunciations of "atrocities" committed by municipal presidents, inattention to the basic needs of communities, exploitation of peasants by unscrupulous middlemen, overexploitation of forests, absentee teachers in remote communities, electoral fraud, and cholera epidemics ("Constitución del Consejo" 1991). In the spirit of opposition to the quincentenary celebration, indigenous peasant representatives also called for a movement that would unite all Mexicans: workers, youth, women, union members, and political parties. But these other groups were not well represented at the assembly and never would participate in the Guerrero Council, which would remain devoted to the needs of peasant communities.

The manifesto of the Constituent Assembly makes an explicit connection between these community needs and indigenous rights in its list of the council's goals. The form of the list suggests that the council never distinguished between basic peasant needs and indigenous rights. The definition of self-determination in the manifesto reinforces this impression. Self-determination, it reads, "implies the inalienable right to our territories and the exclusive use of resources, both those found outside and within [these territories]; the right we have to elect our legitimate representatives according to our customs and traditions; the right to the application of justice according to our customs; the right to conserve our own worldview, our language, our forms of social and labor organization, and educational processes and what we understand by development, understood as everyone's right, not just those privileged by wealth." This last point is emphasized by the promise that "we will also fight, organization by organization, town by town, region by region, so that the government will provide us the productive and social infrastructure it provides to mestizo towns and to those who supposedly generate wealth in this country, the rich." In other words, indigenous rights recognized in ILO Convention 169 will be realized when basic peasant needs are met. A new claim to identity as indigenous does not take the place of older peasant claims, especially when we realize that both are literally grounded in a claim to land, or "territory," in indigenous movement discourse.

Martín Equihua, a mestizo founder and later director of the council who was also a leader in the Alliance of Autonomous Peasant Organizations of Guerrero (Alianza de Organizaciones Campesinas Autónomas de Guerrero), stressed the compatibility of the two kinds of claims in a report to the alliance ("Informe a la Asamblea," n.d.). Equihua wanted to assure the alliance's members that their participation in the Guerrero Council in no way compromised their focus on peasant demands. It only added to what they already did: "Since the end of 1990, people have been insisting we again take up the indigenous element as one focus of the struggle and of our organization." The alliance had to define its own position vis-à-vis the 1992 quincentenary celebration, Equihua writes, and, to that end, he participated in the formation of the Guerrero Council. But, he writes, "it is not just an indigenous movement, but it aspires to be an open space for a democratic convergence of rural and urban sectors, taking advantage of the historical moment of 1992, which is why it is called the 'Guerrero Council 500 Years of Indigenous Resistance.'. . . It is not about replacing either the [alliance's] procedures for negotiation or the specific demands of [its] sectors. And much less about creating structures above or parallel to those of the [alliance's] organizations. Instead, it attempts to offer solidarity to those who need it and to take up again the historical or general demands that many times we forget, like repudiation of the external debt, respect for indigenous cultures, self-determination of peoples, respect for human and political rights, and so on."

Equihua's report is interesting for two related reasons. It assures a peasant constituency that an "indigenous" movement is to be welcomed, not feared, as a strategic option. And it suggests that this peasant constituency—which, it is clear, includes *indigenous* peasant groups—still considered itself peasant first and indigenous second, if it considered itself "indigenous" at all.[6] Although Equihua mentions the continuation of the alliance's specific sectoral demands, he mentions "indigenous" only once and in a list of things "that many times we forget." Not only is an indigenous movement perfectly compatible with a peasant organization, he assures alliance members, but it will also subordinate itself to issues that are essentially peasant issues. Although this characterization of the movement was not exactly true, as the Constituent Assembly's repeated references to indigenous self-determination and ILO Convention 169 make plain, it does define the almost exclusively *peasant* demands the council would bring before government officials in the years to follow.

Trust and Honor: Negotiating a Relationship with the State

By early 1992, the council had sent funding proposals to the INI and to the Ministry of Social Development (Secretaría de Desarrollo Social, or

---

6. For example, Equihua specifically names Zanzekan Tinemi and San Luis Acatlán later in the report as active members of the Alliance of Autonomous Peasant Organizations of Guerrero.

SEDESOL, which had authority over the INI) for basic operating costs. It was already negotiating its position between autonomy and dependency on government assistance. It was also already acting as a broker between communities and the government by bringing community demands for services to the attention of a variety of federal and state agencies. This combined role of client and broker would continue to define the council in the years to come.

The council made its national debut in 1992. The key moment of that year was a national march on Mexico City in October, in which the council participated with groups from around the country. The public goal of the march was to protest the Columbus quincentenary, though the ultimate goal was to meet with President Salinas to present their grievances to him in person. On 13 October, the marchers managed to have this personal meeting with the president, who promised that his government would consider their demands in a series of meetings with INI and SEDESOL held over the following two days. The council listed their constituents' needs at these meetings: support for production (fish, honey and beeswax, corn, coffee); road construction (the government agreed to study the reasons for the suspension of construction, for example); and infrastructure (drinking water and electricity systems, hospitals, housing). Government agencies promised more studies and agreed to continue to meet with the council to resolve these issues ("Como resultado" 1992).

For the council's directors, assurances received in this series of meetings were understood as statements of personal honor by President Salinas that his government would fulfill what it had said it would fulfill. The council consistently favored this kind of direct, clientelist appeal to high-level authorities that bypassed regular institutional and bureaucratic channels and that, having secured promises from a political leader, called on that leader's sense of (manly) honor to fulfill them. When these promises went unfulfilled, as they did in most cases, the council would mobilize its membership for another demonstration whose goal, again, was a personal meeting with the man in charge, either the president or, more often, the governor of Guerrero. Like other clients of the government, the council participated in these "rituals of marginality" (Vélez-Ibañez 1983, 22). Thus, in a letter dated 31 May 1993 and addressed to Salinas—the president himself encouraged this personalized contact—the council protested the lack of institutional attention to its demands, and it emphasized honor and trust: "In October 1992, we expressed our needs [*carencias*] to you and we asked for your intervention to provide a solution. *We are convinced you spoke to us truthfully. We didn't sign papers. We believed in your word.*

Don't betray our trust. We have acted and continue to act prudently, as you asked us to, in state politics; it is hard to expect more" (emphasis in the original).

From the beginning, financial ties connected the council with the government and with the communities the council served. An emphasis on personal ties to officials complemented the group's financial dependence on the agencies the officials represented. After the October 1992 march on Mexico City, the council continued to meet with government agencies to follow up on the demands the group had presented to President Salinas. It acquired an official status as an "civil association" (*asociación civil*) in early 1993, equivalent to nonprofit status in the United States, which facilitated the transfer of government funds to the council; already in 1992 the council received grants from the INI to pay its eight or nine directors (about 400 pesos each, every two weeks—the equivalent of about 50 dollars). And the council in 1992 had already assumed the role of an administrative agency to channel the many demands community members brought every day to its office in Chilpancingo.

The group's role as a broker between the federal government and indigenous communities continued in 1993, with the INI promising to give the council a total of 120,000 pesos for the year, which included salaries for directors and money to cover the rent of the office space. This money came with the condition that the council provide the INI with reports on all its activities, "so that INI can be informed and, if needed, provide an opinion on a possible reorientation of these activities" ("Convenio de concertación" 1993, 4). The other condition was that the council be responsible for finding alternative funding sources nationally and internationally, since the INI was to "gradually reduce the financial support for the execution of its projects" (4).[7] The council was especially anxious to secure funding for its State Congress of Indigenous Peoples in September 1993. The 1992 congress had been a success: attendance by community members had exceeded expectations and had helped to raise the political profile of the council in Guerrero. Minutes from meetings of the directors in 1993 reveal their central concern with the upcoming congress, even as they also continued to meet with government agencies regarding the demands made in Mexico City in 1992.

---

7. By the end of 1994, Martín Equihua became a PRD federal congressman and gave part of his salary to the council over the next few years. In 1997, Marcelino Díaz de Jesús, a council founder from the Alto Balsas region, took Equihua's place as a federal congressman and also gave a substantial part of his salary to fund the group's operations.

The number of these meetings seemed endless and appeared to accomplish little on the ground. Part of the trouble was due to the kaleidoscopic nature of the bureaucracy responsible for attending to indigenous peoples, which included agencies as diverse as the Ministry of Agriculture and Water Resources (Secretaría de Agricultura y Recursos Hidráulicos, or SARH), the Ministry of Planning, Budget, and Urban Development, the Ministry of Communications and Transportation, the State Health Service, the Ministry of Fisheries, and the National Solidarity Program (Programa Nacional de Solidaridad, or PRONASOL), the federal government's umbrella program for development coordinated by SEDESOL. Although there was coordination among the agencies and each was responsible for a separate aspect of community development, there was also enough overlap to confuse responsibilities. Thus one agency was in charge of building preschools; another in charge of building primary and secondary schools. One agency was in charge of road maintenance in one region, another in another, and PRONASOL took charge in yet other cases.

In one meeting, the state branch of SARH reported that it had received fifty-one solicitations for support that required the participation of four different government agencies. Each of these solicitations needed community approval and technical studies completed that would confirm project viability, and communities would need to contact yet another agency to fund these studies ("Minuta de acuerdos" 1993). Meanwhile, community petitions for services such as health centers were held up because they had been filed incorrectly. And the council had to draw up technical proposals for community electrification on its own since the Federal Electricity Commission had neither money nor technicians to do this work.

"Give Me What Belongs to Me": Promises Deferred

The council's frustration with a situation in which the group had achieved some measure of success as an official "interlocutor" without then being able to move the government toward concrete action finally became intolerable. At eight in the morning of 30 August 1993, the directors and more than 150 members of Guerrero Council took over the INI's central offices in Mexico City, locking out workers who arrived later that day and paralyzing the agency's regular operations. The building was finally "liberated" at 6:30 that evening when the council left ("Minuta de la reunión" 1993). For those ten and a half hours, the council aired its grievances and made more demands on the government, while INI officials expressed anger and bewilderment, insisting that the council follow proper procedures. The council's takeover and heated words demonstrated the group's strong sense of entitlement to services promised but always deferred; promises of a revolution long left incomplete but not, as result, without rhetorical force. My source for the following discussion is the candid INI record of the meeting ("Minuta de la reunión" 1993) that took place during the takeover between the council's directors and INI officials, including Guillermo Espinosa Velasco, the director general himself.

What is most remarkable about this meeting is the degree to which the council and the INI failed to understand each other. Martín Equihua informed the INI that the takeover was the result of the lack of response by federal and state agencies to the demands presented to President Salinas on 13 October 1992. The council's demands that day in August 1993, Equihua said, were for the government to fund the group's upcoming congress and to fulfill the promises it had made to them in 1992. They wanted to meet with the governor of Guerrero and with the heads of the all the agencies in charge of development. They also wanted to discuss the establishment of a special fund for indigenous peoples in Guerrero. Marcelino Díaz de Jesús expressed his frustration that even simple requests for an ordinary typewriter were not heard, and another director said that Guerrero's indigenous communities "have waited a long time, that the years pass and they don't have roads, that there aren't resources for social services, that they are tired of [empty] promises, and that they [the agencies] should abide by the President's word" ("Minuta de la reunión" 1993, 2).

Throughout the meeting, the council's directors brought up "new" demands that were outside of the 1992 agreement they had come to discuss, something that INI Director General Espinosa Velasco obviously found quite irritating. Equihua began the meeting by summarizing the projects currently in progress, stressing that the council had exhausted its appeals to all the government agencies in charge. When an INI official then read out loud the agreement reached with President Salinas and the advances made since that meeting, the council's directors told him to stop; they knew that document all too well and that was not why they were there. After admitting that they had continued to add new demands, making it appear that nothing had advanced, Pedro de Jesús Alejandro added that "government authorities have no sensitivity toward the demands of indignous peoples and there is discrimination and a paternalist attitude" ("Minuta de la reunión" 1993, 3). Roque Nava emphasized that bringing up these additional demands was justified because they had been backlogged for decades, that a dam in Chilapa had still not been completed because the community needed a geologist and technicians. The INI director general responded by insisting that the council not continue to discuss added demands that were not part of the original agreement. In response, Julieta asked that a schoolhouse be built in Citlaltepetl, while Ismael asked that the road between San Miguel Tecuixiapan and San Francisco Ozomatlán be completed. Espinosa Velasco insisted that they stop adding demands "since, this way, the agreements with different agencies are not consolidated, and there is the complaint that in each meeting different petitions are presented" ("Minuta de la reunión" 1993, 4).

For the INI, the council's additional demands far exceeded the scope of the meeting. For the council, they were statements of the facts of indigenous lives that the INI needed to address. The meeting minutes read like tragicomedy, with the council presenting one excessive concrete demand after the other and Espinosa Velasco repeatedly insisting (with increasing impatience) that they needed to present "concrete proposals" and "concrete documents." To which Isaac responded that Zacapexco and Ahuehuetic, two of the poorest towns in Guerrero, needed gas-powered corn mills. At the beginning of the discussion, Mauro asserted that "the people who have taken possession of the INI building are likely to do anything because the instructions of President Salinas de Gortari are not being carried out" ("Minuta de la reunión" 1993, 2). Espinosa Velasco repeatedly asked the council members why they continued to hold the INI hostage when it was clear, in his view, the INI was negotiating with them in good faith. The takeover was necessary, said the council members, as an act of strength—not to mention as a demonstration of the group's level of frustration, something Espinosa Velasco could not either understand or admit. Official insistence on following proper, institutional procedures blocked real social change since groups like the council were constantly in meetings with one agency or another, chasing paper along a particular trail. On the other hand, when the president or the governor or even the INI director general personally met with council members, the ritual of these meetings worked to strengthen the official's authority in a political system structured by hierarchy and deference.

Throughout the INI takeover meeting, council directors asked for more flexibility with normative rules, so that their proposals might be accepted without necessarily complying with the INI's requirements. Director General Espinosa Velasco responded to these requests by repeating that the institute was willing to help with their demands by interceding with the various agencies, "but always under the operative and normative scheme of the Institute because it is not possible to give exceptional treatment to some indigenous peoples to the detriment of others" ("Minuta de la reunión" 1993, 2). Nevertheless, and in the very next sentence, Espinosa Velasco agreed to give the council 30,000 pesos for its congress. He also personally set up a meeting between the council, the governor of Guerrero, and the heads of six different agencies, to be held in Chilpancingo upon the council's return.

The takeover had achieved something that could not have been achieved by following proper institutional procedures. Luis Roniger (1994) suggests that a patron-client relationship can be understood as a "type of representative democracy."[8] So long as they are basically reciprocal and mutually beneficial, patron-client exchanges can allow individuals to make decisions and can "reconcile public and private authority and formal and informal rules of the game" (Roniger 1994, 10). The INI benefited from this exchange when the council acknowledged, through the takeover, that the institute was important to indigenous peoples. The council's direct appeal legitimated the INI, which could be considered especially welcome for the federal government in a historical moment when criticism of the government was widespread. The council was able to secure resources it needed and its own importance as a client and broker was acknowledged.

More important, however, was the symbolic identification established between the state and the council when services and resources were provided (Günes-Ayata 1994, 23). Like populism, clientelism works to smooth over the contradictions inherent in an unequal relationship using a rhetoric of solidarity and "an ideological emphasis on the voluntary nature of the attachment" (Roniger 1994, 4). Clientelist exchanges may provide those subordinated with a little more than they previously had—and even with a sense of some autonomy—while leaving them excluded politically and economically from the benefits provided by the government and the economy. Ironically, the most insidious thing about clientelism is the hope it generates, the "feeling of being protected, of being able to depend on some 'patron,' be it an individual or an organization" (Günes-Ayata 1994, 22). However rarely it improves indigenous lives, the bureaucratic and personalistic "anti-politics and hope-generating machine" can be seen to do the important work of keeping the poor in their place (Ferguson 1990; Nuijten 2003). Thus, even though the council gained a little through its

---

8. Others would argue that clientelism is the opposite of constitutional, representative democracy and that it contradicts the logic of public accountability and the protection of individual and collective liabilities and rights. In practice, most democratic political systems comprise some combination of this constitutional ideal and a clientelist reality, which is what Roniger suggests when he refers to clientelism as a "type of representative democracy."

personal appeal to Espinosa Velasco, this only set the group up for the next round of appeals that would last the rest of the decade. Each time, the council would attempt to hold authorities to their promises and to win better, long-term concessions, and each time its attempts would be stymied, sometimes through government inaction, sometimes through violence. The council's leaders well understood the group's dilemma, as their official history notes:

> Thanks to a tradition of organizing in the peasant sector, which had the most influence on the organizing process before the rise of the Indian movement, [the council] used both pressure and negotiation to obtain resources and services from the government because this marked the strategy for consolidating production autonomy and food self-sufficiency. However, this worked against political projects because most of the time we fell into the dynamic of clientelist processes. Besides, getting [financial] resources instead of political rights has been easier thanks to the same organizational trajectory of an important group of leaders, whose actions have been oriented toward obtaining resources or services. *For this reason, the council found itself caught up in the inertia of prioritizing public works, submitting paperwork, and soliciting services as an intermediary and not as the political interlocutor for the communities.* (Consejo Guerrerense 2001, 63; emphasis added)

Indian Patriots

The council's relationship with the government did not change much after 1 January 1994, when the Zapatista National Liberation Army (EZLN) led an armed uprising of indigenous campesinos in the southeastern state of Chiapas. What change there was largely came in the form of an increased visibility for all indigenous groups in Mexico, which they took advantage of in March 1994, for example, by marching en masse to Mexico City to meet with President Salinas.[9] Although the council took up the EZLN's cause, it did not support its violent means and in fact used the EZLN armed

---

9. Although important for gaining visibility, involving community members, and legitimating the movement, these marches drained the energies of the council's leadership: "The council's directors were consumed with treating the sick, with food needs, and money for gasoline . . . as a result, the negotiations [with the government] stalled since the only priority was to solve the urgent needs of the marchers" (Consejo Guerrerense 2001, 62).

uprising as a foil to legitimize the council's peaceful pursuit of justice for indigenous peoples. The council had always proclaimed its respect for the law, but its words meant something different in a situation of armed conflict with an indigenous guerrilla group. Still, the council's words did not protect it. On 14 September 1994, as its directors and more than one hundred community members were marching in central Chilpancingo to demand the release of government funds, mounted riot police surrounded the marchers, running their horses into the crowd, hitting people with their clubs, and kicking them with their spurs. The attack left up to fifty people injured, some severely (Monge 1995).[10] Even the council's obvious signs of patriotism could not protect them: "They fell on us savagely, even as we [were] singing our National Anthem with our brass bands, and raising, as a last resort, our Mexican Flag" ("Declaración del Consejo," n.d.). After all of the council's protests in the capital that had proceeded without incident, this explosion of police violence was a reminder that the government was edgier than usual in the aftermath of the Zapatista uprising. In response, the council would continue to be very clear that it worked within the law, and it demanded that the government work within the law, too.

The council's leaders consistently made patriotic references to the citizenship rights held by all Mexicans, as did "Roberto" when I interviewed him on 27 January 2000:

> *Roberto:* We know we are going to have to put on demonstrations to extract an agreement. The government doesn't want to make it easy. And we aren't used to asking for charity from the government. We are . . . we are accustomed to restoring and demanding the dignity of our grandparents. Many of our grandparents died, in a very dignified way. They preferred to die before being subjugated to the Spanish yoke [or] the Yanqui yoke. . . .
>
> When we ask for resources, they always tell us, "There isn't anything." They give us the runaround, until we demonstrate. For example, in 1999 the governor had authorized the release of 2,750,000 pesos. And they didn't want to free this until we did. . . . We blocked a street behind the Capitol to demand that the resources be handed over immediately.

---

10. The major in command of the riot police was never prosecuted for this attack, and he turned up several months later as the officer in command of forces that massacred peasants at Aguas Blancas in June 1995.

> *Rebecca:* And they did it.
>
> *Roberto:* And they did it. And that very day. And the checks were ready, they had already been written. It was just [their] whim. And we put on a good demonstration. And, really, the proof of this is that the things we get, that the communities get, the organization gets, are not [because we say,] "Give me, please." No. Give me what belongs to me, because the public budget for us in this country is ours, it's the people's. It belongs to the whole population.

This sentiment was echoed by the council in a letter to the editor of the newspaper *La Jornada* (Mexico City) on 15 March 1994: "We went [to Mexico City] to exercise our constitutional rights to public assembly and free expression. We went with the Constitution in our hand and our feet solidly placed on the asphalt." This is an appeal to what Carlos Vélez-Ibañez (1983, 21) calls the myth of "national integration" that expresses the myth of universal access to the state and integration into the nation: "The central myth in Mexico that underlies all formal sectors is the proposition that everybody in a highly stratified and hierarchical system has equal access to economic resources or is represented politically, regardless of status." The council's leadership was well aware that the group was a client of the government in an asymmetrical relationship and they knew, as a result, that the myth of universalism was only that, a myth obscuring the reality of their continuing marginalization. That they continued to make appeals on the basis of this myth testifies to the power of postrevolutionary nationalism to shape political discourse even—and especially—in a neoliberal age of the spun-off, privatized nation-state.[11]

And yet there is more to this situation than the hegemony of a particular ideology. For the council's members, leaders included, approached the government with a sense of their own empowerment, their own entitlement. As "José," a council director, told me on 24 January 2000, the INI "began because indigenous peoples were being harmed: 'those poor Indians.' And then it decided what indigenous communities needed and should have. This is indigenista policy. The Guerrero Council is an example of an 'indigenous policy,' in which indigenous peoples decide for themselves what they need and how they will carry out their own policies." "Isidro" echoed this idea when I asked him what "autonomy" meant to

---

11. The connection between postrevolutionary nationalism and neoliberalism is discussed in greater detail in chapter 4.

him. He was one of the leaders of an organization of Nahua towns close to Chilapa that came together in 1999 to form an asociación civil called "Seojtli Llankuik" (New Path). For Isidro, interviewed on 10 April 2000, "autonomy is deciding for yourself what you want to do, as an individual, as a community, and not doing what others, like political parties, tell you to do." This sense of autonomy and power has been crucial to the mobilization of indigenous peoples long subject to the whims of government at all levels. As we will see in chapter 4, the government would use this same language—of self-determination and self-reliance—to withdraw even further from its responsibility toward the citizenry. In other words, the council's populist strategy, openly encouraged by the state, could only fail.

Communities and the Council: Meeting Local Needs

From 1995 to 2000, the Guerrero Council continued to act as a client and a broker. Important new regional movements for autonomy that were connected to the council got started in 1995, such as a community police and justice system in San Luis Acatlán and the declaration of an "autonomous" municipality in Rancho Nuevo de la Democracia (discussed below).[12] But the group's core work in Chilpancingo—getting government moneys to the communities that needed them—remained unchanged. In this respect, the EZLN's militant strategy had no effect on the group whatsoever. As the Zapatistas increasingly promoted a version of autonomy radically in opposition to the state and federal governments, rejecting government support, the council continued to mobilize its members to press the government to fulfill its obligations to them. What did members of the council think of this work? Documents, meetings I attended, and conversations I had with individuals suggest that community members had a

---

12. The Community Police (Policía Comunitaria) is based in the municipality of San Luis Acatlán, but includes communities from the municipality of Malinaltepec; these are mostly Tlapaneco and Mixteco, though there are Nahuas here, too (there are Nahuas everywhere in Guerrero, actually, thanks to the Mexican and then Spanish colonization of the region). For the Community Police, which is a regional indigenous justice system based on the reeducation and reintegration of criminals into their communities, the overwhelming issue was the violence that the State of Guerrero did nothing to stop, and that in many cases it actually incited. Banditry was regular and rampant; when the municipal and state governments did not respond to repeated community requests for public security, the communities responded by forming their own regional police force and justice system in 1995 (Gutiérrez 1997; field notes, 31 May 2000). The Community Police continues to operate in the region and includes more communities every year despite hostility from the Mexican army and the state police. For a detailed discussion of the Policía Comunitaria, see Johnson 2005, 2007.

pragmatic approach to organizing and to autonomy that was focused much more on concrete local issues than on the nation or nationalism.

A report written by the Independent Peasant Organization of Indigenous Communities (Organización Campesina Independiente de Comunidades Indígenas, or OCICI), a member of the council based in the predominantly Nahua Chilapa region, sheds light on how members viewed the council's work of shuttling back and forth between presidents and governors and agencies. The report focuses on the marches to Mexico City, beginning in 1992 and ending with the hunger strike in 1994, but also mentions the rallies, the council's state assemblies, and the police brutality suffered in September 1994. Even though the OCICI's council members were "tired of coming and going to government offices carrying papers and more papers, so that they would give us a concrete response to our petitions for drinking water, the opening and maintenance of roads, community electrification, construction of town halls, municipal fields, brass bands, and irrigation canals for productive projects," they did it over and over again ("Balance del Primer Informe" n.d.). The report concludes this fatiguing list of interminable bureaucratic procedures and shocking violence on a note of triumph, by proclaiming that "this is how we managed to get our demands met; the infrastructure projects and the services that our towns now have, made possible through the work of the Guerrero Council 500 Years of Indigenous Resistance, [through] blood, sweat, and tears. It wasn't easy! But we did it!" Given the basic subsistence and survival needs of many indigenous communities and given the government's long history of neglect in the countryside, the OCICI's feeling of triumph—even after all the runaround—makes sense. This was the first time they had seen any kind of improvement in their towns.

One day while at the council's offices in Chilpancingo, I had occasion to witness how the council could ease, without removing, the onerous difficulty peasants had navigating a complicated bureaucracy to get projects completed at home. I could see how, despite its obviously vulnerable position as client of and broker for the government, forced to "carry papers and more papers," the council really *worked* for the people. Two Tlapaneco men had arrived from the colonia Las Palmas in the town of Totomixtlahuaca, about nine hours' drive away in the municipality of Tlacoapa, to present an accounting for a project they had completed with money the council had secured from the state. Accompanied by "Néstor," a council director (also Tlapaneco), we all went to the state government offices, where a woman with a reputation for being strict, Néstor informed me, reviewed the Las Palmas paperwork. One of the problems for communities under state government review is the state's reluctance to accept the receipts the communities present for materials they have used because such receipts are not bills, or *facturas,* official documents used only by certain licensed businesses (and there are not many of these in remote rural areas). Communities must also have all signatures and fingerprints in order. It turned out that there were two or three sets missing from the salary reporting forms. Worse still, the state government had in its records that the project was related to road improvement, when, in fact, the community had used the funds to bring piped water to their homes. Néstor checked his own records and saw that the funds had been issued explicitly for roadwork.

Las Palmas had proposed the road improvement project a year earlier, in February, during the dry season, but had not received the money until half a year later, when it was already raining. Not able to work on the road when it was under water, they decided to use the money to put in pipes to carry water, for the first time ever, to their homes—and there was a great deal of water to pipe during the rainy season. Not being as flexible as Las Palmas, the state was not going to accept this situation. The problem with the signatures and fingerprints could be solved easily, but Néstor and the men decided that what they needed to do was "prove" somehow that Las Palmas had really used the state's money to improve a road.

Coincidentally, in the council's office that same day was another man who was in Chilpancingo to give an accounting of his community's project, which happened to be for road improvement. He had photos. Could the men from Las Palmas buy his photos from him? The man looked nervous. What if he needed them to show the government how his community had used the money? Néstor told him that since he had the negatives, he could develop more photos here in Chilpancingo, and they would give him money to do this. But the man did not understand how he could do this, or he just did not want to give up his photos, and he refused to hand them over. As a result, the men from Las Palmas had to return home, get everyone organized to start work on the road, find someone with a camera to take their photo, and then come back to Chilpancingo to hand in their "revised" documents to the state. It was going to cost them more time and money but in the end it *would* work out for Las Palmas and for the council. Without Néstor to shepherd their case through the appropriate office, speaking and reading Spanish fluently and knowing how the process worked, Las Palmas would probably not have been able to get a second chance to revise its paperwork. More important, the community would never have received the funding it did to complete its piped water project in the first place.

It is this kind of practical, on-the-ground work that drew communities to the council and kept them there. Coming from the same kind of communities that needed projects completed, Néstor and other directors like him traveled the indigenous regions of Guerrero to tell people how the council could benefit their towns. And individuals from the towns traveled to Chilpancingo to see what kind of help they might receive for a pressing need. "Hermina," for example, had come from Metlapilapa, also in the municipality of Tlacoapa, to give an accounting of moneys spent on a stove project. She showed me photos of the adobe stoves, which men in the community had learned to make after attending a workshop in San Luis Acatlán. Sixteen families now had these new, closed stoves with flues for smoke and places for a pot and a *comal* (cast-iron griddle) to cook tortillas—a real improvement on the typical arrangement of three rocks over an open fire.

When, on 25 January 2000, I asked Hermina how she had applied for funds for this project, she told me about how her husband had fallen down a hill—and almost died, in fact. He had to be hospitalized in Ayutla for two months; the hospital bills had totaled 3,000 pesos (about 300 dollars), an astronomical sum for most rural Mexicans. Fortunately, her husband had always helped out "the Party," so they went to Chilpancingo to see the Party (she was referring to the council itself) and ask for money to pay his bills. They met with Néstor, who told him the council could not get money for him as an individual, but they could get money for his community. Why didn't he solicit moneys for a canal irrigation project, and why didn't she solicit a stove-making project? They followed Néstor's advice. Soon after their return home, they received a letter from Néstor on council letterhead requesting their presence to pick up the checks for their projects. They had initially come to Chilpancingo asking for 3,000 pesos for one man, and they left with 42,000 pesos for an entire community. As a result, said Hermina, her entire community "was now with *this* Party."

There are several related things going on here. Community members understood the close relationship the council had with the state government, which led them to consider the group a political party. They did so not just because the council appeared to bestow its largesse on loyal members, just as any political party would, but because several prominent council directors openly supported and represented political parties like the PRD and the PRT. From town leadership to municipal presidents to federal congressmen, council directors were always visibly connected to political parties. Their active participation in the political system contrasted strongly with the EZLN's refusal to engage the government on these terms based on the argument that the entire system was corrupt. Their participation in party politics was further evidence of how much the council leadership differed from the grassroots, *la base*.[13] It also reflected and reinforced the populist claims they made on the government, the appeals to the myth of national integration, since they were engaged in the same system of power. Community members who were not council directors were generally more concerned about the viability of their pueblo and its customs than they were with the nationalist and populist claims made by the leadership based in Chilpancingo. But by no means were community members limited in their vision by the pueblo's boundaries.

Seojtli Llankuik had participated in the council since 1999 to get projects completed, though individual communities benefited earlier from their participation. Cuamanotepec, for example, was able to build a basketball court in 1994 and received electrification in 1995, thanks to support from the council.[14] At Isidro's invitation, I attended a meeting of Seojtli Llankuik on 7 February 2000, where I heard about the issues these Nahua communities considered most pressing and saw what they called "autonomía" in action. High on their list of priorities was the restoration of their culture and customs, especially the *bandas de viento* (brass bands) and dances.[15] The bands were expensive to equip, dancers needed costumes, and for many years these cultural expressions had not existed. The community members at this meeting also spoke of the importance of continuing to put on fiestas and make offerings at hilltops to honor and propitiate both Catholic saints and the natural forces their tradition recognized. There was a long and impassioned discussion of these communities' shared history, which they recognized as being at least 500 years old, and of how that history united all of them and should *keep* them united to benefit them

---

13. Since 2000, however, community members who had participated in the council but not in politics have become active in mainstream parties and elections as candidates, a trend that appears to be spreading. Some of the implications of this new trend are discussed in the conclusion to this volume.

14. Fourteen communities participate in Seojtli Llankuik. All are satellite communities (*anexos*) of a larger, "head" community (*cabecera*), San Jeronimo Palantla, from which families left to settle its outlying lands.

15. Participants at the 7 February 2000 meeting of Seojtli Llankuik spoke Nahuatl and also Spanish, so that I could understand. Isidro acted as my Nahuatl translator, too. The *bandas* and *danzas* traditions are shared by Guerrero's four ethnic groups, and each group considers these to be *indigenous* traditions, which they are, though in their origins there is a good deal of European tradition, too. This is especially true for the dance of the Moors and Christians (*danza de los moros y cristianos*) and the dance of the twelve friars (*danza de los doce frailes*), both of which are popular in indigenous towns, but have Spanish origins.

The community projects in and around Cuamanotepec include a town hall, health center, school, basketball court, church, and water tanks.

all. Their shared culture and history formed the basis for Seojtli Llankuik's political work, pressuring the municipal government to make funds available for their projects and participating in the Guerrero Council, "the mother of all the organizations."

It was at this point that the meeting shifted from the poetic language the participants used to discuss their past and their customs to the concrete language of bureaucracy and forms, as Isidro spoke of the various requirements each community needed to fulfill in order to solicit funding. He reminded them how important it was to know and follow bureaucratic procedures; that this knowledge was as much about their rights as about the projects the communities wanted completed. Isidro was an ambitious man: in a later conversation, on 10 April 2000, he told me that he hoped to increase the size of Seojtli Llankuik "little by little," so that in ten years, he guessed, it would be strong and represent most of the Chilapa region.

The logic of this kind of regional organization, based as it is on the shared strength of communities to confront a distant and unresponsive municipal government, often leads to the conclusion that what indigenous peoples need are their own municipalities. This demand dates back to the

The demand for new indigenous municipalities at the Intercultural Encounter (Encuentro Intercultural) march in Chilpancingo, April 2000.

colonial period, when different communities vied for cabecera status to be in charge of their administrative affairs and to avoid paying tribute as subordinate towns (Lockhart 1992; Gibson 1964).[16] In her public lecture at Chilapancingo on 10 February 2000, Danièle Dehouve, a French ethnohistorian who had been working in Guerrero since 1967, drew an interesting parallel between the contemporary indigenous demand for re-municipalization and the redefinition of territory that took place in Guerrero in the eighteenth century, when many indigenous towns first petitioned to become cabeceras. Both are evidence of a long-term desire to reach beyond the pueblo to connect to a larger and more powerful political space.[17]

---

16. A cabecera in colonial times was roughly equivalent to a municipal seat now, though there were many more cabeceras then than there are municipal seats today. As with San Jeronimo Palantla, however, communities still remember the colonial cabecera, and it continues to have cultural and political relevance.

17. Dehouve (2001, 289–91) connects this desire to be part of a larger, more powerful political entity to the demise of the anthropological myth of the stable, homogeneous community: "The administrative units that appear in the territorial division of the state correspond to the highest level of development of the collective interest. In effect, a small town (*comisaría*) is the result of the action of numerous subterranean groups in cooperation; as they build a school, participate in cargos, and build a chapel, the men take part in a collective action whose goal is the recognition as an official administrative category. . . . In this sense, the existence of an administrative unit is the manifestation of a complex of interests that come together to reach a collective goal. Its disappearance or change of form manifests, in turn, the evolution of the interest groups and the cooperation that sustained them. . . . An administrative unit, at any moment of its development, is a theater for the expression

The issue of new municipalities dominated community discussions during the council's "Intercultural Encounter" (Encuentro Intercultural), held in Chilpancingo in April 2000. "Librado," whom I had first met in February, was attending as a delegate from Seojtli Llankuik. On 9 April, he told me that those gathered in the Nahua tent had talked about the creation of new municipios because "municipal presidents don't follow through on what they say they will do." His community had been waiting for three years for the municipality to build a road, and so far only one kilometer (less than two-thirds of a mile) had been completed. Librado showed me the paper and the card the municipal engineer had signed (three different times), along with the accompanying signatures and fingerprints of community members in charge of the project—all as proof of the community's responsibility and the municipality's lack of responsibility. Communities wanted more responsive governments and were talking about forming a new municipality for *every* Communal Lands Commission (Comisaría de Bienes Comunales), each of which is typically located in an old cabecera.

Creating Order Out of Disorder

> The biggest lesson we learn from rural organizations in [Guerrero] is that it is possible to construct medium- and large-scale social development projects that go beyond the domestic and community level. Despite the setbacks and losses, the actions of Guerrero's peasants prove that the "economy of the subject" continues to be a shared Arcadia.
>
> —ARMANDO BARTRA, *Los herederos de Zapata* (2000)

For many council members, the central problem was that the municipal governments then in place did not attend to indigenous communities, and that, if or when they did pay attention, it was only briefly, just before an election. Worse still, these governments were often in the hands of caciques who ruled despotically with the blessing of the state government. To demonstrate efforts to build community governance that are often at odds with established structures of state government, this section recounts the findings of three trips I took to different regions of Guerrero. The first trip was to Apetzuca, a Tlapaneco community in the municipality of Acatepec, established in 1993 after decades of bloody conflict between neighbors. It is about a six-hour drive east of Chilpancingo high in the mountains, at an

---

of opposing forces. . . . In this process, the new localities as well as the old ones change constantly in their form and membership. Old and new form a system, not a collection of independent entities."

altitude of 3,200 meters (about 10,500 feet), where farmers grow corn and opium poppies on incredibly steep inclines. The second was to Rancho Nuevo de la Democracia, the mostly Mixteco "municipality in rebellion" on the Costa Chica near the border with Oaxaca. And the third trip was to Totomixtlahuaca, a large town of mixed ethnicity in the municipality of Tlacoapa, deep in the Sierra de Malinaltepec, about a five-hour drive south of the city of Tlapa.

The politics of indigenous regions cannot be explained—as the government would like to explain them—solely as leftist agitation, since "in this process the decision by indigenous communities to look for an option distinct from what the PRI represents is of fundamental importance" (Flores Félix 1998b, 124). Moreover, most rural conflicts have long histories that often involve interethnic enmity, competition for land, corruption by authorities, religious intolerance, or some combination of these. Thus, for example, in the Montaña municipality of Copanatoyac, a minority of Nahuas—descendants of the original Aztec colonizers—have long held power (as members of the PRI) in the midst of a majority of Mixtecos.[18] The Nahuas live in the municipal seat and control the party directorships of the PRI and PRD, which has given them direct access to greater economic and political resources. This status quo was first challenged in the 1990s, when Mixtecos who had been active in the Communist Party of Mexico (PCM) in the 1970s and now were in the PRD became local representatives of the Guerrero Council and succeeded in bringing in government

18. Politics and culture have always been intimately connected: "As the people in power, [the Nahuas] reproduce the process of domination of the peoples that live in the region, which began with the expansion of the Aztec Empire under Tizoc in 1487. This domination was endorsed by the Spaniards and reinforced by the current political system based on the strict centralization of power that rewards loyal local representatives.... According to this logic, today in the majority of indigenous regions it goes against an unwritten law for an inhabitant of a community outside of the municipal seat to govern the municipality, especially if the community is inferior to the one in power, as is the case of the Mixtecos whose access to the government of Copanatoyac was vetoed for a long time" (Flores Félix 1998b, 107). Abel Barrera, director of Tlachinollan, a highly respected human rights organization based in Tlapa, told me on 4 April 2000 that almost every indigenous community in the Montaña region is divided between the PRI and PRD, each bloc with its own teacher, school, and comisario in separate buildings. "Indigenous teachers are deeply involved in this process of fomenting divisions. For the PRI, the traditional system of cargos worked and works fine because the community elders followed party leaders, who brought certain benefits, of course. In its attempt to take power from the PRI, the PRD has organized a defamation campaign against the traditional system saying that this system is of the PRI. These are indigenous teachers, PRD, who are a new generation seeking power for themselves and for the party and attempting to destroy the indigenous community's social fabric. In our teacher training program at the UPN [Universidad Pedagógica Nacional, in Tlapa], we are trying to raise the consciousness of PRD teachers about the importance of indigenous culture, but it isn't easy!"

funds for development projects. As a result, "Mixteco communities, by means of their assemblies, ordered their authorities to tell the local leader of the Guerrero Council that they had decided he should be their next municipal president" (Flores Félix 1998b, 107). He ended up winning the post in 1996, though his tenure was not without conflict. Mixtecos living in Ocoapa, the second most important community in the municipality, and in Potoichán, the second most important community among Mixtecos, were upset when he did not fulfill their demand to separate from Copanatoyac and form their own municipality.[19]

From among the poorest in Mexico, five new municipalities have been created in Guerrero since 2001, three of which are predominantly indigenous. Of these three, Cochoapa el Grande is now the poorest municipality, while José Joaquín de Herrera, in ninth place, and Iliatenco follow close behind.[20] The fission of existing municipalities tells us that there are two complementary, if sometimes contradictory, political processes going on at the same time in indigenous regions. On the one hand, indigenous communities are constantly "working out more precise referents that define their social group through the demarcation of territories like the community or the municipality" (Flores Félix 1998b, 129), a highly centrifugal process that privileges the local. On the other hand, as the case of the Guerrero Council or Zanzekan Tinemi in Chilapa reveals, many indigenous communities are constantly seeking to build alliances across community and municipal boundaries that can support community life and expand their members' options for a better future in the face of a world dominated by capricious global markets for their goods and labor.[21] Speaking with me on 20 November 1999, José Leonor Sánchez Capistrano described these two processes in terms of autonomy and self-determination: "Autonomy exists already in our pueblos, our local governments practice autonomy daily. What we're missing is self-determination. This is bigger than autonomy; it's a political force that goes beyond our pueblos, the political strength to speak [directly to] the government. Self-determination is something that has yet to be recognized by [higher] governments, but autonomy is our daily practice." This potentially complementary set of

---

19. Both Ocoapa and Potoichán were cabeceras in the colonial period and received tribute from their subject towns, a power Ocoapa retains in the present day, and which it clearly wants recognized in Mexican law (Flores Félix 1998b, 110).

20. See http://www.secof.guerrero.gob.mx/?P=readart&ArtOrder=ReadArt&Article=5/ (accessed 15 August 2008).

21. Abel Barrera suggested to me on 4 April 2000 that this desire to reach out beyond the pueblo also helps to account for the major presence of political parties in indigenous communities.

processes (local autonomy with political self-determination) is reflected in the epigraph to this section. Armando Bartra (2000, 427) goes on to argue that "socially successful" peasant organizations in Guerrero share a common project—an economy of the subject—that works contrary to the economy of the market because their project "preserves and stimulates economic activities, perhaps not competitive within an international context, but publicly useful when it comes to satisfying the multitude of legitimate, if unprofitable, necessities." As discussed below, indigenous communities—hardly stable and never static—are always searching for ways to satisfy the multitude of their economic, social, and political needs.

I went to Apetzuca at the invitation of Néstor, Roberto, and Pablo, all council directors who were representing more the Revolutionary Labor Party (Partido Revolucionario del Trabajo, or PRT) than the council. Julia, a college student from Malinaltepec, came along, too; she had plans to study in Mexico City one day. Pablo was a protégé of Sabino Estrada Guadalupe, former president of the Alto Balsas municipality of Copalillo, north of Chilpancingo, where the PRT had successfully challenged the PRI in the 1980s, and where Pablo himself had once served as president. Roberto had been in the council since the beginning, thanks to his involvement in the struggle to establish the new municipality in the late 1980s, while Néstor (a friend of Roberto's since childhood) was a sociologist who had worked in the federal government's Popular Cultures Department (Departamento de Culturas Populares) until he joined the council full-time as a director. Also traveling with us was Basilio, a mestizo PRT ideologue from Mexico City who regularly visited his *compañeros* in the council as part of his work to build up the party in areas where it had historically been strong (the PRT had been instrumental in the establishment of Acatepec, but had since lost the presidency of the municipality to the PRI). The council directors were going to Apetzuca to speak with the current PRI municipal president and with local leaders to discuss the creation of a municipal *delegación,* a field office where residents could take care of government business (picking up government-issued checks, getting free meals for children, dealing with legal matters) without having to walk all the way to the main offices in the town of Acatepec. This was a trip focused on making local government more responsive to residents: the PRT would represent these residents, and this would help the party in the area. These men regularly made such trips to bring more people in to the PRT and the council, though it often appeared that the PRT took precedence.

We left Chilpancingo before dawn in a pickup truck on 5 February 2000, according to my field notes, some of us in the cab and the rest of us shivering in the bed of the truck as we climbed into the mountains. Around sunrise, we stopped at a small town to buy *atole* (a hot corn drink) and *memelas* (tortillas with beans) from women carrying baskets of these provisions, which we ate more to warm ourselves than because we were hungry. It was dry and quite cold up that high (between 2,500 and 3,000 meters, or 8,200 and 9,850 feet); the cold was made worse by the lack of a back window in the cab, shot out by someone trying to assassinate the municipal president in Copalillo. As we shared stories about ourselves and where we were from, the tone shifted easily from serious to darkly funny. At one point, the dirt road dipped down into a ravine and Pablo, who was driving, pointed out a stand of trees on our right. This was the place where hundreds of community members had lynched five men back in 1993. Had I heard of it? The photos of the naked men hanging from trees had gone around the world. No, I answered, I had not. "Well," Pablo said, "these communities were so fed up with the robberies, assaults, and rapes committed by these guys that one day they just took justice into their own hands. By the time the police knew what was going on, it was too late. And what were they going to do, arrest the communities?" Laughing, he added, "So, now there aren't any more assaults!"

For years, the communities in this part of the Montaña region had suffered at the hands of bandits protected by their connections to extralocal power; in this case, three of the dead were members of Antorcha Campesina, a right-wing peasant organization based in Puebla and connected to Raúl Salinas de Gortari, brother of the president (Gutiérrez 1998, 36). Appeals to the state police for protection went unheeded—indeed, the police themselves very often perpetrated violence against campesinos.

> With a rope around the neck, the body of a man completely naked is hanging from a tree with few leaves, tall, its trunk about 40 centimeters [16 inches] in diameter. It's almost a meter [3 feet] from his feet to the ground. This is a grove off to the side of a dirt road in a steep region, hills and canyons covered with dry plants, in one of the poorest regions of the Montaña in Guerrero. Behind can be seen trees separated by one or two meters. From the ones closest hang the bodies of another four men, with some parts barely covered by pieces of ragged rope.
>
> To the side, on lower and flatter ground, a crowd observes the hanging bodies, as if they are protecting them. Some people are very close to them, at the foot of the trees next to some rocks. There are hundreds of peasants wearing the hat that is typical of the region.

They remain quiet. It's likely that many of them were at the lynching. The day before, residents of three towns gathered at this place where they had long been terrorized, since this was the site the bandits had used for their activities, and in the last five years there had been robberies, rapes and assassinations. No one had stopped them, until the towns had come together. (Gutiérrez 1998, 330)

In the aftermath of the lynching, police arrested six local authorities even though it was clear that they had not participated in the killings; their "confessions" were taken in Spanish, which none of them spoke well, being mostly monolingual speakers of Tlapaneco. It was universally acknowledged that the communities were the guilty parties but, as Pablo had joked, how could they arrest three communities? The local authorities were later released. The state and federal governments responded by increasing state police and army patrols, but this "has not solved the problem of public insecurity and the conflicts have worsened, because there are more problems now with the abuses of authority committed by the police and the military" (Gutiérrez 1998, 37). The militarization of the countryside in Guerrero has increased substantially over the last several years, officially to combat the growing power of drug cartels.[22] It is indigenous peasants, however, who experience the worst abuses at the hands of these representatives of the state and federal governments: rapes, robberies, and assassinations,

---

22. Because Guerrero now has the distinction of being one of the world's major growers of opium poppies, the drug wars associated more with Mexico's northern border have moved to this southern state. When a former high-ranking state PRI official was publicly gunned down in Acapulco in June 2005 and a "guerrilla army" no one had heard of before claimed responsibility, the rumor was that in fact a drug gang was behind the assassination. At a presentation by the Guerrero Institute for Human Rights on 7 April 2000 in Chilpancingo, Abel Barrera spoke at length about the close connection between drugs and the government. "Drug traffickers are now part of the political structure," he said. "Prosecutors, police, judges, they are all tied up with drug trafficking." The directors of the prisons are also connected to drugs. "What we have here is a mafiacracy where the PRI controls the political, police, and judicial posts that protect the drug trade. And there is a diabolical pact between the army and narcos, where the army protects the local bosses [cacicazgos] involved in drug trafficking by arresting the 'troublemakers' fighting the bosses." Worse still, poor peasants struggling to survive grow poppies, which brings devastating consequences as violence, community conflicts, and arms trafficking increase. "The towns are the most defenseless," Barrera added, "since they can't demand that the army leave. The army uses the presence of drugs as an excuse for being there *and* it participates in the sowing and harvesting of the poppies!" Those opposed to poppy cultivation in their communities are often the victims of threats and assassinations by armed groups of their own neighbors connected to drug production networks (Flores Félix 1998b, 92). The recent increase in public violence related to drug gangs in Guerrero is most likely related to the change in parties at the state capital. The PRD won the governorship and a majority in the state legislature in early 2005, wresting power for the first time ever from the PRI and likely upsetting the delicate balance of power the PRI had established over the years with drug cartels.

the vast majority of these crimes remaining unreported or uninvestigated (Tlachinollan 1998, 1999; Gutiérrez 1998, 75–90).

By the time we arrived in Apetzuca at 10:30 that morning, we discovered that the municipal president had postponed the meeting until the following day and that he had invited the communities himself so that it would be his meeting to hold, not theirs. It was an old story, the capriciousness of local leaders. What could we do? We stayed to talk with Roberto and his friends who had come to meet us, sitting by a sacred site along a stream that the council was working with the INI to protect, and eating a lunch of meat stew and tortillas washed down with Pepsi.[23] It was a gloriously crisp and sunny day, which we all enjoyed, regardless of our disappointment about the postponed meeting. As we descended to Chilpancingo, we went through deep-green pine forests, still relatively plentiful, and looked out over valleys hundreds of feet below. Seeing the fields people tended on perilously steep hillsides subject to constant erosion, I was reminded of the extreme poverty of the place, this "region of refuge," as Aguirre Beltrán put it long ago. Refuge from the Spaniards perhaps, but hardly from privation.

And yet the story of Acatepec was one of success. Since 1906, the communities of this municipality had fought the blatant theft of their lands by neighbors in Zapotitlán Tablas, then the main town in the municipality of the same name, to which they had belonged. Despite repeated appeals to the state and federal governments and despite the legal and well-documented possession of their lands, the people of Acatepec remained for decades at the mercy of the caciques of Zapotitlán Tablas, who had the support of officials in Chilpancingo and Mexico City and had always acted with impunity (Martínez Rescalvo 1991). A new generation of Tlapaneco leaders who came of age in the 1980s—the same generation that Marcos and José Leonor spoke about in Acatlán—organized the communities around Acatepec to petition the state for a new municipality. The time was right—the time of Solidarity and self-determination—and the petition was accepted. This eased some of the problems people have faced over land, and it certainly boosted the leadership of the movement, but it did not solve the basic problem of poverty caused by poor land. And just as this "isolated" region has long been connected to extralocal power, it continues to be subjected to violence perpetrated by the state.

23. It never ceased to amaze me that, no matter how difficult it was to reach a town in these remote regions, I could always count on getting a bottle of either Coca- or Pepsi-Cola (towns appeared to have exclusive contracts with one or the other company's bottlers). Held in high esteem, Coke and Pepsi confer prestige on those able to buy them.

Steep mountain milpas in the Montaña region suffer from the constant erosion of topsoil, which means a constant need for fertilizer. This situation keeps peasant farmers dependent on government subsidies, often controlled by corrupt local officials.

In the municipality of Rancho Nuevo de la Democracia, I encountered similar stories of neglect and abuse by authorities and there, too, the communities had decided to create a new municipality, one "in rebellion," which meant it was not officially recognized; at the time I visited, it encompassed communities from the mostly Mixteco and Amuzgo (and some Nahua) municipalities of Tlacoachistlahuaca, Xochistlahuaca, and Metlantonoc. Suffering from a long list of economic and political grievances, Rancho Nuevo declared its independence in 1995 after the mestizo municipal president of Tlacoachistlahuaca refused to recognize indigenous community leaders elected by community assemblies and imposed his own choices. In 1998, 90 percent of the economically active adults in the Rancho Nuevo region earned no wages, which certainly contributed to its status as the poorest region of Guerrero and therefore of the country (Rodríguez W. 1998, 121). Mestizos dominate politically and economically, holding the best lands and controlling the region's commerce. The declaration of a new "autonomous" municipality in 1995 was initiated by a Mixteco takeover of the municipal offices in Tlacoachistlahuaca that lasted seven months, followed by the unofficial relocation of those offices

Rancho Nuevo de la Democracia meeting, December 1999. Gender differences are manifest: Mixteca women seated on the ground wear "traditional" dress and most typically go without shoes or wear flimsy plastic slippers, while the men are seated on benches at the back and dress more like mestizos—they also wear shoes or sturdy sandals.

to the town of Rancho Nuevo (formerly Rancho Viejo). By 2000, state government harassment—including the arrest of a Mixteco leader—and disputes within the PRD, with which leaders of the Rancho Nuevo movement were affiliated, had divided the leadership of the new municipality.

I had traveled there with a group of council directors who were active in the ANIPA, which hoped to register these communities as new members. The goal of the trip was to introduce community members to the legal instruments that protected them as indigenous peoples so that they would know how to defend themselves in their legally precarious position. Our group included Pedro de Jesús Alejandro, his brother Carlos, Martha Sánchez Néstor, her brother Daniel, Marcelino Díaz de Jésus, Isidro from Seojtli Llankuik, Carmelo from the ANIPA offices in Mexico City, and José, a wealthy accountant from Acatepec who was living in Chilpancingo (he would be elected Acatepec's municipal president in 2002, and Daniel would go there to work as his assistant). On a sultry day in December, we all caravanned in a car and a pickup truck to the Costa Chica. In Ometepec, we stopped at the INI offices and traded the car for one of their pickup trucks; the director of the Indigenous Coordination Center there was an avowed ally of the council's. The rest of the trip took four hours driving in the dark over one of the worst dirt roads I have ever encountered, one that, like many in the Montaña, becomes a river of mud during the four to five months of the rainy season, impassable even for four-wheel drive trucks. In their climb to the mountain valley where Rancho Nuevo was located, our two trucks crawled along at five to ten miles an hour. We passed through one *pueblito* after the other, arriving late that night at a mission run by Ekumene, a Catholic lay organization. The mission had electricity and running water, thanks to the river nearby; both luxuries were especially welcome after the long, hot, and very dusty trip.

Greeting us was Dionisia, a small Mixteca woman in her early twenties with bright, intense eyes, who moved and talked quickly. Her participation in the PRD had won her the respect of community members; she was one of only four women in the council's leadership. With a high school degree and fully bilingual, Dionisia had gone far beyond her local community and then returned better prepared to stir up trouble. Clearly, she relished this role. And just as clearly, she owed her success to her mother, who had encouraged her to run away to get more education. "My father didn't want me to leave the village to study," she told me on 16 May 2000. "*No one* left to study and definitely not a girl!" After completing two years of primary school, she arranged to live with an American nun living in Tlacoachistlahuaca. When the nun and her Mixteca assistant left to missionize in the pueblos, Dionisia stayed home to learn Spanish from the assistant's sister. She went on to San Luis Acatlán to finish high school, worked in Ometepec for a while as a bilingual teacher, and then returned home to find that her mother had died and her father, who had been active in the PRD while she was away, was no longer angry with her. When the local PRD representative to the Congress of Guerrero was looking for a secretary, Dionisia was the only one in Rancho Nuevo who could do the job. She began to visit communities, helping them fund local projects, and she opened two stores with her savings from teaching. Dionisia gained a following, thanks to her visibility and connections, which by then included working with the council, and also to the jailing of a key figure in the autonomy fight. As part of her initiative to raise the consciousness of her neighbors about their legal and political rights, Dionisia had helped bring the ANIPA to Rancho Nuevo. Over two days, we met with community members in the new municipal hall, for which the council had helped Rancho Nuevo obtain state funding, but which, it would emerge during the meetings, was a cause of tension within the community, already divided by intraparty rivalries.

According to my field notes for 4 December 1999, we began the first day of our visit at dawn. Walking toward the municipal hall, I could see we were in a large valley crossed by the slow-moving San Pedro River and dotted with small homes near the river and up the hillsides. Wood smoke rose from the houses, muting the sunlight and turning the scene a blue gray. Cattle grazed a scrubby field lit up with orange marigolds. The beauty of the surrounding countryside contrasted powerfully with the squalor of the community. The smoke drifted up out of windowless, poorly ventilated mud brick houses. People walked barefoot along paths bordered by trash and excrement—human and animal—and many of the younger children had the distended bellies of chronic malnutrition.

The ANIPA had paid local residents to slaughter a cow one day and a pig the next in order to feed all the participants attending the meeting. Several local women worked to prepare huge quantities of stew and tortillas, lending the whole affair a festive tone that first morning and adding to the excitement of registering everyone's name in the ANIPA's roster before the meeting was convened. Present were 180 people from seven communities, the men sitting at the back on benches, the women and some men sitting up front on the dirt floor, all listening intently every time Dionisia translated the proceedings from Spanish to Mixteco. Pedro de Jesús Alejandro began with an overview of the rights indigenous peoples have in domestic and international law, speaking about the fight for autonomy in municipalities and in production projects. "We need to know our political rights," he stressed, "in order to defend ourselves." He also took the time to remind everyone that the Guerrero Council had helped build the municipal hall where they were sitting and that it had worked to get a key leader of the Rancho Nuevo movement out of jail, for which the PRD alone was taking all the credit. But it was clear that people were getting impatient and wanted to talk about corn mills and money for crops, things they needed right then.

It was at this point that a man in a Cleveland Indians cap stood up out of the crowd to express his confusion about the purpose of this meeting. His main concern was with a check the council had given to Dionisia's community to build the municipal hall. "This group [the council] stole the money from the other communities just like what happened before," he said in Spanish, stirring up the crowd and completely shifting the focus of discussion. Another man stood up to express his distress and confusion about funds that Dionisia had given him—20,000 pesos. His community had heard Rancho Nuevo had 100,000 pesos to distribute; when he returned with much less than this larger amount, people in his town accused him of theft. Martha and Pedro jumped in at this point, with Dionisia's assistance, to explain that the council distributed 200,000 pesos (about 20,000 dollars) to each microregion within the council and that this total sum had to be divided among the towns within that region; in Rancho Nuevo, this money was to be shared by seven towns, distributed under the direction of the president of the microregion's committee. Because each town had different projects to fund, however, it could receive more or less than its neighbors, a situation that in a climate of constant suspicion led to conflict and hostility. This president had to show how the money was spent, with his paperwork all in order, to prove to the state government that the council was not simply taking the money without any accountability. Martha spoke forcefully and clearly: "This has not been done. The money from the state now comes in two parts, with one half distributed first, then an accounting must be completed, then the second half is distributed, then a final accounting. The council needs this accounting completed by the different communities so we can release more funding. Otherwise, we can't give out more money. The whole council is going to be in trouble because of this building, because you still haven't shown how the money was spent!"

The real issue was not so much about money as about party politics. Martha was speaking directly to Marcelino Isidro de los Santos, the leader of the Rancho Nuevo movement and a PRD loyalist who had been jailed in

Ometepec. Upon his release, which was won through the combined efforts of the council and the PRD, Marcelino showed no interest in sharing leadership with Dionisia, acting instead to create his own following based on his status in the PRD. The money mattered because the council gave out more than the PRD did, but the conflict over money was really a conflict over local legitimacy, with Marcelino and his friends attempting to link Dionisia and the council with the PRI government. What first appeared to me as confusion about what the council was and what it did was in fact an expression of political reality. That is, what little money enters these communities is almost always tied to some kind of political obligation, to either a cacique, a party, or both. The distribution of funds always implies some kind of political loyalty, even if this loyalty is often coerced. In Rancho Nuevo, it was understood that either you were with Marcelino or you were with Dionisia; there was the PRD and there was the council— even though both were in the same party. In the meantime, the basic problems of a subsistence economy supplemented with migratory work to Michoacán and Sinaloa (much of the town was empty for long periods of the year) remained unaddressed, and the people's needs were largely ignored.

The meeting became more and more heated, with accusations flying and the presence of the ANIPA and its agenda entirely ignored. Finally, the municipal vice president stood up to ask for calm and for an end to the accusations so that the meeting could continue. Several men and women began to cry in shame and remorse that people in the group had said such bad things about Dionisia, and they asked for her and our forgiveness for interrupting the proceedings. Dionisia remained stoic throughout, translating when she had to and never betraying any emotion. She told those gathered that all was well, that it was normal for there to be disagreement, and that she was fine. We were then able to continue.

But all was not well and the community's internal division would persist, eventually weakening the autonomy movement there so that today it no longer exists as such. Party politics were at fault, but more insidious still was the overwhelming poverty of communities desperate to retain whatever meager resources came their way. Under such circumstances—and this is demonstrated in rural communities throughout Guerrero—party rivalries create and exacerbate internal tensions that often end in violence.

I encountered the idea of "Guerrero bronco," Guerrero as an inherently violent place, in my travels throughout the Montaña region. When I went to Totomixtlahuaca ("Toto" for short), it became still clearer to me how violence is just as much the result of the absence as it is of the presence of the government in the lives of *guerrerenses*. Both the absence and presence of the government contribute to a pervasive structural violence that affects every aspect of daily life—even a trip down a dusty rural road (Farmer 2005, 139–59). I quote below from my field notes for 19 April 2000:

> The ride from Tlapa started out all right, crowded and packed into the back of a truck like cattle, sure, but the road was *paved*. Two hours into the trip, however, the pavement gave out and the dusty *terracería* (dirt road) began ... and *how*. I've never been that dusty, inside and out. Cough, cough. There was a pleasant camaraderie among the passengers, all of us joking about our hair and eyebrows and moustaches being white with dust. About an hour and a half before Toto, a truck going back to Tlapa passed us carrying a family and a scary story. Evidently, just up ahead of us in the crossroads a group of robbers had assaulted a couple of trucks and had cut off a man's finger. *And we were going to pass by there.* The news was taken seriously enough that ... in the pueblo of Paraje our driver stopped to inform the local delegation of the Policía Comunitaria [Community Police], but either they were too busy or too scared (opinion was divided among the passengers), and they did not want to accompany us. The Policía Comunitaria patrols these roads regularly, but Toto doesn't participate, which may explain why they declined our invitation. We did have one young guy with a new-looking rifle riding shotgun, however.
>
> Everyone worked fast to hide their money while we were stopped. It was Easter weekend, after all, and hundreds were traveling to Toto's big annual fair in honor of the local saint, both to celebrate the religious holiday and to stock up on all manner of household goods. Several of the passengers were coming home for the holiday and were bringing cash and gifts for family. It was the perfect time to be a bandit. I put my passport and money in a black plastic bag and put this at the bottom of my backpack, keeping 100 pesos plus change in my pocket as bait, hoping this would work. One of my neighbors pulled a Bible out from his bag and started reading. He told me that every time he has prayed to God, he has had his prayers answered. "God protects those who have faith," he said, and I hoped I might be included, too. I was scared, and I still don't feel very safe after all the stories of violence and murder I've heard today. The rule of law is fragile—if it exists at all in this region. There is so much regular robbery and murder that goes unpunished here. No one believes

that jailing or the police are worth anything since the police don't investigate and the criminals are always getting out of jail. So, it is not uncommon for communities to carry out their own justice by trapping and executing criminals themselves. A young woman whose father was brutally tortured and murdered told me that when they went to the police demanding justice, the police told them to bring the corpse to Tlacoapa (the municipal seat) and they would investigate it! And this is pretty typical, apparently. According to the daughter, her father was murdered because he wouldn't sell his nice 9 mm pistol or his burro to this guy who had already been in prison in Acapulco. This was two years ago and the murderer is still her neighbor. I was also told that the truck carrying government checks for families was robbed last week, or so said the police. The money never arrived.

The only phone in town hasn't worked for two months, and they only just now got a replacement, but it hasn't been installed yet. I'm interested in the relationship of the state with indigenous peoples, but I have to ask: Where is the state here? The primary school teacher is supposedly in charge of the phone but hasn't gotten around to doing anything about it. Felícitos says he is teaching his kids to read because they don't learn in the *primaria* here. In communities that participate in the Policía Comunitaria, there is some justice and order but in others there is only a fragile order and little justice. So, where is the state here?

When we had first met in Chilpancingo, Felícitos had invited me to visit his family in Totomixtlahuaca over the Easter weekend. He and a friend had come to the council's offices to complete the accounting for a road project—which had become a piped water project in the months between the planning and execution stages. This was the first (and only) time I traveled without friends, but I was curious about the council's work in Toto, and there was no other way to get there that weekend. I came bearing gifts—toiletries and dried food items mostly, in addition to cigarettes and alcohol for the men—that I was told would be especially welcome in a place with inflated prices. But these gifts were nothing compared to the generosity of my hosts wherever I went.

Felícitos was in his mid-forties and had a large family of eight children, ranging from three or four years old to their early twenties (and married). They all lived in a large, two-room mud brick house with dirt floors and an outdoor kitchen, where food was cooked over three rocks, and wood smoke billowed everywhere. There were two double beds, but most of the children and I slept on cane and *petate* (straw mat) beds laid on top of sawhorses. The home was lit by a lightbulb or two and had a corn mill, a radio, and, of course, piped water; these amenities and the size of the house meant that Felícitos was relatively well off. Not only did he grow corn and beans but he also grew sugarcane, which he processed into *piloncillo,* a hard brown sugar he could sell for a good price when there was no corn or beans to eat. He had also once been elected comisario of Toto's communal lands, testifying to his status in the community. Even though his wife, Susana, worked hard all day cooking and milling (there was a community corn mill in the home) and washing in addition to caring for the children and the chickens, she appeared happy, as did the children and Felícitos. Although the son of a Tlapaneca woman and a Mixteco man, Felicitos spoke only Spanish, but understood a little Tlapaneco. Susana spoke Tlapaneco and Spanish was her second language. Their children spoke only Spanish. "They make fun of Tlapaneco," Susana told me. "'Blah, blah, blah,' they say, and they don't want to learn."

Mixtecos and Tlapanecos and later Nahuas have long lived together, if not always harmoniously, in Totomixtlahuaca (Nahuatl for "bird in the field"). Augustinian friars established an important monastery there in the late 1600s, which rivaled the one in Tlapa and which demonstrated the importance of Toto as a religious and tributary center, even under Mexica domination and likely even earlier (Ramírez Celestino n.d.). This distinction probably reflects the town's blessed location: high up in the Sierra de Malinaltepec in a lush valley irrigated by the Totomixtlahuaca River, where farmers can grow a variety of produce year round.

And yet electricity had only recently been introduced to the town, and the road I had traveled was also relatively new (both introduced within the previous five or six years). Before the road was built, people had had to walk or ride animals to travel anywhere, and the festival market had been much smaller—only three or four stalls, compared to dozens in 2000. Even in 2000, there was a noticeable lack of newspapers or magazines for such a large town. In Totomixtlahuaca, as in other indigenous towns I visited, the leadership was a new generation of men in their twenties and thirties who, like Felícitos, had at least a high school education and who were the first leaders to make more intimate connections with the wider world. Felícitos had attended high school with Roberto, the council director who had gone on to complete some university studies when Felícitos's money had run out. This extralocal personal connection to the council in

Chilpancingo had made a difference for the people in Felícitos's colonia: now, at least, they had clean water to drink. But, in general, Toto was ignored by local and state powers. The night they held a big outdoor dance, for example, the town had to contract police from other municipalities for security. And a bridge that would keep Toto connected to Tlapa during the rainy season was still unfinished a year after construction had begun (Felícitos said the municipal president had taken the money needed to finish it). As a result, when the water rose, trucks could not cross, effectively cutting the town off from the north. This repeated inattention by outside authorities ("Las autoridades no cumplen"—The authorities don't fulfill their obligations—I was often told) made the council and the PRD welcome support options for residents who otherwise would have had no other options at all, short of armed rebellion. Even with the road in place, which certainly helped, people still had to pack themselves into the back of rickety trucks and be driven for hours over roads where they were at risk of toppling down steep mountain cliffs, being robbed, or both. They laughed sardonically at these conditions, but the radical difference in standards between urban and rural areas continues to be outrageous.

"A Point of Equilibrium"

The formation of the Guerrero Council is itself a response to many years of marginalization. As Néstor put it on 27 January 2000, "We know that it is the state's responsibility to provide the resources for development, [but] all the resources it provides go to the municipal government and the municipal governments don't attend to [the people]. And that's why it was necessary to create the Guerrero Council . . . as a point of equilibrium, really." For community members, the group was a reliable broker, "a point of equilibrium," between them and the state. Marcos Matías Alonso, in the epigraph to this chapter, argues that "local village demands are now part of a national demand," yet I found that these demands remained quite distinct. Even though the council's leaders tried hard to act as a bridge to unite them, to bring indigenous peoples visibly into the realm of the nation that had always excluded them from decision-making power, there were always obstacles in the way of this project. Moreover, the council's peasant populist strategy only strengthened the clientelist webs that ensnared it in its relationship to the state and federal governments, making real autonomy impossible. The council's official history laments that a key problem internal to the group was an "ideological inconsistency" that was a result of the variety of political affiliations it represented (Consejo Guerrerense 2001, 61). In fact, the group was united ideologically around a discourse of peasantness tied directly to a populist vision of the nation-state, a vision that had even less basis in reality in a neoliberal moment than it had ever had. Paradoxically, the peasant populist strategy shared by the various organizations within the council led to a disintegration of the movement as a whole, as each group approached the government with its own demands: "Despite the unity and common front of the Indian peoples of Guerrero in the council, the immediate interests of each collective, with its particular culture, its times for action, and its own dynamics for getting resources, meant that each of them pursued their own project to the detriment of unity, to the point that, at times, they were not compatible with the rest" (62).

The centrifugal force of localism within the movement, though closely related to the council's peasant populist strategy, also has to be understood within the larger context of neglect and abuse only touched on above. Even when the council attempted to expand the scope of its action, to act outside of the narrow confines of populism and clientelism as it did through participation in the ANIPA, the immediacy of local concerns sabotaged the leadership's efforts. This is what happened in Rancho Nuevo, and it was evident, too, in the council's takeover of the INI offices in Mexico City, when the litany of local needs overwhelmed whatever dialogue might have been possible between the group and the central government's representative. Roberto described this situation when I spoke with him on 27 January 2000:

> All of this, you can see, isn't easy. . . . It isn't easy to work here as an organization to put all these cases in order, because it gives you a headache, because on one side there is indignation, and on the other the impotence you feel because the [government] agencies don't take responsibility for finding a solution. There are various cases, the case of Narciso, for example. He's also Tlapaneco. He's been arrested and his two children had to stop going to school. One was in second grade, the other in sixth. The boy and the girl had to stop going because their dad is in jail. And the mom is sick. And the other [child] is full of worms, of amoebas, malnourished. Just really awful conditions. And [because of this] we asked for a pardon, because they deserve it. As decent as the life of a high official is in this country, the indigenous deserve equally decent treatment. But this doesn't happen.

In an indigenous peoples movement, then, what comes first, the nation or the village, *la patria o el pueblo?* Or is it possible to take these together into a coherent national strategy that would allow indigenous peoples to intervene at all levels of politics and in a variety of policy decisions that affect all Mexicans? The council's leaders embodied the integration of village and nation; leaders like Martha and Pedro and Marcelino were also able to integrate the transnational level into a cosmopolitan definition of what it means to be an Indian in Mexico. The dire situation in indigenous communities almost guaranteed that these individuals were exceptional, but the real obstacle to the full emergence of indigenous peoples in national life was located in the nation-state itself, an issue discussed in chapter 4.

FOUR

OPPORTUNITIES AND OBSTACLES: CONTEXTUALIZING THE
GUERRERO COUNCIL'S WORK IN THE 1990s

The Guerrero Council gained strength and national presence at a time when the Institutional Revolutionary Party (PRI) was in decline. This was no coincidence. As we saw in chapter 1, the PRI government's withdrawal from the countryside—a result of the party's strong shift to neoliberal economic policies in the 1980s—meant that peasant groups could no longer appeal to the central government for economic assistance as campesinos. Indigenous peasant groups like the council turned to the new, international discourse of indigenous rights that emerged in Mexico in the early 1990s to make economic and political demands on the government. Facilitating this turn was the federal government's adoption of a discourse of rights that provided an unprecedented opportunity for the council. This new discourse was directly connected to neoliberal economics and justified the federal government's withdrawal from the large social assistance programs that had long characterized it as "revolutionary." Under President Salinas, the Mexican state shifted its nationalist message to fit the new economic program, drawing on old images of the Indian and matching them up with a new economy of self-sufficiency and individual choice that nicely complemented the indigenous movement's own emphasis on self-determination and autonomy. The government's new discourse was an explicit affirmation of the popular self-determination the council had made one of its central goals early on. From affirmation to real respect was, of course, not usually the path government officials took when it came to the self-determination of popular groups. Nevertheless, the proliferation of the discourse gave the council a legitimacy it would not otherwise have had. Salinas and his assistants exploited a rhetoric of populism that made the Indian the privileged subject of a state program whose political purpose was "to appear to further social justice and thereby legitimate the regime" (Dresser 1991, 35). As Rosalva Aída Hernández Castillo (2001, 299) notes, "During the transition from a mestizo Mexico to a multicultural Mexico, the nation-state again assigned itself the right to legitimate certain indigenous identities and to deny others."

In effect, the "self-determination of indigenous peoples" was defined in a way that legitimated only a particular kind of indigenousness, one necessarily tied to the local, peasant community. This was the kind of Indian implicitly defined in the criticism expressed not only by officials of the National Indigenous Institute (INI), but also by indigenous activists inside and outside of the council—that several of the council's directors were not representative of indigenous peoples. They were out of touch with an indigenous reality, said the critics, and were more concerned with personal political power than they were with the grass roots (*las bases*). The basis for this criticism is a preoccupation with keeping Indians in their place. When an indigenous leadership moved easily between the local and the national/global, it disrupted the accepted notion that Indians "really" and exclusively represent only the local. But the preoccupation persisted—in part because the council's attention to peasant and cultural issues could not help but reinforce it—and, as discussed below, it acted as a serious obstacle to the advancement of Indian leaders and Indian issues beyond their communities, effectively closing off national politics to them.

The council faced another related challenge. The pragmatism of community members often meant that they saw the council as just another patron, like any political party, that handed out favors in exchange for loyalty. This was an issue of political consciousness raising (*concientización de las bases*), the hard work that still lay ahead to make the local-national-global project for "self-determination" concrete to millions of indigenous peasants still struggling to survive from one day to the next.

A New Relationship

President Salinas's social development program "Solidarity" (Solidaridad), discussed below, represented his administration's "new relationship" with

Mexican society, a relationship that encouraged presidentialism—the president as the exclusive locus of national power—and discouraged federalism. As such, it was a relationship that threatened the power of local officials and party members, who saw it "as a competitive network to traditional corporatist relationships" (Braig 1997, 266).[1] The international context was important here, too. For at the very moment that the central government embarked on far-reaching economic reform, it was also signing international human rights and free trade agreements. Harvard-trained Salinas and the technocrats who surrounded him were determined to have their country enter the First World community of nations. To do so required at least the formal acceptance of the nominal standards that measure a country's membership in this community: respect for human rights and respect for the free market. Salinas pushed hard for NAFTA, and he created the country's first National Human Rights Commission (CNDH).

Mexico and Norway were the first countries to ratify the International Labor Organization's Convention 169 on Indigenous and Tribal Peoples, which few indigenous people in Mexico even knew about at the time.[2] The convention is a landmark international human rights instrument that codifies for the first time in history a series of rights specific to indigenous peoples. It also provides for self-identification as a measure of indigenous identity, which moves significantly away from the assumption that an "acculturated" Indian is an oxymoron. Beginning with Article 2, the convention uses strong language to support indigenous rights: "Governments shall have the responsibility for developing, with the participation of the peoples concerned, co-ordinated and systematic action to protect the rights of these peoples and to guarantee respect for their integrity." That only thirteen countries ratified ILO Convention 169 in the 1990s, and only seven since, suggests that nation-states are wary of signing on to an instrument that could lead to important changes in their relationships with the indigenous peoples within their borders. That Mexico led the world in ratifying the convention sent a strong signal of support for the new generation of collective rights.

But there is another side to the convention that is rarely discussed and that is strongly connected to Mexico's neoliberal opening. Like the Salinas government's reform of Article 27 of the Constitution, which ended

---

1. Although the Solidarity program ended with President Salinas's term in office, in 1994, its language of participation has remained.
2. As of August 2009, twenty countries had ratified the convention: Argentina, Bolivia, Brazil, Chile, Colombia, Costa Rica, Denmark, Dominica, Ecuador, Fiji, Guatemala, Honduras, Mexico, Nepal, Netherlands, Norway, Paraguay, Peru, Spain, and Venezuela.

land distribution to the peasantry and allowed for individual title to lands in the ejido, ILO Convention 169 is an attempt to ensure "a better investment climate for everyone," as the World Bank put it in the title of its 2005 World Development Report. Although the convention declares that "the rights of the peoples concerned to the natural resources pertaining to their lands shall be specially safeguarded," it also makes provision for the legal dispossession of these natural resources: "In cases in which the State retains the ownership of mineral or sub-surface resources or rights to other resources pertaining to lands, governments shall establish or maintain procedures through which they shall consult these peoples. . . . The peoples concerned shall wherever possible participate in the benefits of such activities, and shall receive fair compensation for any damages which they may sustain as a result of such activities."[3] Proper consultation with indigenous communities, granting them unspecified "participat[ion] in the benefits," and paying them "fair compensation for any damages" are all that is necessary for a rights-holding government to legitimately exploit their land and resources. Consent is not necessary, as Article 16 makes clear: "Where the relocation of these peoples is considered necessary as an exceptional measure, such relocation shall take place only with their free and informed consent. Where their consent cannot be obtained, such relocation shall take place only following appropriate procedures established by national laws and regulations, including public inquiries where appropriate, which provide the opportunity for effective representation of the peoples concerned."

One is left to wonder what "effective representation" might mean in the context of the structural violence discussed in chapter 3, especially given that the convention also makes it clear that it uses the term *peoples* idiosyncratically, without legal weight: "The use of the term 'peoples' in this Convention shall not be construed as having any implications as regards the rights which may attach to the term under international law." José del Val Blanco, an anthropologist who was director of the Inter-American Indigenist Institute (part of the Organization of American States system) when I spoke with him on 12 June 2000, said of this strange paradox, "If I recognize the rights of a group as a legal subject, I call them a people, but then I don't accept them as a people. . . . I give you this right and then I put in a page of qualifications that really take away this right. I'm revealing the lie and dissimulation of the very Convention. And this is the *most*

---

3. See Article 15 of Convention 169, http://www.unhchr.ch/html/menu3/b/62.htm/ (accessed 10 August 2008).

that has been gained [by indigenous peoples]!"[4] In one of its last articles, the convention further qualifies its potential impact, noting that "the nature and scope of the measures to be taken to give effect to this convention shall be determined in a flexible manner, having regard to the conditions characteristic of each country." Moreover, indigenous peoples cannot speak directly before the ILO because they have no standing there. Instead, they must get a union or a business or a central government to speak for them and no documents are permitted except those presented by one of these three recognized parties.

Mexico's ratification of Convention 169 in 1990 kicked off a decade that combined government support for the rights of indigenous peoples with the opening up of the country to foreign private investment.[5] The use of human rights discourse as a means of legitimating an economic system was rarely acknowledged in public either by government officials or by indigenous activists. Instead, both more often spoke in similar terms about

---

4. Del Val Blanco went on to suggest that such ambiguity will have far-reaching effects in international law: "The recognition of indigenous peoples as peoples implies a further reformulation of international law that has been ongoing since the third generation [of collective rights]. But this is a trap. Because Convention 169 is the beginning of the reformulation of international law. Now people and territory will no longer mean what they meant before. There are going to be peoples that have territories but they are neither peoples nor are the territories theirs. Before, since 1917, it was the Wilson Doctrine: one people, one territory, one sovereign state. Period. That was it. Convention 169 is one of the first international instruments of collective rights that is a sneaky reformulation, in my opinion, of the categories of international law." It is "sneaky" (*tramposa*), del Val Blanco argued, because instead of protecting indigenous peoples, it protects corporations. He told me a story to support this assertion: "Before [Convention] 169, as most of these [indigenous] territories were legally undefined, none of the transnationals [corporations] wanted to go in because it was going to generate a set of problems that would impede their working adequately with their own shareholders. I had British Petroleum in here telling me 'You control'—this is verbatim, mind you—'you control the Indians of America? It's just that in our last British Petroleum shareholders meeting our shareholders proposed the necessity of attending to the themes of indigenous peoples and ecology. So, we want to develop some projects so that our shareholders will allow us to expand in America.' *Verbatim.*"

The ambiguity of the convention's language reflects a moment in history when three competing imperatives dominate the globe: free trade, state sovereignty, and human rights, more or less in that order. Central governments have increasingly been forced—by public opinion, local elites, transnational capital—to balance these imperatives in their policy decisions and the convention responds to this need.

On 13 September 2007, the UN General Assembly voted to adopt the United Nations Declaration on the Rights of Indigenous Peoples, 143 votes in favor, 11 abstentions, and 4 opposed (the United States, Canada, Australia, New Zealand). Unlike Convention 169, the declaration is not legally binding but does carry "considerable moral force." See http://www.iwgia.org/sw356.asp/ (accessed 8 July 2008).

5. "Net flows of FDI [foreign direct investment] to Mexico in the 1990s were the highest among Latin America's largest economies and were surpassed only by Brazil in 1996–2000" (Máttar, Moreno-Brid, and Peres 2003, 133).

the respect for indigenous autonomy and culture and about the importance of consultation, participation, and dialogue. President Salinas's Solidarity program was the quintessential expression of this language.

Participatory Solidaridad

Solidarity's emphasis on "personal responsibility" encouraged popular organization by groups like the Guerrero Council. Moreover, the government's definition of *participation* emphasized the cultural practices of Mexicans, especially indigenous peoples, as inherently positive elements in Mexico's journey toward modernization. President Salinas had done field research in rural Mexico in the 1970s and had seen the effects of government development policies on peasant communities. He learned from this experience that government spending in the countryside was not nurturing support for the political system among the poorest of the poor (Cornelius, Craig, and Fox 1994, 6). What was needed was a new kind of government program that *could* nurture this support, and that is where Solidaridad came in. Here was a program that would finally take into consideration the needs of the people whom it was supposed to help by actively soliciting their participation in the implementation of local development projects.

Participation was not a new idea in Mexican development policy; the government had implemented similar programs in the late 1970s and early 1980s that encouraged community involvement, as we saw in chapter 1. The difference in the late 1980s was that the Mexican government faced a new combination of internal and external pressures to change. On the one hand, the PRI faced a formidable electoral challenge for the first time. On the other, the International Monetary Fund required the federal government to cut back or eliminate its system of general subsidies and replace this with more targeted programs of poverty alleviation. The response to these pressures was a program that would attempt to "achieve more with less" (Braig 1997, 252). Promoting community participation was one way to do this because it would demonstrate the government's desire to be more inclusive and flexible while saving money by contracting out labor costs.[6] Because President Salinas himself had inaugurated Solidarity in the early days of his administration, a direct connection constantly emphasized in program materials, Solidarity further helped to strengthen a Mexican

---

6. The Salinas administration boasted that federal social spending as a result of Solidarity was 1.7 billion dollars in 1991, almost double the 680 million dollars spent in 1989 (Dresser 1991, 5). The 1991 figure, however, represented only one-tenth of the total debt service bill for the same year, and worked out to just over 15 cents per day spent on each of

tradition of presidentialism (Bailey 1994, 107). The president and "the people" were at the center of Solidarity's rhetoric, united against an old-fashioned and ineffective bureaucracy; that is, the old welfare state (Braig 1997, 263). It was classic populism, "run out of the president's private pocket, its beneficiaries . . . selected on personalistic and partisan grounds, and, most fundamentally . . . immune from any democratic means of control or accountability" (Dresser 1991, 3).

It was the way in which *participation* was defined by the government that made the concept appear to be especially virtuous. This definition focused on the positive cultural attributes of Mexicans, particularly indigenous peoples (also called "the poorest" or those with the "greatest needs"). Salinas and Solidarity officials spoke of these groups' cultural cohesiveness and resilience as emblematic of *Mexican* strength. President Salinas (in Braig 1997, 253), for example, said that the "solidary Mexico" had "its origins in the forms of labor and cooperation that *we Mexicans* have practiced, in the natural course of events, to solve our basic problems." Echoing Mexican anthropologist Guillermo Bonfil Batalla's notion of a "deep Mexico" (and Alfonso Caso's earlier assertion that "Mexico is without doubt, in a very real sense, an indigenous country"), Solidarity officials asserted (in Braig 1997, 253) that "it is the original Mexico, the other Mexico with the great culture of its people, the communitarian Mexico, with which Solidarity is working." As another official stated, "Solidarity has found a method (co-responsible participation) for channeling Mexico's vast cultural knowledge in ways that can overcome bureaucratic-administrative barriers. . . . In sum, Solidarity is betting on an alternative development strategy that is participatory and co-responsible" (González Tiburcio 1994, 68, 76). In other words, the "solidary Mexico" was to replace the old, clientelist, paternalistic Mexico "with one based on participation, transparency, and reciprocity" (Braig 1997, 253). One Solidarity official went so far as to assert that full recognition of Mexico's traditional cultures was "the only valid basis for national integration. This situation places the historical tension between tradition and modernity in a new context" (González Tiburcio 1994, 69). Indigenous cultures were to act as a kind of bridge to a modernity that was to be uniquely Mexican, resting "less on simple mimicry of developed Western models and more on respect for and inclusion of the strengths of traditional cultures" (69).

---

the 17 million Mexicans considered to be in extreme poverty, which included most indigenous people (11). Moreover, overall government subsidies (for food, transportation, water, etc.) declined by nearly two-thirds from 1989 to 1990 (13).

And yet Salinas's modernization project deliberately disparaged the "revolutionary tradition" that valued Mexico's peasant culture. His reform of Article 27 of the Constitution, eliminating land redistribution to the peasantry, was a clear indication of this disparagement, as was his government's single-minded promotion of NAFTA. As Luis Hernández Navarro (2003) comments, "NAFTA was designed and negotiated explicitly to reinforce a complex of reforms destined to drain the rural population. It was the lock that would seal these changes. Luis Tellez, a man who played a key role in the Salinas agriculture reforms, announced [in 1991] that the treaty would expel around half the rural population from its lands in a period of 10 or 20 years."

The use of a "culture of participation" in Solidarity's development discourse was a cynical ploy to soften the blow of neoliberal restructuring. But it was also another phase in the development of indigenismo. It is not insignificant that government officials found it necessary to make an appeal to an indigenous Mexican identity in the face of a major economic restructuring. Given the history of indigenismo in Mexico, we should not be surprised at this appeal. It looks identical to statements Alfonso Caso made back in the 1950s that proclaimed the indigenous roots of Mexican culture. This was nationalist language that emphasized, in particular, how Mexico was *not* like its bullying northern neighbor. Given Salinas's Harvard education and his administration's keen desire to connect Mexico to the United States more closely than ever before through NAFTA, a nationalist appeal to indigenous difference made even more sense: Maybe it *looked* like the government wanted to be just like the United States, but, really, it was completely Mexican/Indian. In the 1990s, an appeal to the strength of an indigenous identity was now a part of an official policy that devolved a good deal of decision-making power to indigenous groups.[7] Indigenismo had endured two decades of criticism as part of a widespread critique of government authoritarianism after the Tlatelolco massacre in 1968, and Solidarity was the inheritor of this critique.

Policy Change in the INI and Indigenismo

A sign of indigenismo's continuity and change under Salinas was his appointment of Arturo Warman as INI director general. Warman is a

---

7. Diane Nelson (1999, chaps. 8, 9) discusses a similar convergence in Guatemala of neoliberal economic restructuring, decentralization of federal government functions, official recognition of Maya difference, and Maya demands for autonomy.

distinguished anthropologist who was a leader of the young cohort of indigenistas who criticized the fundamental premises of their profession, beginning in earnest in 1970 with the publication of *De eso que llaman antropología mexicana* (This Is What They Call Mexican Anthropology; Warman et al. 1970). Luis Villoro (1996, 12) specifically names Warman and Guillermo Bonfil Batalla as authors whose work epitomized this criticism. That Warman was director general of the INI in 1990 signaled the government's real commitment to a new relationship with indigenous peoples. Warman was a respected anthropologist and not a career bureaucrat, which signaled that the government would take indigenous issues seriously.[8]

The principal criticism of indigenismo was that its emphasis on integration would lead to the "ethnocide" of Indian peoples in Mexico. There was no respect in the INI for preserving the cultural traditions of indigenous peoples, said critics, and even less respect for their ability to make decisions about the things that affected them most. By the 1970s, an indigenous movement was influencing the direction of INI policies as never before, a point Félix Báez-Jorge (1977, 54) strongly makes: "In effect, indigenous reactions beg[a]n to seriously concern the State, which in response . . . decided to channel them institutionally." One of the ways the government did so was to organize the First National Indigenous Congress in 1975, held, symbolically, in Pátzcuaro, Michoacán, where President Cárdenas had convened the first Inter-American Indigenist Congress in 1940. The 1975 congress was a response to an Indian congress, held in San Cristóbal the year before, that was the idea of the state government of Chiapas but that the Catholic Church actually organized. The Mayas who attended the Chiapas congress adopted strong resolutions denouncing stolen lands, official corruption, and the exploitative conditions in which they lived (Báez-Jorge 1977, 54). A second congress was held in 1976. Despite the presence of the heavy hand of the central government, all these congresses were forums for indigenous criticisms of the regime and represented "a strong current that challenge[d] and express[ed] fundamental contradictions to the theoretical positions and concrete actions of indigenismo" (55).[9]

---

8. By 1992, however, Warman supported Salinas's privatization of the land-reform system and, as the new agrarian attorney general, oversaw its implementation in the countryside (Fox 1994).

9. The indigenous congresses appear, however, to have had no direct effect on the indigenous organizing that led to the formation of the Guerrero Council. In all of my conversations with activists and supporters, no one ever mentioned the congresses held in the 1970s. I suspect in part this has to do with the relatively conservative nature of the Catholic Church

The first significant policy change within indigenismo occurred during President López Portillo's term (1976–82), and its key word was "participation." In chapter 1, we saw how López Portillo's social program COPLAMAR deliberately promoted a new kind of regional participation in rural warehouses among indigenous communities. This was part of a larger shift toward the government's incorporating critics and criticisms within the state apparatus and government policy. In the INI's *Report of Activities, 1976–1982,* "The New Indigenista Politics" (La nueva política indigenista) is the title of its first chapter, which begins by acknowledging the impact of indigenous organization on government policy: "Corresponding to the advance in the awareness of these [ethnic] groups is the determination of the current government to rethink indigenista policy from the premise of the organized participation of the Indian peoples themselves" (INI 1982, 17). Moreover, the INI also acknowledged that this participation depended on the defense of indigenous lands and rights and the strengthening of their economies—all of which would "sustain their free determination oriented toward conserving and developing their ethnic identity that invigorates the diverse profile of Mexico's personality in the concert of nations" (19).

The Agrarian Myth: Opportunity with Strings Attached

The more things change, the more they stay the same. Although "indigenous participation" was a new phrase for the INI and offered a new opportunity to indigenous groups like the council, it was interpreted within the government's populist conception of indigenous culture as "tradition-bound." The conception worked to legitimize a social program and a government that in fact were not interested in eliminating the fundamental inequalities that structured indigenous and peasant lives. We saw in chapter 3 how the government could continue to play on a theme of participation while incrementally handing out small concessions to the council. The repeated meetings with President Salinas, as the council's directors well understood, were not about participation but about promoting the centralization of federal power, an important part of Solidarity's strategy. The precondition for the council's participation in indigenous economic development was the group's support of presidential power.

---

in Guerrero, which has no tradition of liberation theology comparable to the one in Chiapas, for example.

The "new" indigenismo the INI promoted recognized the elitism and cultural bias of the "old" ideology and claimed to have superseded it. Solidarity's flagship program set up specifically for indigenous economic development, the Regional Solidarity Funds (Fondos Regionales de Solidaridad, or FRS), was supposed to epitomize this ideological shift. Like other community-based Solidarity development programs, the funds comprised community groups and government officials working together on a variety of local development projects—mostly agricultural but also infrastructural—conceived and directed by community members themselves. The goals of the Regional Solidarity Funds included more autonomy for groups and communities in the management of funds; the diversification of and increase in production; and the establishment of projects that made money and created jobs for communities. INI publications stressed the importance of community decision making and the "new relationship" in all aspects of the institute's programs, but especially within the Regional Solidarity Funds, which even in 2000 continued to be the focus of the INI's regional work.[10] A 1993 FRS publication, for example, explains that "the eradication of poverty in Indian regions requires a change in the distribution and assignment of government resources, in the rules, mechanisms and norms for the assignment of these resources, besides a profound modification of the structural relationships that the state has had until now with indigenous peoples. This signifies a modification of the economic, cultural, and political bases so that this part of the population can gain access to justice and equality" (SEDESOL/INI 1993, 6).

Although this is ambitious language, the front cover of this FRS publication tells us something about the kind of indigenous projects the government supported. It is a drawing of a middle-aged man in full Indian regalia, wearing white cotton pants, a white shirt, and sandals. There is no indication of what ethnicity he represents. He is standing in a cornfield, one hand on his hip, one foot raised on a rock, and he is looking confidently straight at the viewer with a slight smile. Another Regional Solidarity Funds publication cover shows a drawing of an older and a younger man, both looking off-center and both dressed as "indigenous," hats beribboned as they are in Chiapas. The younger man has one hand on his hip and looks very serious. A stone carving of a face is prominent in the lower right corner. The strong suggestion in these cover illustrations is

10. As of August 2009, the Regional Solidarity Funds remained in place, probably because they had years of relatively autonomous existence all over the country that would not be easy to end abruptly, especially by presidents keen on establishing their populist credentials in tough economic times.

that the Regional Solidarity Funds support traditional, rural, peasant indigenous culture; indeed, that all these terms are interchangeable.[11] The 1993 operations manual reinforces this suggestion when it states that indigenous peoples are poor because of agrarian problems, the overexploitation of natural resources, migration, and "the exploitation to which they have been subjected" (SEDESOL/INI 1993, 6).

The trouble with the Regional Solidarity Funds was they did not relieve exploitation. In theory, each group receiving a loan from their regional fund had two years to pay off the loan, including interest. In fact, this usually did not happen. What happened instead was that the productive projects the fund supported through its loans rarely realized any profit, the members in the project spent the money on immediate necessities, and there was nothing left to return to the government. Lourdes, a Nahua woman who directed a women's producer collective based in Huitzuco that received fund money, described the situation to me on 17 April 2000: "The government doesn't follow strict rules, so why should we? Indigenous communities are not prepared to make profits on their projects because they can't even feed themselves yet. Every time some quantity of money—say, 2,000 pesos—is destined for a particular project, maybe 1,500 pesos goes to the project—to buy chicks or thread to make hammocks, but the rest goes to buy food. So, very often the proposed project never takes off because there's never enough money to take care of a community's basic needs and create a viable, long-term project. The INI's projected returns for the funds are unrealistic in this miserable world." Néstor, the council director mentioned in chapter 3, argued on 27 January 2000 that the funds had a negative effect on the indigenous movement, contributing to the weakening of the council and its attempts to raise the consciousness of (*concientizar*) community members:

> Unfortunately, because of the extreme poverty, what our *compañeros* and *compañeras* do is they go to the fund over there. And then they

11. The National Indigenous Institute loved to fund small folkloric projects that were "islands without connection to something bigger and more inclusive," Abel Barrera told me on 11 April 2000. The INI in Guerrero funded two such projects, the preservation of a sacred site in Acatepec and a program to train community members in the repair of musical instruments that Juan, a member of the council, had proposed, acting entirely on his own. The ease with which Juan obtained this funding as an individual was impressive, given the struggles the council was going through. "All I had to do," he explained to me on 24 January 2000, "was talk with Don Pepe in the delegation, and he helped me with all of the paperwork. This was a lot easier than when I asked an engineer there if the INI brokered agreements with seed companies to give indigenous farmers discounts. This guy was indifferent to my question and to how important it was that we don't have these discounts." Community cultural issues always trumped larger economic ones in the INI.

don't believe, they don't believe in the organization [the council] because here there aren't the resources. So what the INI does is put in these funds and creates division, creates distrust within the organization. And the municipal governments do the same; it's the same official party. They put together these resources and then they go and give away misery, really. A kilo of cornmeal, some sandals, a ceramic griddle, that's it. It's all they give away. And all of this takes place as part of a constant electoral process.[12]

Like other groups financed by the fund, Lourdes's group took the money it had borrowed (200,000 pesos) and lent it to individuals and communities not in the fund. Eduardo Portillo, an INI anthropologist, told me on 3 April 2000 that an unpublished analysis by the INI of the funds revealed that 60–70 percent of them were disorganized and were losing money. Violeta Hernández, an INI researcher in Mexico City who studied regional producer groups, confirmed this, adding that no one really knew how many loans were actually paid back to the funds since there was little evaluation of projects and no real follow-up.

As Lourdes said, the idea behind the funds (100 percent recovery of principal plus interest) was completely incompatible with rural reality. In one of the program's promotional brochures—"Our Regional Solidarity Funds!"—hand-drawn cartoons tell the story of Martín and Felipe, both obviously Indian in their white cotton clothing and sandals. They comment on the year's poor harvest and ask each other why they find themselves in such a condition. Their answers are interesting for what they omit: "We aren't well organized. We let a few decide for everyone. We don't participate in community meetings. We lack money to produce what we need, and if we aren't well organized, it's hard to get money." The funds are the solution to these problems because they "strengthen the autonomy of our organizations! We can build ourselves up out of our own resources!" Moreover, it is important that only organizations and not individuals participate in the funds because organizations "form part of the tradition

---

12. In 1999, the council received 2,750,000 pesos (about 275,000 dollars) from the State of Guerrero, which administered the funds for the federal government. The council divided up this money among its 11 microregions, each of which received approximately 250,000 pesos, which was further divided and given to communities. Most community projects received an average of 5,000 pesos, a fifth of which usually had to be spent on transportation costs for the project committee members to travel to Chilpancingo to apply for the funds, pick up the checks, and then account for all costs incurred. Communities often did not pay the labor costs included in the project proposals, opting instead to use the funds for a different project (like repairing a church), and so ended up donating their labor.

of our people."[13] Missing here is any discussion of factors that made it highly unlikely a rural community could build itself up out of its own resources: widespread soil erosion, landlessness, and the small size of most plots, to mention just three. Indeed, it is estimated that 79 percent of ejido lands are not even suitable for agriculture (Morett Sánchez 2003, 122). The language of the brochure ignores this reality to focus on the self-sufficiency of indigenous producer-entrepreneurs ("Help yourself and we will help you!" the brochure exclaims), who, with the funds in place, now have the opportunity to make decisions for themselves and carry out their own projects.

My conversations with indigenous activists and INI employees strongly suggested that this situation was not about to change. Limited to a reduced, folkloric vision of indigenous peoples and their "development" for the ideological reasons discussed above, the INI was in no position to tell indigenous peoples what to do to improve their lot. In the meantime, indigenous organizations were carrying on business as usual (clientelism, party politics, lack of accounting), and there was little even an aware and sympathetic INI observer could do about it. When I was in the Alto Balsas region at Lourdes's invitation, I saw better how the INI's participatory development model was out of the INI's control, even if the INI preferred not to admit this in public. Lourdes's group, Indigenous Women in Struggle (Mujeres Indígenas en Lucha, or MIL) had a close relationship with the CCI–Chilapa director, Juan Carlos Barrios, who had supported the inclusion of two women delegates from MIL to participate on the board of directors of the Alto Balsas Regional Solidarity Fund. Although Lourdes considered Juan Carlos an ally, she did not trust him and the group kept up friendly appearances while not telling him exactly what they were up to. Juan Carlos and I accompanied Lourdes and a few women from MIL on a visit to a Nahua ejido near Copalillo that was hoping to get the INI's support to develop the natural springs they owned into an ecotourism site.

As director of an Indigenous Coordination Center, Juan Carlos was always traveling around his region, attending one meeting after the next with indigenous organizations. As we rode in his pickup truck to the ejido,

13. Geronimo, a council director from the Alto Balsas region, where there was a Regional Solidarity Fund run mostly by groups that were also in the council, complained about having to fund only organizations when it was often individuals who needed funding, especially since there was very little credit available to peasants. "This is why we need to disconnect ourselves from the INI," he told me on 3 May 2000, "to act on our own and get our own funding sources." Channeling money only to organizations under the pretense that they are more "traditional" and "indigenous" is one way of limiting credit in the countryside.

he seemed to relish this life without vacations. "New times require new ideas," he told me on 17 April 2000 when I asked him about the INI's role in indigenous communities. "We have to make it possible for communities to participate more in program decisions. With other government agencies a technician makes decisions from a desk. Here [in the INI] the people decide." Earlier that day in the unfinished house that MIL was using as an office, Juan Carlos had met with Lourdes and the group, offering them advice about the group's projects and scolding them for buying a new truck: "It's much newer and better than mine," he teased, even though it was smaller and the only truck they had. All the women nodded in agreement with him that maybe they *had* acted too impulsively buying a new truck when they could not really afford it. They had used a 9,000-dollar grant from the Global Fund for Women to pay for the truck and to set up the office, which migrant remittances from the United States were also supporting, but they were still heavily in debt. But, as Lourdes told me later that same day, speaking in private,

> Juan Carlos was in my house at my invitation and he may have his ideas about what we should do, but we will do what we want no matter what he says. There is no way we are getting rid of the truck! This is all part of the game we are playing because we need the 300,000 pesos the INI has promised to set up a new fund based in Copalillo, and we need his support for the work we are doing. To get this, we need to hide things from him we know he won't like. Like the 200,000 pesos Mujeres [MIL] got from the fund [in Alto Balsas] that we're using to capitalize the organization and that we won't pay back as we're supposed to. Altepetl and Zanzekan Tinemi and even CPNAB are using their own moneys as they like and are not going to pay them back, so why should we?

The funds had become unofficial mini bank accounts from which each group drew moneys to lend to communities, all the while urging them to pay back their loans because, as Lourdes said without a trace of irony, "we want to encourage a culture of paying back, of self-sufficiency. People are so used to getting government money on a continuous basis but the money doesn't get invested in a long-term solution, it only encourages dependency on the government."

"Here the people decide," Juan Carlos had told me. But the way they were deciding was not exactly through the harmonious democracy of equals the INI promoted in its brochures. In fact, as I heard from "Yvette," a young Nahua woman from Chilapa who was a council member through her association with Zanzekan Tinemi, the funds were mirror images of the larger political system in Mexico. "The fund in Chilapa is controlled by only a few organizations, like Altepetl and Zanzekan [Tinemi]," she told me on 9 April 2000, "and these groups don't let other organizations join because they're not interested in sharing the money. Many groups get money through connections they have through family or *compadrazgo* [fictitious kin] but they aren't accountable for the funds, they don't make any profits and the fund loses money all the time. Juan Carlos knows this but he can't do anything about it because if the INI cuts off funding it will be threatened with a protest by the groups in power." In other funds, like the one based in Ometepec, political parties were heavily involved. Benito, a council director from Xochistlahuaca, had attempted to have Amuzgo folk art projects funded, but "we got tired of being there," he said on 25 January 2000. "They told us 'this won't work because it isn't profitable' but then they turned around and lent money to someone without a project. The PT [Workers Party] got involved there and supported everyone who got funded, so that if you wanted to get anything you had to be in the PT." The general impression of indigenous "participation" in development projects was of institutional chaos: an INI out of control and most indigenous groups constantly losing money. An unpublished 1999 interview with Eligio Pacheco Marín, CCI–Tlapa's former coordinator of boarding schools (a Tlapaneco from the Montaña who worked under Maurilio Muñoz in the 1960s), provides the perspective of an old indigenista disappointed with INI initiatives, which remained limited in their scope and success: "[In the late 1980s] we entered a crisis during which the CCI didn't have enough of a budget to attend to the more than 200 communities in the region. We couldn't attend to the entire region so we focused on ten or five or three communities and we currently haven't expanded this work" ("Entrevista" 1999). As we saw in chapter 2, the INI has always been financially limited in its ability to make a significant impact in Mexico's poorest regions—Muñoz himself lamented this back in the 1960s—so Pacheco Marín's complaint sounds familiar. A conversation I had with Violeta Hernández, an INI researcher in the Department of Social Studies, further suggests that an ideology of folkloric poverty was behind the reduced scope of the Institute, since it permitted a willful ignorance of the population to which it was charged to attend, much like the notion of the "closed corporate community" had long restricted anthropological understanding of indigenous community dynamics. Hernández herself is a Zapoteca from Oaxaca. Speaking to me on 29 June 2000, she bemoaned how the

INI's limited knowledge of and limited impact in indigenous regions were intimately connected:

> Curiously, after fifty years, the INI does not have a demography department. What does this mean? It means that we don't know our own universe. Even if the census gathers data on the population of indigenous language speakers I think there are many people who don't express this variable but who nevertheless are indigenous. And this is worrisome because the INI doesn't know its own population—it doesn't know it beyond indigenous speakers. Anthropology uses a series of variables that constitute an identity: dress, customs, all of that. But the INI does not use these variables in its universe. We need to think about demographics as something more integral, that the universe is much broader and complex than just speakers of a language.

She continued with illustrations of how this limited perspective was put into practice:

> A little while ago there was a meeting in Morelos to hand out resources and money. A man approached me and said, "Listen, Licenciada. I'm indigenous and I'd like you to register me on your list." Then the official in charge asked him if he spoke an indigenous language and the man said, "No, no, I don't speak it, but my parents do speak it. I mean, I lost it for a lot of reasons, but that doesn't exclude me from the group because I am an Indian." It's possible that, in that moment, he was an Indian because they were handing out credits, but when an official disqualifies someone because he doesn't speak a language then that's a problem with our knowledge.[14]

---

14. Indigenous language usage can be understood as a proxy for indigenous community membership; it is this connection that bothered Violeta Hernández because it implied a reduced definition of who counted in a "universe" that was more complex when it came to Indian identity, which I understood somewhat better at the end of our conversation. Violeta told me that she spoke Zapoteco, which she learned from her campesino parents. She did not say that she was "Zapoteca," but she did say that on the Census she noted she spoke a native language and that she does not deny her background. When I asked her whether she described herself as Zapoteca, she said she did. "I was discriminated against as a child by other kids for speaking Zapoteco, but my father always stressed to me how good it was to speak a language others could not understand—he said that was why they made fun of me. It was so important to me that he did this." I was struck by how her connection to Zapoteco was key to her Indian identity, but that, as a professional working in the INI, she seemed almost reluctant to admit this to another professional—as if I might not believe her

> In 1997, we conducted a national survey of employment in indigenous zones—this included a question asking about self-identification. We fought to get a similar question included in the Census that didn't just ask about language. Well, after years of working on this we were told for political reasons that this wasn't possible. They said that it couldn't be included because there wasn't money, because one question involves a lot of investment. But this was obviously a political decision because before they had never included questions [on the Census] related to disability—in no other one except this one [in 2000]. And this is because Mrs. Nilda Patricia, the wife of President Zedillo, wanted questions about disability. It's too bad she wasn't interested in Indians, too, because this might have given us the opportunity to include more questions! There are three questions on the Census related to Indians and seven related to disability. The question about self-identification appears only on the Ampliado [expanded version], but this is applied in only a few regions and isn't nationally representative.

The result, Hernández argued, was a situation in which reality eluded the abstract pronouncements of government officials, and indigenous peoples suffered the consequences.

> The problem here in Mexico—I don't know if it's true in other countries but I don't think so—is that you construct models but you never know your target population. I'm telling you, it's like that—Kafka, Fassbinder, all of them come up short when it comes to describing what happens in this country! For example, when I need credit to grow corn, they will lend me money at a time of the year when I don't need it. So I'll wait until the crop grows and when the official arrives again it will be after the harvest and I still won't have the resources when I need them. It's like nothing is in accordance with reality because you design things on the basis of abstractions without knowing your world.

Given the way that folkloric poverty worked to provide ideological support for a bounded cultural conception of indigenousness, it makes

---

because she lived and worked in Mexico City? She knew intellectually that a focus on language limited our understanding of indigenous identity, but she seemed to have internalized the idea that language alone had the power to mark someone indelibly Indian.

sense that the INI promoted "participation" as the keystone of its development work. Speaking with me on 27 January 2000, Néstor commented on the effects of this participatory development model in indigenous communities:

> We aren't getting to the bottom of what development is . . . its basis. We are leaving behind something superficial, something visual, something, some visible things. Like the government does. A government likes to build an ejido center, big, nice, painted all pretty. And with lightbulbs, fancy, see, and expensive. And this is the same thing that the council has been doing for several . . . really, until now. They are mistakes. We are putting in roads, we're putting in electricity, we're putting in schools, we're asking for town halls, sports fields, and even stores. This, let's say, this isn't crazy, but it isn't development itself.

He explained in some detail a plan he and others had developed for the Montaña that focused on rural infrastructure, like irrigation canals and the production of organic fertilizer to replace dependence on commercial fertilizers. His main point was that in order to talk about development, "to talk about politics, to talk about rights, first the people need to be fed, so that they can think, so that they can have opinions, so that they can contribute ideas and contribute proposals."

As Néstor pointed out, the council's work—superficial development—had great value for the government, which maintained its centralized control while the basic conditions of inequality persisted: "In any case, this is good for the government. It's good for the government that we ask for these kinds of public works. Because we are doing them a favor. We are including . . . what it is their responsibility to do: build schools, build roads, build town halls. It is the government's responsibility to do this. And by doing it ourselves, we're taking a weight off them."

Néstor appreciated the function of the agrarian myth in government social policy. Key to the myth is the affirmation of an ethnic/peasant essentialism as the foundation of the nation. An ethnic politics based on populist imagery fits easily within neoliberalism and poses no threat to the larger system of power—it is "apolitical." The government benefits from the language of popular participation since this translates in practice into a withdrawal of state responsibility for the poor even as government officials claim a primordial bond with them. An exclusive focus on the local community and its basic needs—a function of the desperate situation of indigenous people in Mexico—accompanies this essentialism and neatly fits the narrowed scope of government development policy. As discussed in detail below, the local community continues to define who Indians are.

Traitors

What we're talking about here is a structural abyss created by the West to destroy all forms for building an indigenous leadership of individuals, on an equal level, with whom we can argue. *There is no dialogic equality.*

—JOSÉ DEL VAL BLANCO, DIRECTOR OF THE INTER-AMERICAN INDIGENIST INSTITUTE, JUNE 2000

Who legitimately represents Indians? What level of organization is legitimately indigenous? These were crucial questions for a sprawling organization like the council that incorporated different kinds of leadership at a variety of organizational levels, from the barrio, to the region, to the federal legislative district. At every point along the way, the group encountered critics who insisted that only the peasant community truly defined what was properly Indian. Although it is true that Indian elites have long articulated the needs of Indian peasants in a relationship that has sometimes been "distant, ideologized, paternalistic, and even arrogant" (Varese 1996, 60), we need to be careful about simply disparaging their efforts. Often framed as a sincere concern for the grass roots (*las bases*)—who are considered the most real of all—the reduced definition of indigenous leadership and organization easily translates politically into a reduced scope for change in indigenous lives. This is a pervasive discourse shared even by indigenous activists who constantly justify their position in the movement by referring to the connection they continue to have with their pueblo, their home community—while at the same time suggesting that others who no longer have such a connection can speak for no one. The insistence on a narrow definition of the legitimate Indian is a key part of the "structural abyss" that José del Val Blanco insists acts to limit the creation of an effective indigenous leadership.[15]

It is important to note that the authority of indigenismo's community-bound Indian endures today in part as a legacy of Cardenismo, when the

---

15. Kay Warren (1998) shows how Guatemalan mestizos use a similar discourse to delegitimize the leadership of the pan-Maya movement in that country. David Stoll's examination of Rigoberta Menchú's personal testimony and his attempt to cast doubt on her leadership because of the inconsistencies he found there also draw on notions of an authentic Indian properly placed in the local community. See Arias 2001.

federal government advocated for indigenous communities as never before. Keen on building a corporatist Mexico of loyal social sectors, President Cárdenas initiated the first Regional Indigenous Congresses (Congresos Regionales Indígenas) in the 1930s that mobilized hundreds of young Indian delegates around the country to advocate for their towns within the terms provided by the central government (Dawson 2004). Similarly, Cardenistas in Chiapas privileged young male bilingual Mayan leaders who defended community identity (and their own interests) against mestizo depredations (Rus 1994). Beginning in the 1950s, the INI continued this local advocacy, all the while allowing "local elites to monopolize power with the consent of federal officials, as long as they supported federal officials on certain key issues" (Dawson 2004, 158). This history of local advocacy and co-optation by the state and federal governments complicates the desire for authentic local representation since it strongly suggests that even those most connected to their pueblos have not been entirely accountable to their communities. Indigenous elites, with the open support of the government, have often used their close ties to the community and their defense of local "tradition" to benefit mostly themselves and their kin (Rus 1994; Gutiérrez Ávila 1999). Within this historical context, the desire for real accountability uncompromised by outside interests is certainly understandable, but it is also by no means clear that it will come only from those who have remained in the community.[16]

The association of place and authenticity has dominated anthropological discourse from its beginnings. We saw in chapter 2, for example, how the INI's official discourse struggled to force "the Indian" into a local and isolated place, despite abundant knowledge to the contrary. Akhil Gupta and James Ferguson argue that this kind of thinking continues and "often haunts contemporary anthropological approaches to local communities, where 'the local' is understood as the original, the centered, the natural, the authentic, and opposed to 'the global,' understood as new, external, artificially imposed, and inauthentic" (Gupta and Ferguson 1997a, 7). My

---

16. The political history of the municipality of Xochistlahuaca illustrates the conflict between those—often those better educated—who act as brokers for communities with municipal and state governments and those who are community leaders (Gutiérrez Ávila 1999). Though they can support the community leadership, brokers by no means have the best interests of their communities always at heart, and they almost always struggle among themselves for this position. As community members consistently told me, the communities themselves remain the most neglected in all of this. A communitarian discourse of legitimacy is a defensive position against the reality of municipal, state, and federal control over community affairs without real community representation.

conversations with INI officials illustrate the political implications of such an approach.

Agustín Ávila, the INI's director of Justice Programs, made the connection between place and authentic representation immediately clear. An anthropologist who had done fieldwork throughout Mexico and who had served as a consultant to the World Bank and the Indigenous Fund, Ávila was also a historian who studied the evolution of Mexico City's oldest colonias from the sixteenth through the nineteenth centuries. When I spoke with him on 29 March 2000, he had served as director for almost a year and a half, though he had worked for the INI off and on for many years. As director of Justice Programs, Ávila was in a key position to comment on and promote new legislation that could potentially recognize new forms of indigenous self-government. He began the interview with the premise that "the great majority of indigenous peoples from Mesoamerica to South America—it is different in the North—are structured by a pattern of community organization. Meanwhile, on a higher level there aren't organisms that represent the group [of communities]." He continued: "There *are* organizations that say they represent everyone, but, well, every day here I get three or four that tell me, 'I represent all the Indians in Mexico.'"

Then he explained with a concrete example he thought I would understand: a proposal to create a Pluriethnic Autonomous Region (Región Autónoma Pluriétnica, or RAP) in the Alto Balsas region. I had heard about this proposal from the council, but it always seemed like an idea the government would passively resist, as it had the State Fund for Indigenous Peoples (Fondo Estatal para los Pueblos Indígenas). I knew the region's indigenous groups did not work together harmoniously and that political parties played a role in maintaining divisions among the Nahuas there. But I also knew it was one of the most organized and well-funded indigenous regions in Guerrero, with its own Regional Solidarity Fund, a legacy of the mobilization against the dam in the early 1990s. Nahuas in the council were highly active in this fund, and it was they who proposed the pluriethnic region. If there was anywhere a RAP would work well in Guerrero, it would have to be in the Alto Balsas. For Ávila, however, the history of division there meant a Pluriethnic Autonomous Region was impossible: "It could be good, but it doesn't correspond to today's reality." When I asked him why, he answered with a question:

> Because, what are its bases? Of representation, for example. Be careful now, because we can fall into a dynamic of "Of course, I'm conscious of and clear on the issues, so I can assume the representation

of all the rest. And I do what I feel like because I am a leader and representative of everyone because I name myself representative." To the extent that there is an effective process of representation, and an effective leadership, and an effective accounting, it will work. But without this, it will only be a nice idea. I don't believe them, when there are these artificial processes.

Ávila's caricature of the RAP proposal for the Alto Balsas essentially disparaged the Nahua leaders who had years of experience negotiating at all levels of the government, and who were ideally prepared to attempt this new organizational form. He also dismissed out of hand the region's ability to keep the leaders accountable for their actions. The whole idea of an extralocal organization was, for him, artificial. To emphasize its artificiality, Ávila claimed that this Nahua proposal was exactly the same as the Supreme Councils of Indigenous Peoples (Consejos Supremos de Pueblos Indígenas) the government organized in the 1970s to channel indigenous dissent. "With the best of intentions they wanted the indigenous to have their own structures, broader structures of representation. What happened? Again, the problem of representation is fundamental. Without this, we're talking about fantasies or manipulation." The analogy with official creations is spurious at best, but he extended it by equating the Nahua proposal for the Alto Balsas with the worst tendencies of indigenismo: "It ended up by imposing on indigenous peoples what we thought was best for them: 'We think it is best to have a broader-based organization.' 'We think you have to wear shoes instead of sandals.' 'We think you need to go to school.' This is indigenismo's historic problem."

As a historian, Ávila knew that the fragmentation of larger indigenous political units into discrete communities, especially in the Central Plain, was itself an artificial process that began with the Spanish Conquest (Díaz Polanco 1997). He ignored this to focus on the reality the community supposedly represented. Insofar as the level of the community could be incorporated into new legislation, he asserted, then "the real bond between the law and the population will be more effective and will achieve an impact. I believe that customary law, before everything, and the structures of community organization, only these allow the people to attend to and resolve their problems, manage their coexistence, defend themselves against the exterior."[17] Ávila used an image of an inherently fragmented indigenous

---

17. José Luis López, the INI's chief lawyer in Guerrero, asserted in an interview on 8 April 2000 that the Guerrero Council was weak because "it doesn't have a presence in the

Mexico to emphasize how much fantasy was involved in proposals for indigenous organizations that transcend the local: "Imagine: in Mexico, there are around 60,000 indigenous localities distributed among sixty-two languages—not to mention the issue of situating the languages according to their morphological structure." There was, in other words, something *necessarily* centrifugal about indigenous communities that kept them apart; it did not matter that throughout history these communities had always found ways to organize together. Ávila focused on the community alone, concluding that "an adequate policy would strengthen and constitute the communities, strengthen the self-reconstitution of communities. In this sense, the essential element is that a policy allows communities to select their future path. It has to be built in relation to the reality of indigenous peoples. Any other way generates artificial options."

It follows from this logic that an indigenous leader of an extralocal organization is unreal and unrepresentative. Even José O. Ávila Arévalo, or Don Pepe as he was also known (no relation to Agustín Ávila), followed this logic when we spoke on 5 April 2000. The only anthropologist on staff in the INI's Chilpancingo offices who worked closely and sympathized strongly with the Guerrero Council, Don Pepe and Renato Ravelo Lecuona had helped organize the council in 1991, but he was highly critical of the council's leadership, contrasting it with the good leadership found in indigenous communities. The obligatory and prestige-oriented *cargo* system, in which community leadership positions rotate every year, was the example Don Pepe believed the council's leaders needed to follow. He reproached them for living a good part of the time in Chilpancingo and for not being elected directly by the communities each year: "The leaders who were in charge at the beginning have not changed and they live here, not in their communities. There's a lack of democracy because they don't change positions." And, he added, "they're mixed up in politics."[18]

My conversations with Don Pepe almost always turned to the subject of indigenismo's failures and his disillusionment with the INI, where he had worked since 1978. He criticized the council and the INI for many of

---

communities," which was false and demonstrated how easy it was to dismiss the leadership in Chilpancingo using localism as an exclusive measure of indigenous political strength.

18. Speaking with me on 5 April 2000, two mestizo activists close to the council were blunt in their characterization of the council's leadership. Both were disappointed that it had strayed from the grass roots, and they pointed to Pedro de Jesús Alejandro and Marcelino Díaz de Jesús as examples of this: "They're both fat now, with a nice new truck, a new lifestyle."

the same reasons: according to him, both were out of touch with traditional indigenous communities. Like Agustín Ávila, Don Pepe believed that indigenous representation was most real and most uncorrupted at the community level. But the community is a difficult place from which to launch and sustain a sophisticated indigenous leadership capable of pushing for changes at all political levels. The lack of information about the outside world, for example, is obvious to visitors in many, many indigenous communities, as I saw when I visited Totomixtlahuaca (Toto), an important town on a central route that connects the Montaña region with the coast. Toto's only telephone was broken, and I never saw a single newspaper for sale. Although there was reception, not everyone could afford a radio, much less a television. The situation was worse in rural areas, especially mountainous ones, where the cost of electricity was relatively high and many communities had neither radio nor television reception.

In San Luis Acatlán, the Light of the Montaña Union of Ejidos and Communities (Unión de Ejidos y Comunidades Luz de la Montaña, or LuzMont) has organized coffee producing communities in a region that is not that remote, but that still presents serious obstacles. The group's description of the situation its leaders face is common in Guerrero's indigenous regions (Ravelo Lecuona and Ávila Arévalo 1994, 92): "In this zone of the Montaña, there are no communications media as there are in the city, where one can become easily informed through the television, radio, or the press. In this zone, there is no possibility that people, even if they'd want to, could be informed. In order to inform people, the Union's delegates have had to wait until the community holds an assembly, and when it does, only a minority of producers, who besides live very dispersed, attend. . . . Communication is an indispensable issue for an organization that wants to be democratic, but in this region there is no infrastructure to take advantage of. The conventional means for transmitting information are the community assemblies, but these are insufficient because of the quantity and frequency of information that is generated in the Union. In the Union, in one or two months many things can happen. The Union advances quickly, but the people in general very slowly" (92).

Another issue is that community government is not always democratic, as I heard on 2 June 2000, when I attended a workshop organized by Tlachinollan, a human rights NGO in Tlapa. Indigenous community members analyzed the human rights situation of their communities through role-playing and small group discussion. When the women and men in attendance were asked to describe "traditional democracy" in their towns, they listed the various cargos ("comisarios," "fiscales," "topiles," "principales," etc.) and affirmed that, in the best of cases, the leaders who served as these were honest and fulfilled their duties. In some communities, however, only the principales decided, without community participation, while in others, this lack of democracy had prevailed until a younger, educated generation took charge and changed political decision making to include the community. A related issue is the exclusion of women from formal community governance structures, though this is often also the case in regional organizations like the council.

In sum, the community remains a romantic place of origin for the real Indian, but it is a place with inherent limitations for nurturing a well-informed and agile leadership. Community leaders have a certain kind of knowledge appropriate for the issues their communities face, but these issues are qualitatively and quantitatively different at a regional and national level, as the leaders of LuzMont note above. Suggesting that only community leaders are legitimate leaders is a way of keeping Indians in their place politically, economically, and spatially. As Gupta and Ferguson (1997b, 47) note, "The enforced 'difference' of places becomes . . . part and parcel of a global system of domination." The need to denaturalize cultural and spatial divisions, they suggest, is part of "the political task of combating a very literal 'spatial incarceration of the native' within economic spaces zoned, as it were, for poverty" (47).

José del Val Blanco had the most incisive critique of this "spatial incarceration." He had worked at the INI as director of Research and Cultural Promotion under Arturo Warman; when I spoke with him, he was director of the Inter-American Indigenist Institute. He came highly recommended by both Pedro de Jesús Alejandro and Marcelino Díaz de Jesús, the council's directors who were most involved in national and international affairs, because he strongly supported the formation of a national indigenous leadership. Del Val began our conversation on 12 June 2000 by pointing out the aesthetic of poverty that dominates images of Indians, which he called "an aesthetic cult of indigenous misery." So, he said, "you have the sandal, the colorful skirt [*huipil*], the white cotton cloth, the braid, the hat. The religious fervor, of course; the marvelous fiestas. And this is what the indigenous are." Indians cannot legitimately define for themselves a different way to be Indian. "But do Mexicans think that the Catalans [for example] don't define their culture and their identity? Well, more strongly than Mexicans do! But it turns out that they're not poor. And yet when an Indian puts on a tie, he stops being Indian. And this is a discourse in the world. If a Tojolobal puts on a tie and hat and a Hugo Boss suit, he's no longer an Indian. He's a traitor." This identity with poverty means, in structural terms, that governments do not create the conditions that allow indigenous leaders to occupy official posts. Education programs for indigenous students are limited at high levels; what are emphasized instead are training programs like those Solidarity offered.[19] The logic, said del Val Blanco, is "to train them to make their survival a little better, but they'll remain poor peasants." And, as poor peasants, what they only represent are other peasants, not ideas as such: "This is a structural abyss that we're imposing on them here. When an Indian speaks, we don't listen to what he says, but to whom he represents. 'This one doesn't represent many.' Indigenous peoples are not recognized for their words, but for their representativity that is determined by how many people they can bring to a demonstration." Del Val Blanco reframed Agustín Ávila's concern with so-called artificiality: "So, the problem in this sense is that if an indigenous leader develops himself and no longer depends exclusively on his base to become an indigenous thinker about the indigenous problem, we make him into a traitor, we don't trust him—and we end up destroying him."

There is a dilemma here that Carlos Zolla, INI director of Research and Cultural Promotion, outlined very clearly from his perspective as a government official. On the one hand, he told me on 23 February 2000, "the legitimate leaders of communities or organizations are leaders with a partial representation in terms of territory or population. And so an honest indigenous leader can go to a meeting in Geneva and, of course, voices emerge that say, 'Well, you represent the Mayas of Campeche, but I'm Cora, or I'm Paypay. I didn't elect you.'" On the other hand, "a kind of 'jet-set' indigenous person is created, no? Bureaucratized, that only aspires to shine in the international field, with trips and hotels, things like this. Something that also weakens any movement, any indigenous movement. This is a problem ... this is a problem that needs work. And the *indigenous* need to work on it a lot." In other words, within the dilemma that has been constructed, there is no way an indigenous leadership can ever have much of an impact in forums dominated by nonindigenous. In both cases Zolla outlines, indigenous peoples do not represent ideas or positions,

---

19. The numbers reported in the *Diario Oficial*, 15 March 2000, say it all. The INI's total two-year budget for higher education scholarships was 600,000 pesos (about 60,000 dollars) in 2000. This included support for graduate studies, but only in indigenous languages, while college students received a maximum of 10,000 pesos (about 1,000 dollars) per year. Few students were funded; in 2000, for example, from Chiapas, one of the states with the highest percentage of indigenous people, only seven students received this scholarship. On the other hand, the Regional Solidarity Funds *each* received up to 936,100 pesos annually—and there were ten funds just in Guerrero.

only themselves or other indigenous, which means they cannot represent anything of consequence—both sides of the dilemma are defined by their limited representativity. Worse, Zolla says that it is up to indigenous peoples to solve this dilemma, when it exists as such because officials like Zolla and Ávila perpetuate it.

The trouble is that indigenous groups and leaders also perpetuate the folkloric poverty—local, peasant, poor—that defines a legitimate Indian. They do so, of course, while they also continue to push against the barriers that maintain a strict definition of indigenousness, by acting at all political levels. And they do so because most indigenous peoples in Mexico are poor peasants. But the discourse of Mexican populism that still equates the real Mexico with the countryside meant that the council framed the legitimacy of its claims around a discourse of peasantness. The council's directors who were no longer strongly connected to this peasantness— Pedro de Jesús Alejandro and Marcelino Díaz de Jesús and Martha Sánchez Néstor—I heard called, by other indigenous leaders, "Indios nailons," Indians who were synthetic like nylon (and, really, synthetic in the original sense of the word). The ANIPA was often disparaged by council directors and mestizo sympathizers who did not participate in the ANIPA as an organization of "professionals" disconnected from the base. Benito, for example, the Amuzgo director from Xochistlahuaca (Xochis) who was a generation older than Martha and who openly challenged her ability to be a leader, made explicit the connection between authenticity, localism, and language when he spoke with me in Chilpancingo on 25 January 2000:

> Martín Equihua was not very indigenous . . . like Marcelino, Pedro, they don't speak their own language. Not even Martha knows how to speak Amuzgo or Mixteco. These people are half mestizo sometimes, like when Martha was in Xochis and she was ashamed to speak Amuzgo. And the language of her father didn't interest her, either. Most of the people who come from the countryside have suffered and have lived that life themselves. The people who come from there, like me, we're not interested in being a congressman. But for them [Pedro, Martha, and Marcelino] this is what interests them the most. They're the ones most involved in the PRD, with the ANIPA, and all of that. We've [his own group from Xochis] participated in the ANIPA on various occasions but after we saw that only ten or fifteen compañeros were in charge, we knew this wasn't the will of the people. It's like a political party, and, right in the Amuzgo region, it is dividing people. The compañeros from the ANIPA go and hold

their own meetings without letting me know. I would say that of the council's eleven regions, eight "speak the same language," and we have the same goal, the struggle directly with the people [*la lucha directa con la gente, con los pueblos*]. And the other regions are more involved with political things: Alto Balsas and Rancho Nuevo.

Benito also told me, however, that he had been president of the PRI in Xochistlahuaca, and as an agronomist with a university degree he had worked for seven years in the Ministry of Agriculture and Hydraulic Resources (SARH), thanks in part to the assistance of a member of the Echevarría family working there. It did not bother him that his own experiences with party politics contradicted his criticism of other directors.

I could detect more ambivalence in this criticism in my conversation with a council director, Roberto, on 27 January 2000. When he asked me whether I could help him contact an NGO to get funding, I asked him whether any council directors had already made these contacts in their travels abroad. "Yes," he answered, "but these are 'nylons.' We're from the grass roots [*la base*]. It's the nylon Indians who fly around up there, the Indian travelers, as [Subcomandante] Marcos says [laughing]. And we haven't gotten to that yet. We are sustained by the grass roots. We have to create this area. We haven't created it yet." Even Pedro, despite his impeccable national and international credentials as an indigenous activist with an invaluable store of knowledge derived from his long experience, felt compelled to defend himself in a public forum I attended on 29 October 1999 against charges coming from a Yaqui activist that he did not represent anyone and was just an intellectual. "I don't consider myself an 'intellectual,'" he responded. "My community elected me to represent them, and that is what I do."[20]

20. Given the immediate needs of communities on the ground, it is understandable how international travel can be a risky business for indigenous leaders if tangible results for community members are not forthcoming. There is also, however, the risk involved in how others *perceive* this travel, as discussed above. "I was in Panama for the Third Intercontinental Meeting of Indigenous Women," Lourdes explained on 16 April 2000, "in New York for Beijing+5, and I travel nationally to different conferences and workshops. But we have to be careful as a group that all this travel—making connections with other women's groups, NGOs, and foundations, this is all important—but it shouldn't take us away from our community work." Daniel Sánchez, Martha's brother, shared similar concerns about a trip he had recently taken to Canada: "My trip to Winnipeg, paid for by the Canadian government—I went representing the ANIPA—was a total sham," he said on 13 April 2000. "No recommendations, no resolutions, no agreements were reached at all. Nothing on paper to take home, even." The danger that indigenous leaders can get used as props in high-profile meetings that promote dubious benefits for indigenous communities is real; this is the trouble with "consultation," as Daniel noted. But Daniel also appreciated the potential benefits

When Pedro asserted this, he denied the possibility that an indigenous activist might be an intellectual who no longer lives primarily in his community, but for whom the cause of that community remains paramount in all he does. A few of the council's directors expressed their concerns about this situation, including Martha Sánchez Néstor. Her work in the National Indigenous Women's Coordinating Committee of Mexico (Coordinadora Nacional de Mujeres Indígenas de México) brought her out of her hometown to advocate for indigenous women all over Mexico; she was also executive director of the Plural National Indigenous Assembly for Autonomy (ANIPA), based in Mexico City. Her ethnicity alone subverted ideas of an essential Indian: Martha was Nahua and Tlapaneca by birth, but Amuzga by choice since she grew up in Xochistlahuaca, in the heart of Amuzgo territory. She was always traveling between Chilpancingo and Mexico City, and often traveled abroad to speak about indigenous issues. She maintained close ties to home and participated in local community politics to oust a corrupt municipal president, but most of her work was in the state and national capitals and this was how other activists attempted to dismiss her contributions to the council. Martha's concern, meanwhile, was the regionalization of the council that was a direct result of the emphasis on representativity: "Everyone is in their region and no one is in the office coordinating the group's work," she told me on 5 May 2000. "If someone is always in the office then she or he is criticized for losing touch, for not doing the work in the region. No one is really in charge of the *group's* direction."

One of the worst crises the council faced involved the entwined issues of localism and Indian identity. The Party of the Democratic Revolution (PRD) had approached the council before the 1994 elections to ask the group to nominate one of their members as a congressional candidate. In the aftermath of the Zapatista (EZLN) uprising, with indigenous issues now part of a national debate, the PRD saw the advantage of an opposition party fielding an indigenous candidate for a national office (this was through the system of proportional representation each party is allowed). The council's directors nominated Martín Equihua, the mestizo council leader who had years of experience organizing peasants in Guerrero. From a strategic perspective, selecting someone with excellent political and social connections

---

of his trip: "I met representatives from Guatemala and Bolivia and I shared experiences with Canadian Indians. You know, these alliances *could* be so important. I mean, what if those from Canada spoke out against the policies and tactics of the Mexican government, and we did the same here about the Canadian government?"

across the state was smart. Equihua had demonstrated his commitment to the council, he was a leader everyone respected, and he was a centering force in a movement with strong centrifugal tendencies. "The trouble started," Martha went on to say, "soon after he became a federal congressman, however, and he reneged on the oral promise he had made to the council to give the organization 50 percent of his salary and to step down after three years to allow Pedro de Jesús Alejandro to occupy the position." Not only did he refuse to make good on his promise, but he also publicly denounced his fellow leaders. By 1996, the council voted to expel Equihua from the organization, and with him went the organizations and leaders he had been supporting all along; much of his congressman's salary had gone to these groups, who turned around and affiliated themselves with the PRI. All of the council's remaining directors I spoke with about Equihua expressed surprise and dismay over what they considered an epic betrayal of his friends.

What is interesting, given that there were obviously indigenous groups and leaders loyal to Equihua, is how the council's official history of this betrayal focuses on Equihua's ethnicity. One of the main reasons the group chose him to be a PRD candidate was that "not being indigenous he didn't take the side of any of the regions" (Consejo Guerrerense 2001, 69). This even outweighed the negative political consequences of choosing a mestizo as the PRD's "indigenous" candidate, a choice other indigenous organizations in Guerrero apparently criticized. But the council's history equivocates, arguing that "the council's gravest error was that it never added the condition that this congressman had to belong to an indigenous community, so that if he ever went wrong someone could have complained about it and subjected him to the rules of the community" (70). Although the history appears to be concerned with Equihua's problematic mestizo identity, it is really about what it means to be an Indian. The Indian's inherent localism is seen, on the one hand, as a limitation for a multiregional organization like the council, but, on the other hand, this same localism is understood positively, as the source of a communitarian ethic that keeps leaders honest. Equihua never acted as a "lone mestizo," without any obligations, however; he had always been closely connected to the leaders of peasant organizations, who had come out of communities and were well respected in the council for this very reason. Indeed, the council's remaining leaders felt especially betrayed when their Indian compañeros left the organization to follow Equihua. Ironically, Marcelino Díaz de Jesús replaced Equihua as the PRD's Indian congressman in 1997 and he served out his term without any major incident, although in 2001 he, too, had been publicly censured by the organization for improper conduct because he had signed a letter supporting President Vicente Fox Quesada (2000–6) in the name of the council. He had not consulted the other directors about this and then never apologized for having neglected this responsibility.

In sum, the mestizo leader was not disconnected from obligations to others, nor was the Indian leader necessarily bound by a communitarian ethic. But the council's history ignores these facts to concentrate on a particular construction of the parochial Indian inherently bound by his community. The trouble is not that such an Indian does not exist, but that cosmopolitan Indian leaders insist, even at the risk of contradicting themselves, that such an Indian is the only Indian that counts. The need to be truly representative meant that the council's directors tended to overlook larger issues of coordination and consciousness raising that transcended the community, the region, or even the nation. The imperative to represent the local is dangerous for the political reasons to which Agustín Ávila inadvertently alluded above. It acts to limit both a broad-based indigenous organization and the creation of a cosmopolitan leadership that is best equipped to deal with the complex issues impacting indigenous peoples: regional and national economic development; constitutional and international law; and human rights. The community alone cannot protect itself. A multiregional association like the council can act as an important intermediary and protector, so long as its leaders keep this larger, inclusive project—of development, of law, of rights—always in view. The leaders based in Chilpancingo tried to translate the terms of this project for local community members so that they could appreciate the long-term goals of the organization and more equally participate in their realization. Making the translation effective, however, was itself a long-term goal often at odds with the leadership's own discourse of localism.

Overcoming Localism in Order to Protect It

At the Intercultural Encounter of Indigenous Peoples (Encuentro Intercultural de Pueblos Indígenas) that the council staged in the middle of Chilpancingo in April 2000, about 500 people representing Guerrero's four different ethnicities participated in discussions about the meaning of autonomy and self-determination. They also came to share their culture with each other, to play music, and to dance. It was great fun. But it was also quite serious, with the council's directors devoting an entire weekend to explanations in five different languages of international and national laws affecting indigenous peoples. An event like this was the only time in the year that community members could hear about and discuss these laws and their rights as indigenous peoples. My conversations with participants, perusal of meeting minutes, and general observations suggest that the work of consciousness raising (*concientización*) was just beginning.

The form of the encounter included four different tents representing each ethnicity. The subjects of the discussions rotated throughout the weekend and a council director was in charge of explaining the issues and soliciting feedback from community members. Directors talked mostly about ILO Convention 169, the changes to Articles 4 and 27 of the Constitution, the San Andrés Accords, environmental issues, the autonomy movements in Rancho Nuevo de la Democracia, and the Community Police (Policía Comunitaria) in San Luis Acatlán. These were to be discussions in the language corresponding to an ethnicity. But when, on 9 April 2000, I asked Melchiades, a member of Seojtli Llankuik, what had transpired under the Nahua tent, he told me he had not understood much that was said because it had been presented in Spanish. He was not sure, for example, what the Community Police really was. He asserted that the government had to fulfill its obligations to indigenous peoples "because of the law they were talking about . . . the Constitution [Article 4]. . . . The government needs to listen to us." Isidro, however, whose Spanish was better, told me that the Nahua tent liked hearing about the Policía Comunitaria and wanted something like this for the Chilapa region. And he was fully prepared to hold more workshops back in their communities: "We'll take back what we have learned to sow ideas."

Melchiades, meanwhile, confirmed what I had observed: that little, if any, interethnic dialogue had taken place. "We don't understand each other and each group prefers to speak its own language," he said, even though he had spoken fine Spanish with me. All the while we talked, Pedro de Jesús Alejandro was making an impassioned speech on the main stage, peppering it with references to national heroes like "Nuestro Generalísimo José María Morelos y Pavón." I asked Melchiades what he thought of the speech and he told me he thought few people understood what Pedro was saying. Nevertheless, during their discussion period, Nahua attendees clearly articulated the issues they believed were important, issues shared with other ethnicities, and these were duly noted by council directors. The practical absence of the municipal government, for example, and its broken promises—an issue that made the idea of an autonomous municipality like Rancho Nuevo very appealing. The rejection of political parties, for the same reasons, because they did not help. The desire to implement and have respected indigenous law and custom. The Amuzgo representatives also liked the idea of the Community Police because they could not trust the state police. They liked ILO Convention 169, too.

This consensus across ethnic groups that did not speak to one another came about because most, if not all, attendees were members of organizations within the council. The Mixtecos were largely from the municipality in rebellion, Rancho Nuevo de la Democracia, while the Nahuas were from the Alto Balsas region and from groups like Seojtli Llankuik that had years of organizing experience within the council. The Tlapanecos had a similar experience, including within the Community Police itself. The Amuzgos alone were relatively new to the council, but were strong traditionalists, a trait I suspected made them highly receptive to discussions about autonomy and self-determination. My suspicion was confirmed by Doña Florencia, an Amuzga master artist, who told me on 9 April 2000, "I no longer believe in political parties, but the Guerrero Council supports traditional ways like organic fertilizer and traditional authorities, which I like." Thus, even though the council's directors were preaching to the choir, these groups were in a particularly good position to take this information home and disseminate it.

This was not the case, however, in the day-to-day work the council did either out of its central office or in the regions. As Ricardo, an Amuzgo director, told me on 5 January 2000, "The most urgent issue, the most necessary for most Indian peoples, is productive projects, more than justice." According to Martha Sánchez Néstor, the great challenge for the Guerrero Council was overcoming a community focus on the money the council could channel toward a local project. The problem was, she explained on 26 January 2000, "that without a political consciousness of indigenous rights, communities will just go to whichever group will give them what they most need at that moment. A consciousness of rights can go beyond the party system." The council derived its legitimacy among communities from its ability to deliver, however. Whereas council directors may have seen their participation in a clientelist relationship with the government in the context of a national project for indigenous rights, community members with immediate needs did not see this larger context.

A client/broker relationship was familiar and often worked in a community's favor, after all. Martha's concern, shared by other directors, was that a client/broker was *all* the council really was. A consciousness of rights could work to strengthen the entire movement because individuals and communities would have the confidence to speak out against abuses; they could also then balance their short-term needs with long-term goals. Florencio, a council director who helped found the Community Police, spoke at length with me on 16 May 2000 about the pressing need to raise the consciousness of communities around the issue of the privatization of ejido land. The reform to Article 27 of the Constitution allowed ejidatarios to sell their plots, and many in the San Luis Acatlán region were doing so. Florencio made the connection between this problem and the need for a larger project of economic self-sufficiency: "Six or seven ejidos rejected privatization, but the others accepted [it] because they lacked information. Ninety percent of peasants are very poor and they are going to sell their land to ranchers. But then these peasants will need to work, and they will become renters on their own land. Now the Policía Comunitaria are paid by the communities, and if the communities don't have money, neither will the police, so we need a new proposal to guarantee self-sufficiency in the region." The consciousness-raising campaign Florencio had in mind was still only a proposal, but it had the following elements: "We need a consciousness-raising campaign about ecology and health," he explained. "We need regional meetings where the leaders will meet and explain to others why we need change. Do you want change? Well, begin to change yourselves first. Stop being egoists, stop being greedy. Each one needs to go back to your pueblo and tell people about what's happening. People need information first in order to analyze their options."

Florencio's proposal reminded me that the local/global split divided the group's leadership from communities, which is not to say that the leadership was unrepresentative. The cultural distance between the two showed how much most indigenous people are still forced into a place of poverty, as an effect of the "structural abyss" José del Val Blanco described. The central government's programs for poverty alleviation, especially Solidarity, may have extolled the virtues of indigenous participation, but they were never meant to eliminate the poverty that defines Indians. In effect, indigenismo remained the same the more it changed. The government offers only so much before it withdraws again in order to maintain the inherently unequal relation of power it has with indigenous peoples.

Beyond Folkloric Poverty

> The main ideological role of populist discourse has been to mobilize grassroots support in defense of the agrarian myth, while at the same time depoliticizing this process, an objective achieved historically by means of linking "popular" culture with nationalism and simultaneously delinking both from politics.
>
> —TOM BRASS, *Peasants, Populism, and Postmodernism* (2000)

In Mexico, the legacy of indigenismo serves an important political function. Even though a self-consciously political indigenous movement has discredited this national ideology of cultural assimilation, the particular kind of Indian indigenistas constructed as real—poor, isolated, and culturally distinct—remains a potent symbol. But the marginalization of Indians in Mexico has much more to do with politics than with "tradition" and Indian culture, which indigenistas privileged. The focus of most community members on the autonomy of the pueblo has a long history, beginning with the Spanish Conquest. It is also the result of the subsequent marginalization of the local community in Mexico's centralized political system—not the result of an isolationist culture. When Indians act in ways to open up their political identity to go far beyond the pueblo—as the council's directors did—it ought to be evaluated positively as a step toward their full participation in the nation.

But it is not. Instead, the full force of indigenismo's Indian is brought to bear upon indigenous groups and individuals who simultaneously speak for and beyond the local community. Even those who are most cosmopolitan prefer to minimize the importance of their identity in favor of an emphasis on the virtues of "real" Indians back home. Sensitive to charges of inauthenticity, the council's directors used the indigenista image of the Indian to legitimize the work that they did, consistently linking this image to their populist claims to citizenship rights. Thus only Mexico's real Indians, embodying the nation's cultural patrimony, deserved "to feel and be real Mexicans." Thus, too, cultural identity and political legitimacy are inextricably linked.

As a result, "indigenous issues" still get defined at the level of the community, which permits a kind of political quarantine to keep indigenous peoples and their larger demands on the state safely isolated. If indigenous leaders can only speak for their communities, then they cannot legitimately represent anyone or anything else while still claiming to be Indian and to speak for Indians. The dominance of Subcomandante Marcos as the voice of the EZLN is the best example of the indigenous leadership's isolation from national and international political discourse. Given the logic of folkloric poverty, only a mestizo like Marcos would have the authority to speak simultaneously for Indians *and* for those outside of the community.[21] Just as the nation-state is the privileged political and cultural space, so is the populist Indian sketched out above the privileged subject of this space. Both are constructions of what James Tully (1995, 58) calls a Western "empire of uniformity." As Ludwig Wittgenstein (in Tully 1995, 58) argued, "A *picture* held us captive. And we could not get outside of it, for it lay in our language and language seemed to repeat it to us inexorably." Confined by the picture of the "Indian," the council's and the larger Mexican indigenous movement's citizenship claims on the nation-state can only be limited in their scope and effectiveness.

---

21. Navidad Gutiérrez (1999, 195) notes that "while the Indian peoples certainly occupy a place of relevance in the political scenario, no ethnic intellectual input has been made apparent. And such a vacuum of indigenous ideas, at a public level, is of fundamental importance.... From the beginning of the [Chiapas] conflict up to the present phase of parliamentary approval of a new law on indigenous rights and culture, Indian ideas and spokespersons have been systematically left out." She quotes the Nahua leader Marcos Matías Alonso: "'If people like [Subcomandante] Marcos would withdraw from the negotiating table, another set of results could be obtained, because they cannot adequately synthesize indigenous claims.... Indian peoples cannot be restricted to [being represented by] a nonindigenous man. This cannot be'" (196).

CONCLUSION:
THE EXHAUSTION OF THE INDIGENOUS MOVEMENT:
WHAT COMES NEXT?

It continues to be evident that the organizational weakness of [social] movements acts as a barrier in their struggle. These groups do not have a clearly functioning structure; their discourse and material demands bring them together, which can be an advantage and a disadvantage.

—DAVID VELASCO, DIRECTOR OF THE CENTRO DE DERECHOS HUMANOS, DECEMBER 2005

Folkloric Poverty began with the observation that, by 2000, the national indigenous movement in Mexico—the loosely coordinated organization of many different groups—was in crisis. It then asked why that was so after a decade of unprecedented visibility and achievement. An examination of the Guerrero Council's brief life, a life that exemplified this larger achievement, allows us to understand how several factors contributed to the weakness of a group that was uniquely positioned to advance its agenda at the local, national, and transnational levels. This conclusion reviews these factors to clarify how, taken together, they constituted a significant obstacle to the political power of indigenous peoples in Mexico. In contributing to this analysis, my interviews with council leaders in 2005 also suggest current and future directions—the next phase of the movement, or movements.

At the heart of my argument is a figure that embodies what I call "folkloric poverty," the deliberate and pervasive restriction of the Indian to a space zoned for poverty, a figure elaborated by indigenistas for years: the traditional, authentic Indian, defined only by his community (indigenous women have only recently been taken into consideration, as discussed below). Like folklore more generally, folkloric poverty was an important expression of Mexican national identity in the twentieth century, no matter how confused that expression was. We saw, for example, how indigenistas oscillated between assertions that the Indian was the essence of Mexico, on the one hand, and a stranger to it, on the other. Although, in the 1990s, this oscillation settled mostly on the Indian as Mexican essence, the function of folkloric poverty always remained the same, which was to shore up a Mexican national identity distinct from its neighbor immediately to the north. In the 1950s, such a distinction was important in the context of a centralizing nation-state that promoted the cultural homogenization of its citizens; folkloric poverty legitimated integrationist policies that would bring isolated Indians fully into the nation and thereby strengthen Mexico vis-à-vis the United States. In the 1990s, the distinction was important in the context of a spun-off state whose key functionaries were eager to be economically and culturally closer to the United States than ever before. During this decade, folkloric poverty functioned like Brass's agrarian myth, as part of an attempt to legitimize the regime and its economic policy through the appeal to a shared primordial ethnonational identity. This primordialism, the México profundo, formed the basis of a nationalistic Mexican multiculturalism, which was expressed most clearly in the San Andrés Accords, and which became the slogan of the indigenous movement (as several indigenous groups declared in 1994, "We want to feel and be real Mexicans, part of one living fatherland that is ours").

It was a populist multiculturalism compatible at once with Mexico's neoliberal opening and with the rise of a national indigenous movement that took advantage of the government's rhetorical support for indigenous rights ("autonomy") and indigenous participation. President Salinas's Solidarity program took the place of broad government assistance to the peasantry, setting up instead targeted programs like the Regional Solidarity Funds, which characterized indigenous peasants as self-sufficient small businesspeople who operated best in a free market unfettered by dependence on an onerous government for their livelihoods. Although such a characterization made sense in a neoliberal world where support for "self-determination" complemented the central government's withdrawal from rural areas, it made little sense in the real world of grinding rural indigenous poverty. Nevertheless, indigenous groups like the council appreciated the opportunity that Solidarity and official multiculturalism offered at a time when *peasant* issues no longer appeared to matter to the government, as the official end of land reform confirmed.

Ironically, the danger lay in the fact that government agencies defined *indigenous* issues only as peasant issues, that is, as issues of poor rural communities—as folkloric poverty. The council accepted this definition because it was an organization of peasant groups, but also because the leadership perpetuated the complex of terms—local, peasant, poor—that continues to define the "real Indian." Stuck in this groove, the council appealed to the government as peasants always had, as clients who depended on personalistic ties to those in power for access to basic resources. Although the new language of Indian rights and participation seemed to strengthen this appeal, we saw how endless bureaucratic webs consistently ensnared the group and worked to defer real improvement in indigenous lives. As the council's own history tells it, the group "fell into a dynamic of clientelist processes" because of the "organizational trajectory of an important group of leaders oriented toward obtaining resources and services" (Consejo Guerrerense 2001, 63). This particular orientation was not only an old habit, however. It was also a response to two things that are products of and sources for the idea and image of folkloric poverty: the strong localism of community members, whose personal identities are rooted in their home pueblos (the double meaning of this word in Spanish, both "town" and "people," reinforces this identity), and the widespread lack of basic services and infrastructure in rural communities.

The persistence of localism among indigenous communities combined with official and indigenous movement discourses privileging localism to act as powerful centrifugal forces on the council, dispersing its energies and its leadership in numerous directions. Localism was also the basis for the disparagement and dismissal of any indigenous leaders who attempted to act beyond the borders of their pueblos. If a leader happened to be firmly located in a community and then spoke in a forum outside of this community, what the leader said could be ignored because others would say that this person represented only a particular place. But even if a leader happened to be more cosmopolitan and less connected to a particular place, the leader could be similarly dismissed as speaking only for him- or herself. This placed indigenous leaders in a dilemma that was hard to escape, given the persistence of folkloric poverty as the measure of real indigenousness. For the council's leaders, it was a pernicious dilemma that pitted individual against individual ("los 'nailons'" versus "la base," for example) and remained unresolved. The more a leader was in Mexico

City or abroad, the less the leader was considered a true part of the movement, but the more a leader remained in his or her own region, the less the leader was able to support the movement as a whole. When, on 9 July 2005, I asked Eufemia, one of the council's four women directors, to comment on the reasons for the group's disintegration, she told me that the council "became divided because we lost the trust between the older leaders. We came to lose trust and respect for one another—there was no longer anything like collective rights nor that great unity we'd had at the beginning." When the state government ended its financial support of the council in 2002,[1] most of the directors remained in their regions working locally because they could no longer afford to make the trip to Chilpancingo: there were no other sources of funding available, and the communities were too poor to help much, despite half a century of rural development programs. And so the council had come full circle in just over ten years: first emerging out of the local—and then ending with a return to it.

In assessing the council's weaknesses on 11 July 2005, Pedro de Jesús Alejandro pointed to the leadership's emphasis on material demands. "We had a project focused on peasants and economics [*un proyecto economicista y campesinista*] and not on politics in terms of our rights. Only a handful of the leaders understood or were interested in a far-reaching political program." The council's failure, he told me, "was that we didn't work harder to raise the political consciousness of those in the council, especially those who entered later." Eufemia had made much the same criticism on 9 July 2005, when she said that "a new leadership was needed. In the first year, [the council] could have formed the first generation of leaders and, in the second year, the leadership could have changed to let new leaders enter. But it did not change." Pedro added that no one wanted to step forward to take charge of the group's direction for fear of being the one accused of whatever might go wrong (this fear became especially acute after the expulsion of Martín Equihua). This meant that directors had another incentive to remain focused on their own microregions, usually involved in local party politics.

Néstor was even more frank when I spoke with him on 12 July 2005, asserting that it was the corruption of the leadership that led to the end of the council—though it was not clear to me what precisely was involved in this corruption. Now, said Néstor, "none of the former directors have any legitimacy in the communities because even the honest ones have been

---

1. Until 2002, the State of Guerrero had been giving the group 60,000 pesos (about 6,000 dollars) each month to be distributed among sixteen directors, Eufemia told me.

tainted by association. Even the word *council* is rejected by organizations!" In this situation, he continued, "we [former directors] can only have a role as advisors, not as visible leaders anymore. We will have to support others and train them without actually assuming a leadership role."

Falls from Grace

Among national indigenous leaders, who represent a variety of regions and groups, there is considerable divisiveness precisely because the issues of authenticity and legitimacy remain potent. Those who have chosen to work in the government are pitted against those in academia and those in or sympathetic to the Zapatista National Liberation Army (EZLN), which will have nothing at all to do with the central government. In these conflicts, the populist Indian and the grass roots (*las bases*) remain the final arbiters of authenticity. In March 2005, for example, Luis Hernández Navarro, an editor at *La Jornada* (Mexico City) and a longtime supporter of the EZLN, wrote an editorial criticizing the ANIPA for being "prepared to collaborate with a government of the right. The new administration thus began with the co-optation of a sector of the indigenous movement" (Hernández Navarro 2005). For Hernández Navarro (2005), this "co-optation" meant that the leadership had distanced itself from the real struggle for indigenous rights at the local level: "The road toward conquering the institutions by one part of one of the currents of the Indian movement ended in disaster. The construction of indigenous autonomy from below will be built on the ruins of this collapse."

In response to Hernández Navarro, Julio Atenco Vidal wrote a long letter to *La Jornada,* which was never published, but which remains on the ANIPA's Web site.[2] Atenco Vidal explained that Fox, unlike any president before him, had during his inauguration "manifested his support for the legitimacy of the Indians' struggle for the constitutional recognition of their collective rights, especially the right to autonomy and self-determination, and he pledged to turn the San Andrés Accords into law. Which Mexican head of state had expressed this political recognition before the Mexican nation in such a solemn act? Wasn't this a political opportunity for our peoples and Indian organizations?" Atenco Vidal framed the issue as a choice between political pragmatism and ideological

---

2. For Julio Atenco Vidal's response to Luis Hernández Navarro, see http://www.anipa.org/anipa/respuestajulioatenco.html/ (accessed 8 August 2006).

orthodoxy, noting that Hernández Navarro and Subcomandante Marcos (whom Atenco Vidal calls "el Obispo," the Bishop) disingenuously ignored the "extremely hopeful" possibility that Fox initially offered to indigenous peoples. "Who dared to renounce his claim to ideological purity," Atenco Vidal asked, "in order to take Fox at his word and push him even further in this direction? No one. Stupidly mistaking inaction for politics (which it can never be), we did ourselves in since what we Indians need is precisely high-level interlocutors in the Mexican state. The only thing possible at this time was the fear of political demonization by those 'pure of heart and immaculate image' like Luis and the Bishop." Atenco Vidal accused Hernández Navarro and Marcos of being just like the "reactionary right," of being "equally exclusionist and oppressive of minorities; they do not seek a real sincere dialogue that could lead to the conciliation and reconciliation of majorities. What isn't good for them isn't good for anybody; they only know how to impose their own interests, ideas, projects, policy, and ideology."

One year later, in April 2006, the ANIPA had another response, this time for "Delegate Zero," as Marcos now called himself.[3] Like its 2005 letter, the ANIPA's 2006 missive makes it clear that the EZLN no longer speaks for the "indigenous movement," which now more than ever comprises many different groups with no single leadership. The letter explicitly questions Marcos's authority to speak for indigenous peoples and suggests there are multiple ways to advance the indigenous cause. It is worth quoting at length for the group's characterization of the strife between these two prominent national indigenous organizations:

> A few days ago . . . on 23 April, in the context of the "Other Campaign," Subcomandante Marcos, now self-named Delegate Zero, had the courtesy to show us his great insensitivity and the greater part of the true face behind the mask, when he slipped in again his animosity toward our organization, the ANIPA, and toward the national indigenous movement that would not be (and is not) under his tutelage.
>
> Recently, the Subcomandante has made a great deal of his courage [*ha hecho gala de su bravura*] in the face of everything that is not like him, that doesn't think like him, that doesn't act like him or that doesn't do things as he asks. Behind his mask of a rebel sub "indigenous" [?] leader, he lets us catch a glimpse of the true face of intolerance, arrogance, and pedantry that belongs to those who are most

---

3. For the ANIPA's April 2006 response, see http://www.anipa.org/anipa.respuestaalsub.html/ (accessed 8 August 2006).

> authoritarian, retrograde, and anachronistic. He forgets that the ANIPA is not his enemy but his ally . . . he forgets that the ANIPA is not the one he needs to fight but the one with whom to share experiences and build unity in diversity. The Sub[comandante] forgets that many organizations in the ANIPA gave him our support . . . that many of the ANIPA's members were advisors to the EZLN in the dialogue with the federal government to build the San Andrés Accords; and that these accords had their antecedents in the debates where thousands of sisters and brothers participated in the three assemblies that the ANIPA held before San Andrés, introducing the theme of indigenous rights when the Sub was occupied with other things.

The letter provides examples of the different ways indigenous peoples are attempting to gain control over their lives, from educational to territorial to producer initiatives, and it includes in its list the "efforts and constant struggle of our sisters and brothers of the EZLN." It is careful to single out Marcos himself for criticism and not the movement he represents, which is understood to be one of many possibilities for indigenous mobilization. Like Atenco Vidal, the writers of this letter are vexed by Marcos's disparagement of groups and individuals that do not precisely follow the Zapatista program.

> The Subcomandante has said: "We are not going to do what the ANIPA is doing, pleading with the government to see if it will please notice them and give them positions [in the government]. We don't want these things. We want to get rid of governments. We've been to many states, almost twenty now, and everywhere we've found Indian peoples and city people who are fed up, indignant, and who want to organize themselves outside of political parties."
> We say that there are different ways to conceive of and practice the empowerment of our peoples, our rights, and our cultures. Of course, there are sisters and brothers of the ANIPA who have occupied and occupy political spaces in different government bodies, but it is worth clarifying that these are spaces that indigenous organizations secured as the result of great efforts made in the hope of politically influencing the transformation of our peoples' historical reality. This is one of the many ways that we believe should be recognized and respected by the different actors and sectors of society within the context of diversity, self-determination, and autonomy. In addition, the ANIPA considers public funds to be this—public—that have

their origin in the sweat and taxes of Mexican workers; the ANIPA demands a just redistribution of these funds for the elimination of poverty. This is in contrast to the Sub, whose funding for his transportation, his luxurious truck, and the comforts of spending are of doubtful provenance. Another incongruity?

The letter ends with a scathing attack on and the explicit rejection of Marcos as informal leader of the indigenous movement. "After accompanying the Sub in his romantic revolutionary adventures, today he demonstrates to us that he does not fight for the autonomy and self-determination of our peoples but instead uses the indigenous as a discourse that legitimates his desire for power by maintaining his ego worship in the press.... The real transformation of this country will not be realized by great personalities but by an organized people. 'Never again an indigenous autonomy without indigenous peoples.'"

New Leaders

This explicit and public rejection signals a significant change, in which the EZLN is no longer the only measure of indigenousness and political effectiveness. In a politically pluralistic context, the imperative to "close ranks" around the Zapatistas, a defining characteristic of the 1990s, has lost its power as Marcos has appeared less and less tolerant of the differences he once famously celebrated. Nevertheless, the multiplicity that is indigenous politics today would not have been possible without organizations like the EZLN and the Guerrero Council, which nurtured the development of new leaders and new organizations. For Eufemia, the council's success can be measured by the education of a new generation of leaders like her, who are working now at all political levels. The council, she told me on 9 July 2005, "was my teacher in the process of learning about the rights of indigenous peoples and the movement of indigenous peoples. I was trained in this organization.... There isn't a school for this. How are you going to learn this if not within an organization? Now the new generations are energized to continue this work." With the demotion of the EZLN and the demise of the council, an indigenous leadership has begun to break out of the confinement of folkloric poverty to speak legitimately about issues that transcend the local community. When President Fox took office, he worked closely with indigenous leaders to reform the INI so that by 2003 it became a new federal entity, now called the "National

Commission for the Development of Indigenous Peoples" (Comisión Nacional para el Desarrollo de los Pueblos Inígenas, or CDI). Under President Fox, indigenous leaders attained prominent positions at both state and national levels. Marcos Matías Alonso, a Nahua anthropologist from Guerrero, was general director of the INI for a brief period in 2001–2 and then became a federal congressman. Pedro de Jesús Alejandro was the CDI's representative in Guerrero, followed by another Nahua leader from the Alto Balsas region, while his brother Carlos worked for the state of Guerrero in the Technical Secretariat for Indigenous Affairs (Secretaría Técnica de Asuntos Indígenas, or SETAI). Martha Sánchez Néstor was executive director of the Plural National Indigenous Assembly for Autonomy (ANIPA) for two years, while her brother was in charge of legal affairs for the CDI–Guerrero. This attainment of official positions, especially at the national level, is in striking contrast to the situation I witnessed in 2000 and is an indication of the political evolution of this generation of leaders. To be sure, this leadership remains confined to "indigenous issues," which appear to be defined as local issues even now; the images of folkloric poverty persist, for example, in the Web pages of the CDI (see http://www.cdi.gob.mx). Nevertheless, these positions are part of the transition toward another phase of indigenous mobilization that may yet transcend its political confinement.

Although an increasing involvement in local and state party politics characterizes this new phase—with potential long-term consequences—what is truly new and significant for the future is an emerging leadership of indigenous women. Out of the ashes of the council, for example, the four women who had been directors in the organization formed the Guerrero Indigenous Women's Coordinating Committee (Coordinadora Guerrerense de Mujeres Indígenas), which works with the National Indigenous Women's Coordinating Committee of Mexico (Coordinadora Nacional de Mujeres Indígenas de México), based in Mexico City. These women had worked earlier with the National Coordinating Committee, dividing their time between this work and their work in the council.[4] With the demise of the council, the women took the opportunity to continue their work in a new organization. On 9 July 2005, Eufemia sketched out how they began: "We were participating in forums and workshops where we said that we will throw out the bad customs and we will rescue the good

---

4. There were tensions in the council over the women's dividing their time. Eufemia told me on 9 July 2005 that "the men said, 'Well, where are the women?' and 'Why don't they come to the meetings? Why did they go abroad?' They wanted us to ask permission. No, no, no, no. It was like we were in competition with the men."

ones. And we were thinking about how to create new customs to replace the bad ones we got rid of. For example, how do we indigenous women want to live? Because those who most suffer violence are the women, and not so much the men. Those who suffer twice [as indigenous people and as women] are we women." An indigenous women's leadership was reframing the discussion of Indian cultures, she told me, with serious implications for the future. Not content to accept community culture as given and timeless, indigenous women are opening up a debate about values and customs that threatens male power structures as it also threatens notions of a homogeneous indigenousness. Martha Sánchez Néstor (2004) writes that

> our work as indigenous women has been taken negatively because they say that we are feminists disconnected from community reality, where our people "walk together as equals" [*caminamos parejo*]; that it is not true that men are worth more than women, they assure us, and they have assured us in public events that in our communities there is harmony and complementarity. They say that we indigenous women who use concepts like "gender," "gender perspective," "advocacy," "empowerment," "s/he," "equity," "sexual and reproductive rights"—that these are matters of feminists, who have manipulated us, filling our heads with many bad things that don't have anything to do with community realities.

"In our country," Martha goes on to say, "to speak of women who break the silence, who decide, who choose, and who as a result break with traditional roles, transgress the family norms that form the basis of the society—so say some politicians and others in the Church—is to speak of women who are crazy, who are feminists. . . . If to be a feminist means to fight for the respect and recognition of the rights of the indigenous woman, then, yes, I am an indigenous feminist." Martha is nevertheless quick to point to the dangers inherent to an indigenous feminist critique of indigenous community structures that can easily be used by others to deny the legitimacy of any community authorities:

> It is important to recognize that we [indigenous women] still live subject to the collective decisions [of our communities] and this suggests the necessary reform of our customs and traditions, a highly polemical discussion in Mexico. . . . We say emphatically that while it is true that we suffer the most from extreme poverty, it remains

clear to us that this is not only because of indigenous customs, but precisely because of the Mexican State's low intensity war, with its racist policies that generate violence, malnutrition, illiteracy, and inequality, and that lead to the slow disappearance of our identity as peoples and as indigenous women.

Though careful to condemn the federal and state governments for policies that weaken communities,[5] Martha is writing mostly to criticize a male indigenous leadership that "accepts the presence of indigenous women only when it does not undermine their own voice. We want to push for not only the theoretical recognition [of women] but also for recognition and respect in practice, which in [indigenous] organizations is still a goal to be reached." The emergence of more women in leadership positions strongly suggests that indigenous politics will become even more diverse, representing more than ever the heterogeneity that is Indian Mexico. Martha points in this direction:

> We hear many women with long experience working to make visible the problems and proposals of women from diverse sectors—peasants, blacks, indigenous, youth—we include them as women in a larger movement of NGOs, academics, researchers, consultants, companions. In our experience we've seen that we come from a diverse world, one that allows you to see that diversity in a community is not the same as the diversity in a city, let alone in another country.... I believe our struggle has its own rhythm even though for some it will seem incipient or slow. It comes from the mountains where the echoes generate voices that break down barriers and find themselves with other diverse voices. The challenge here has been to listen to the great number of expressions because there is no homogeneity. On the contrary, we are plural and diverse and this is only an expression of the diverse cultures from which we come.

One senses here a deliberate movement by an indigenous women's leadership away from the folkloric poverty that has most often defined indigenous women in particular as those most local and most poor.[6] But

---

5. See also Sánchez Néstor's essay on the high rates of maternal mortality among indigenous women at http://www.anipa.org/anipa/mortalidadmaternaconvivenciaconmujeresindigenas.htm/ (accessed 10 August 2008).

6. Faced with the idealization of the indigenous past, on one side, and with a racist denigration of indigenous culture, on the other, "organized indigenous women have confronted

the Guerrero Indigenous Women's Coordinating Committee and other women's organizations confront daunting conditions. Indigenous women are often excluded from decision making, Martha points out, and they also have less access to basic health services, which means, for example, that indigenous women are far more likely to die in childbirth than nonindigenous women are.[7] There are significant structural obstacles in the way of real change for indigenous women and, by extension, for the families and communities that depend on these women. With the extreme poverty of indigenous women, it is no coincidence, Gillette Hall and Harry Patrinos (2005, 4) tell us, that "controlling for basic factors known to be strongly associated with poverty, such as age, education, employment status and region within a country, being indigenous still significantly increases one's chances of being poor." Indigenous women are making the connection between women's well-being and the advancement of indigenous peoples more generally; leaders like Martha and Eufemia suggest to me that this is the direction that a national indigenous movement is taking, however slowly.

"A Style of Communication": Old Issues

Indigenous and mestizo peasant movements in Guerrero continue to express old grievances against the same basic power structures in the state: the military and state and municipal governments. In Xochistlahuaca in 2004, Amuzgos united in opposition to the well-established cacicazgo of Aceadeth Rocha and her family (also Amuzgo) began transmitting from the studio of Radio Ñomndaa, La Palabra del Agua, and have suffered various state and federal attempts to shut them down ever since. Then, in late 2007, Rocha started her own "community" radio station out of her house, which daily broadcasts its support for the municipal government ("Panorama" 2008). Thus the fight against caciques, which started in Xochistlahuaca back in the 1970s, is not over. Other groups with names

---

both representations, demanding before the State their right to cultural difference and before the indigenous movement their right to change the cultural forms that threaten their human rights. . . . Indigenous women are providing guidelines for rethinking multiculturalism and autonomy from the perspective of a dynamic culture that is being formed and reformed daily" (Hernández Castillo 2002, 151).

7. In Guerrero's indigenous areas, the maternal mortality rate is more than four times the state average, with 283 versus 70 deaths per 100,000. Guerrero has the highest maternal mortality rate of any state in Mexico. See http://www.anipa.org/anipa/mortalidadmaternaconvivenciaconmujeresindigenas.html/ (accessed 10 August 2008).

that draw on the history of Guerrero's popular radicalism such as Francisco Villa's People's Front (Frente Popular Francisco Villa), the People's Defense Front (Frente de Defensa Popular), the Social Left Movement (Movimiento Social de Izquierda), the Popular Assembly of the Peoples of Guerrero (Asamblea Popular de los Pueblos de Guerrero), and the more famous Peasant Organization of the Sierra del Sur (Organización Campesina de la Sierra del Sur, or OCSS), whose members were cut down in a 1995 police ambush in Aguas Blancas, continue to march on Chilpancingo and Mexico City to demand affordable fertilizer and the completion of infrastructure projects, as well as the removal of the military from their communities (Cervantes 2008). Meanwhile, the Community Police (Policía Comunitaria), based in San Luis Acatlán, is still defending itself from the combined forces of the state and federal police and the military, who indiscriminately interrogate and photograph individuals in an ostensible search for kidnappers who, the police insist, do not exist in the region. The police's region nevertheless continues to grow: from fifty-six participating communities in January 2008 to seventy-two only six months later, a testament both to the effectiveness of the Community Police and to the ineffectiveness of the state police in curbing crime—indeed, to the state's deliberate incitement of lawlessness.

The same combination of state and federal police and the military operates in the municipality of Ayutla, where the Organization of Me'phaa Indigenous People (Organización del Pueblo Indígena Me'phaa, or OPIM) has protested the forced sterilization of thirteen indigenous men in 1998 (and one in 2001) by the local cacique working with the state department of health.[8] The OPIM has also protested the cacique's exploitation of communal forests for his and his group's personal benefit, as well as the embezzlement of funds allocated for community electrification (Gutiérrez 2008). When five municipal policemen were ambushed and killed in early 2008, the military and federal police entered and set up checkpoints throughout the municipality. Not surprisingly, the cacique—who heads a known paramilitary group—accused the OPIM of being a guerrilla group, implying that it was responsible for the policemen's murders.

The long-standing connection between the police and the military and business interests (local, national, international) remains a powerful repressive force in Guerrero that peasants continue to fight. The most famous

---

8. "Me'phaa" is preferred over "Mixteco"—a Nahuatl name—as the self-designation by this ethnicity in Guerrero. The 1998 sterilizations have been the concern of human rights groups in Mexico since they were first reported in 1999 (Overmyer-Velázquez 2003).

example of this resistance is the Peasant Environmentalist Organization of the Sierra de Petatlán and Coyuca de Catalán (Organización de Campesinos Ecologistas de la Sierra de Petatlán y Coyuca de Catalán, or OCESP) in the Costa Grande region. OCESP organized in 1998 to stop Boise Cascade's logging of communal forests, which had been reduced in extent by 40 percent in only eight years.[9] Among other repressive measures, two of OCESP's leaders were arrested in 1999 on charges of drug possession, convicted, and imprisoned for two years. After intense international pressure was brought to bear—Amnesty International named them prisoners of conscience, and they were awarded the Chico Méndez and Goldman environmental prizes—President Fox pardoned the two men. But this did not end OCESP's activism nor the government's repression of the group, which it predictably called a "guerrilla group." By 2008, women ecologists were working in Petatlán with the OCESP to reforest the region and develop conservation, hydrological, and ecotourism projects, proving yet again that "despite the setbacks and losses the actions of Guerrero's peasants prove that the 'economy of the subject' continues to be a shared Arcadia" (Bartra 2000, 428).[10]

In April 2005, a momentous change took place in Guerrero, one expected to have a positive impact on indigenous communities. The Party of the Democratic Revolution (PRD) won the governorship of the state and a majority of the municipalities that month from the Institutional Revolutionary Party (PRI), which had always ruled the state in close coordination with the PRI government in Mexico City. Many of the council's former directors had been working in the PRD at the state and local levels, and it was not unrealistic to hope that the new state government would take indigenous issues more seriously than the PRI had. The trouble was that the new government inherited a legacy of corruption and would have to work with limited resources. The state had a public debt of more than 3 billion pesos (approximately 300 million dollars), about 15 percent of the state's total budget, a result in part of very low rates of tax collection

---

9. The state governor had signed the agreement permitting Boise Cascade to operate on ejido lands in the Costa Grande region; local caciques were also taking their cut of the logging. Boise Cascade left Guerrero in 1999, but the logging continued. See Tlachinollan's Web site for a detailed account of this case: http://www.tlachninollan.org/casos/ecologistas/01marco.html/ (accessed 12 July 2008).

10. As another example of the continuing struggle of indigenous peoples to defend their lands, indigenous peasants in the municipality of Acapulco have, since 2003, actively and legally opposed the construction of the massive La Parota dam, which threatens to flood twenty-one communities and will directly affect 25,000 people, who will have to be moved to other lands. See http://www.tlachninollan.org/casos/parota.html/ (accessed 12 July 2008).

and "excessive and disorderly" state spending (de la Cruz 2005, 2). Moreover, the vast majority of rural development funds had been spent on fertilizer—repeatedly given and withheld by the state as a political weapon—and much of this to nonexistent organizations; as a result, the countryside was severely undercapitalized, with 97 percent of the soils in the state eroded (2). With such troubles, it was going to take a great deal of work for the new government to rid itself of the inertia of the past.

On my visit to Guerrero in 2005, I witnessed how this inertia and the continuing power of folkloric poverty acted to limit the possibility for change in indigenous lives. Authorities from Nación Amuzga, the Xochistlahuaca "municipality in rebellion" that Martha Sánchez Néstor supported, had arrived at the state government offices in Chilpancingo to denounce the continuing violation of civil rights by the officially elected PRI municipal government. The cousin of the former municipal president, Aceadeth Rocha (whose brother was now municipal president), had attacked a member of Nación Amuzga with a machete, and the local state prosecutor's office had done nothing about it. Nación Amuzga represented communities that chose their authorities through community consensus, which valued individuals who have worked for the community in a variety of traditional posts; they opposed the official municipal government's practice

Then: the old state government building or Governor's Palace (Palacio de Gobierno) in Chilpancingo with marchers just outside, 1999.

Now: the new state government complex outside of Chilpancingo, 2005. The former Institutional Revolutionary Party (PRI) government had moved the Governor's Palace from the center of Chilpancingo to its periphery, put a heavy fence around it, installed a central gate manned by guards, and decentralized the buildings themselves. Now, instead of one large building there are several buildings, each housing the offices for a particular region of the state. Protest groups gather there, but they are kept safely outside of the fence and on the steps leading up to the gate, no longer a menace to the smooth functioning of the city.

of imposing its own choice of leadership in the municipality's towns. Thanks to its PRD affiliation, Nación Amuzga's representatives had an appointment to meet with Guerrero's second most powerful elected official, Armando Chavarría Barrera, the secretary general, in the new state government building just outside of the capital. Martha's brother Daniel, who worked at the CDI offices in Chilpancingo and was a member of Nación Amuzga, was the group's official connection to Chavarría; Daniel had also supported Chavarría in the PRD's internal contest to choose a gubernatorial candidate, which did not hurt the group's chances of meeting with the secretary general.

We were all ushered into a meeting room in the Costa Chica building to wait for Chavarría, who arrived like a conquering hero, shaking everyone's hand as he went around the table. Daniel immediately took charge of the entire meeting, clarifying why they were there, what they would say, and what they wanted. Other members of the delegation also spoke and offered their testimonies of the machete attack as just one more abuse they had suffered at the hands of violent and corrupt PRI authorities.

Impressively, right after the first testimonial was given, the secretary general called the state attorney in Ometepec to clarify the facts of the case. The telephone was ceremoniously brought to him at the table, where we all listened in on the high-level conversation and witnessed Chavarría express his concerns to the state attorney; it was a highly dramatic moment. When he hung up, the meeting abruptly ended, with Chavarría promising to look into everything and instructing an aide to give the group 3,500 pesos to pay for their lunch. This amount covered not only lunch but also the costs of the trip and the medical expenses of the injured man. As Daniel told me later, this was "pure populism." I marveled at Chavarría's blatant patronage and Daniel did, too, though not as much. He was careful to tell the group later that they should not be impressed with the money they were given and that they needed to keep the pressure on the government so that it would fulfill its promises. But since when did a top official give an opposition group like Nación Amuzga its attention, let alone so much money? This gesture was going to be hard to resist.

Besides the group's demand for justice, it also requested that the new PRD governor *not* visit Xochistlahuaca soon, as he was planning to do. The PRI candidate for the municipal presidency—Aceadeth Rocha, again—was telling everybody in the municipality that she was very close to the governor and the secretary general, so close that the governor was coming to visit *her* in *her house* to offer his support for her candidacy (which was not true, though it was likely he would visit her in her house because the current municipal president was her brother). She also went around announcing to one and all that she had "two breasts [*dos tetas*], one for the governor and another for the secretary general." The Nación Amuzga representatives feared that if the governor visited the municipality and went to the home of the municipal president—something he surely would do—community members would interpret this visit as evidence of his support for Aceadeth. They would then end up voting for her in the next election despite the well-known brutality and corruption of her entire family.

Thus even in a municipality dominated by indigenous peoples where there was a long history of caciques and despots, and where there was also a history of strong and visible social movements offering an alternative to the status quo—even here, the majority of the population favored the force of official authority, whatever the nature of that authority. Daniel acknowledged that he continued to be the one who interjected, clarified, and guided discussion in these meetings with officials because the others were afraid of state power and accepted its answers without question. "It's a *style* of communication between the powerful and the less powerful that remains prevalent," he told me on 13 July 2005. It is also a manifestation of the enduring effectiveness of folkloric poverty in Mexico today, where indigenous peoples continue to be confined to spaces outside the margins of power in both blatant and subtle ways, despite the mighty efforts of a restricted leadership to break out of this confinement. The future may not be bleak for indigenous peoples in Mexico, but it is certainly freighted with an onerous legacy—ideological and material—that an indigenous leadership, already divided, will be unable to overcome by itself. What comes next, then, will depend as much on the country as a whole as it will on the ability of this leadership to move into new political spaces not zoned for poverty.

references

Abrams, Jim. 1994. "Administration Defends Salinas, Lawmaker Questions NAFTA." Associated Press, February 3.
Acuerdos sobre derechos y cultura indígenas. 1997. Mexico City: Ediciones del Frente Zapatista de Liberación Nacional.
Aguirre Beltrán, Gonzalo. 1976. *Obra polémica.* Mexico City: Instituto Nacional de Antropología e Historia.
Aguirre Beltrán, Gonzalo, and Ricardo Pozas. 1991 [1954]. *La política indigenista en México: Métodos y resultados.* Colección Presencias, 43. Mexico City: Dirección General de Publicaciones del Consejo Nacional para la Cultura y las Artes. (Reprint of *Instituciones indígenas en el México actual,* vol. 2 of Alfonso Caso et al., *Métodos y resultados de la política indigenista en México.* Mexico City: Instituto Nacional Indigenista, 1954.)
Aitken, Rob. 1996. "Neoliberalism and Identity: Redefining State and Society in Mexico." In *Dismantling the Mexican State?* edited by Aitken et al., 24–37. New York: St. Martin's Press.
Aitken, Rob, Nikki Craske, Gareth E. Jones, and David E. Stansfield, eds. 1996. *Dismantling the Mexican State?* New York: St. Martin's Press.
Albó, Xavier. 2002. "Bolivia: From Indian and Campesino Leaders to Councillors and Parliamentary Deputies." In *Multiculturalism in Latin America: Indigenous Rights, Diversity, and Democracy,* edited by Rachel Sieder, 74–102. New York: Palgrave Macmillan.
Alemán Mundo, Silvia. 1997. *Sihuame y la esperanza; La participación en las organizaciones de mujeres rurales en Guerrero.* Mexico City: Universidad Autónoma de Guerrero.
Alonso, Marcos Matías. 1997. "Presentación." In *La autonomía y el movimiento indígena en Guerrero: Homenaje a Sabino Estrada Guadalupe (1955–1996),* 13–26. Mexico City: Convergencia Socialista.
Arias, Arturo, ed. 2001. *The Rigoberta Menchu Controversy.* Minneapolis: University of Minnesota Press.
Assies, Willem, Gemma van der Haar, and André Hoekema, eds. 1998. *The Challenge of Diversity: Indigenous Peoples and Reform of the State in Latin America.* Amsterdam: Thela.
"La autonomía como nueva relación entre los pueblos indios y la sociedad mexicana." 1994. *Memoria* 72 (November; Mexico City).
Báez-Jorge, Félix. 1977. "Indigenismo e impugnación." In *Siete ensayos sobre indigenismo,* 51–72. Mexico City: Instituto Nacional Indigenista.

Bailey, John. 1994. "Centralism and Political Change in Mexico: The Case of National Solidarity." In *Transforming State-Society Relations in Mexico: The National Solidarity Strategy*, edited by Wayne A. Cornelius, Ann L. Craig, and Jonathan Fox, 97–119. San Diego: Center for U.S.–Mexican Studies, University of California, San Diego.

"Balance del Primer Informe de gestión social en la zona Nahua de Chilapa de Alvarez periodo 93–94." n.d. Archives of the Consejo Guerrerense 500 Años de Resistencia Indígena.

Baños Ramírez, Othón. 1998. "PROCEDE: Gateway to Modernization of the Ejido? The Case of Yucatán." In *The Future Role of the Ejido in Rural Mexico*, edited by Richard Snyder and Gabriel Torres, 31–47. San Diego: Center for U.S.–Mexican Studies, University of California, San Diego.

Bartra, Armando. 1985. *Los herederos de Zapata: Movimientos campesinos postrevolucionarios en México. 1920–1980*. Mexico City: Ediciones Era.

———. 1996. *Guerrero bronco: Campesinos, ciudadanos, y guerrilleros en la Costa Grande*. Mexico City: Ediciones sinfiltro.

———. 2000. "Posdata." In *Crónicas del sur: Utopías campesinas en Guerrero*, edited by Armando Bartra, 413–28. Mexico City: Ediciones Era.

Benjamin, Thomas. 2000. *La Revolución: Mexico's Great Revolution as Memory, Myth, and History*. Austin: University of Texas Press.

Bienes Comunales. n.d. Archivo General Agrario, exp. 276.1/818.

Bonfil Batalla, Guillermo. 1996. *México profundo: Reclaiming a Civilization*. Translated by Philip A. Dennis. Austin: University of Texas Press.

Boyer, Christopher R. 2003. *Becoming Campesinos: Politics, Identity, and Agrarian Struggle in Postrevolutionary Michoacán, 1920–1935*. Stanford: Stanford University Press.

Braig, Marianne. 1997. "Continuity and Change in Mexican Political Culture: The Case of PRONASOL." In *Citizens of the Pyramid. Essays on Mexican Political Culture*, edited by Wil G. Pansters, 247–78. Amsterdam: Thela.

Brass, Tom. 2000. *Peasants, Populism, and Postmodernism: The Return of the Agrarian Myth*. London: Frank Cass.

Brienen, Marten. 2007. "Interminable Revolution: Populism and Frustration in Twentieth-Century Bolivia." *SAIS Review* 27, no. 1:21–33.

Briones, Claudia, Lorena Cañuqueo, Laura Kropff, and Miguel Leuman. 2007. "Assessing the Effects of Multicultural Neoliberalism: A Perspective from the South of the South (Patagonia, Argentina)." *Latin American and Caribbean Ethnic Studies* 2, no.1:69–91.

Brysk, Alison. 2000. *From Tribal Village to Global Village. Indian Rights and International Relations in Latin America*. Stanford: Stanford University Press.

Burguete Cal y Mayor, Aracely, ed. 1999. *México: Experiencias de autonomía indígena*. Copenhagen: IWGIA.

Bustamante Álvarez, Tomás, Arturo Léon López, and Beatriz Terrazas Mata. 2000. *Reproducción campesina, migración, y agroindustria en Tierra Caliente, Guerrero*. Mexico City: Plaza y Valdés.

Canabal Cristiani, Beatriz. 1984. *Hoy luchamos por la tierra. . . .* Mexico City: Universidad Autónoma Metropolitana–Xochimilco.

Carrasco Zuñiga, Abad. 1994. "Los Tlapanecos." In *Etnografía de los pueblos indígenas de México*. Mexico City: Instituto Nacional Indigenista.

Caso, Alfonso, Gonzalo Aguirre Beltrán, and Ricardo Pozas. 1991 [1954]. *La política indigenista en México: Métodos y resultados*. Colección Presencias,

42–43. Mexico City: Dirección General de Publicaciones del Consejo Nacional para la Cultura y las Artes. (Reprint of *Instituciones indígenas precortesianas; Instituciones indígenas en la colonia; Instituciones indígenas en el México independiente* and *Instituciones indígenas en el México actual*, vols. 1 and 2 of Alfonso Caso et al., *Métodos y resultados de la política indigenista en México*. Mexico City: Instituto Nacional Indigenista, 1954.)

Caso, Antonio. 1939. *Sociología*. 3rd ed. Mexico City: Editorial Polis.

Castillo Díaz, Ricardo. 2008. "Encuesta nacional ubica a Zeferino entre los tres gobernadores con peores calificaciones." *El Sur* (Acapulco), 6 June. http://www.suracapulco.com.mx/nota1e.php?id_nota=39390/ (accessed 8 August 2008).

Cervantes, Zacarias. 2008. "Marchan en la capital más de mil campesinos; exigen que el gobierno garantice el fertilizante." *El Sur* (Acapulco), 9 April. http://www.suracapulco.com.mx/nota1e.php?id_nota=36257/ (accessed 6 August 2008).

Clifford, James. 1988. *The Predicament of Culture: Twentieth-Century Ethnography, Literature, and Art*. Cambridge, Mass.: Harvard University Press.

"Como resultado de la reunion celebrada el día 13 de octubre de 1992, con el C. Presidente de la República, Lic. Carlos Salinas de Gortari." 1992. Archives of the Consejo Guerrerense 500 Años de Resistencia Indígena.

"Consejo Estatal Guerrero 500 Años de Resistencia India y Popular: Proclama, objetivos, estructura, y programa (propuestas para su discusión)." 1991. Archives of the Consejo Guerrerense 500 Años de Resistencia Indígena. 14 September.

Consejo Guerrerense 500 Años de Resistencia Indígena. 2001. "Pero no pudieron matar nuestras raíces: 10 años de lucha del CG500ARI." Unpublished manuscript.

"Constitución del Consejo Estatal 500 Años de Resistencia India y Popular." 1991. Archives of the Consejo Guerrerense 500 Años de Resistencia Indígena. 14 September.

"Convenio de concertación." 1993. Archives of the Consejo Guerrerense 500 Años de Resistencia Indígena. 1 January.

Cornelius, Wayne A., Ann L. Craig, and Jonathan Fox. 1994. "Mexico's National Solidarity Program: An Overview." In *Transforming State-Society Relations in Mexico: The National Solidarity Strategy*, edited by Cornelius, Craig, and Fox, 3–26. San Diego: Center for U.S.–Mexican Studies, University of California, San Diego.

Cornell, Stephen. 1988. *The Return of the Native: American Indian Political Resurgence*. New York: Oxford University Press.

Cruz, Jon. 1996. "From Farce to Tragedy: Reflections on the Reification of Race at Century's End." In *Mapping Multiculturalism*, edited by Avery F. Gordon and Christopher Newfield, 19–39. Minneapolis: University of Minnesota Press.

Dalrymple, William, 2004. "The Truth About Muslims." *New York Review of Books*, 4 November, 31–34.

Dawson, Alexander S. 2004. *Indian and Nation in Revolutionary Mexico*. Tucson: University of Arizona Press.

Dehouve, Danièle. 2001. *Ensayo de geopolítica indígena: Los municipios tlapanecos*. Mexico City: CIESAS/Miguel Ángel Porrúa.

de la Cadena, Marisol. 2001. "Reconstructing Race: Racism, Culture, and Mestizaje in Latin America." *NACLA* 34, no. 6 (May–June): 16–23.

de la Cruz, Teresa. 2005. "Por irregularidades de René, se adeudan 3 mil 383 millones de pesos: Álvarez." *El Sur* (Acapulco), 15 July, 2.
Díaz de Jesús, Marcelino. 1992. *Alto Balsas: Pueblos nahuas en lucha por la preservación del medio ambiente y su cultura.* Mexico City: Habitat International Coalition.
Díaz de Jesús, Marcelino, and Pedro de Jesús Alejandro. 1997. "El mismo camino, con Sabino." In *La autonomía y el movimiento indígena en Guerrero: Homenaje a Sabino Estrada Guadalupe (1955–1996),* 157–77. Mexico City: Convergencia Socialista.
———. 1999. "Alto Balsas, Guerrero: Una experiencia de lucha autonómica." In *México: Experiencias de autonomía indígena,* edited by Aracely Burguete Cal y Mayor, 143–68. Copenhagen: IWGIA.
Díaz Polanco, Héctor. 1997. *Indigenous Peoples in Latin America: The Quest for Self-Determination.* Translated by Lucia Rayas. Boulder: Westview Press.
———. 1998. *La rebelión zapatista y la autonomía.* Mexico City: Siglo Veintiuno Editores.
Dresser, Denise. 1991. *Neopopulist Solutions to Neoliberal Problems: Mexico's National Solidarity Program.* San Diego: Center for U.S.–Mexican Studies, University of California, San Diego.
"Entrevista realizada al Professor Eligio Pacheco-Marin, Coordinador de Albergues, CCI, Nahua-Tlapaneco, Tlapa, Guerrero." 1999. Unpublished transcript. Archives of the Instituto Nacional Indigenista, Mexico City. 20 December.
Escobar, Arturo. 1995. *Encountering Development: The Making and Unmaking of the Third World.* Princeton: Princeton University Press.
Escobar Ohmstede, Antonio. 1993. "Los condueñazgos indígenas en las Huastecas hidalguense y veracruzana: ¿Defensa del espacio comunal?" In *Indio, nación, y comunidad en el México del siglo XIX,* edited by Antonio Escobar O., 171–88. Mexico City: CIESAS/CEMCA.
Escobar Ohmstede, Antonio, and Jaqueline Gordillo. 1998. "Defensa o despojo? Territorialidad indígena en las Huastecas, 1856–1930." In *Estudios campesinos en el Archivo General Agrario,* edited by Antonio Escobar O. et al., 15–74. Mexico City: Registro Agrario Nacional.
Esteva, Gustavo. 2003. "The Meaning and Scope of the Struggle for Autonomy." In *Mayan Lives, Mayan Utopias: The Indigenous Peoples of Chiapas and the Zapatista Rebellion,* edited by Jan Rus, Rosalva Aída Hernández Castillo, and Shannan L. Mattiace, 243–69. Lanham, Md.: Rowman and Littlefield.
Fabila, Alfonso, and César Tejeda. 1955. "Problemas de los indios nahuas, mixtecos, y tlapanecos de la Sierra Madre del Sur del Estado de Guerrero: Exploración socioeconómica." 2 vols. Unpublished manuscript, INI Archive, Mexico City.
Farmer, Paul. 2005. *Pathologies of Power: Health, Human Rights, and the New War on the Poor.* Berkeley: University of California Press.
Ferguson, James. 1990. *The Anti-Politics Machine: "Development," Depoliticization, and Bureaucratic Power in Lesotho.* Cambridge: Cambridge University Press.
Field, Les. 1994. "Who Are the Indians? Reconceptualizing Indigenous Identity, Resistance, and the Role of Social Science in Latin America." *Latin American Research Review* 29, no. 3:237–48.
Flores Félix, Joaquín. 1998a. *La revuelta por la democracia: Pueblos indios,*

política, y poder en México. Mexico City: Universidad Nacional Autónoma de México.

———. 1998b. "El tigre, San Marcos, y el comisario: Poder y reproducción social en La Montaña de Guerrero." Master's thesis, Universidad Autónoma Metropolitana–Xochimilco.

———. n.d. "'De Nikan para Tech Kixtiske Xtopa Tech Mixtizque': De aquí para poder sacarnos, primero tendrán que matarnos." Unpublished paper.

Flores Lúa, Graciela, Luisa Paré, and Sergio Sarmiento Silva. 1988. *Las voces del campo: Movimiento campesino y política agraria, 1976–1984*. Mexico City: Siglo Veintiuno Editores.

Foley, Michael W. 1991. "Agenda for Mobilization: The Agrarian Question and Popular Mobilization in Contemporary Mexico." *Latin American Research Review* 26:39–74.

Foweraker, Joe, and Ann L. Craig, eds. 1990. *Popular Movements and Political Change in Mexico*. Boulder: Lynne Rienner.

Fox, Jonathan. 1992. *The Politics of Food in Mexico: State Power and Social Mobilization*. Ithaca: Cornell University Press.

———. 1994. "The Difficult Transition from Clientelism to Citizenship: Lessons from Mexico." *World Politics* 46 (January): 151–84.

Gamio, Manuel. 1916. *Forjando patria: Pro nacionalismo*. Mexico City: Miguel Ángel Porrúa.

García, María Elena, and José Antonio Lucero. 2004. "Un país sin indígenas? Re-thinking Indigenous Politics in Peru." In *The Struggle for Indigenous Rights in Latin America,* edited by Nancy Grey Postero and Leon Zamosc, 158–88. Brighton, UK: Sussex Academic Press.

Gibson, Charles. 1964. *The Aztecs Under Spanish Rule: A History of the Indians of the Valley of Mexico, 1519–1810*. Stanford: Stanford University Press.

Gledhill, John. 1991. *Casi Nada: A Study of Agrarian Reform in the Homeland of Cardenismo*. Albany: Institute for Mesoamerican Studies, State University of New York.

González Tiburcio, Enrique. 1994. "Social Reform in Mexico: Six Theses on the National Solidarity Program." In *Transforming State-Society Relations in Mexico: The National Solidarity Strategy,* edited by Wayne A. Cornelius, Ann L. Craig, and Jonathan Fox, 63–78. San Diego: Center for U.S.–Mexican Studies.

Good Eshelman, Catharine. 1988. *Haciendo la lucha: Arte y comercio nahuas de Guerrero*. Mexico City: Fondo de Cultura Económica.

Grammont, Hubert C. de. 2003. "The Agricultural Sector and Rural Development in Mexico: Consequences of Economic Globalization." In *Confronting Development: Assessing Mexico's Economic and Social Policy Challenges*, edited by Kevin J. Middlebrook and Eduardo Zepeda, 350–81. Stanford: Stanford University Press.

Guardino, Peter F. 1996. *Peasants, Politics, and the Formation of Mexico's National State*. Stanford: Stanford University Press.

Günes-Ayata, Ayse. 1994. "Clientelism: Premodern, Modern, Postmodern." In *Democracy, Clientelism, and Civil Society*, edited by Luis Roniger and Günes-Ayata, 19–28. Boulder: Lynne Rienner.

Gupta, Akhil, and James Ferguson. 1997a. "Culture, Power, Place: Ethnography at the End of an Era." In *Culture, Power, Place: Explorations in Critical*

Anthropology, edited by Gupta and Ferguson, 1–29. Durham: Duke University Press.

———. 1997b. "Beyond 'Culture': Space, Identity, and the Politics of Difference." In *Culture, Power, Place: Explorations in Critical Anthropology*, edited by Gupta and Ferguson, 33–51. Durham: Duke University Press.

Gutiérrez, Maribel. 1997. "Una breve historia de la Policía Comunitaria." *El Sur* (Acapulco), 15 September, 18.

———. 1998. *Violencia en Guerrero*. Mexico City: La Jornada Ediciones.

———. 2008. "La confrontación con presuntos paramilitares en El Camalote y las acusaciones contra la OPIM." *El Sur* (Acapulco), 18 April. http://www.suracapulco.com.mx/nota1e.php?id_nota=36851/ (accessed 7 July 2008).

Gutiérrez, Navidad. 1999. *Nationalist Myths and Ethnic Identities: Indigenous Intellectuals and the Mexican State*. Lincoln: University of Nebraska Press.

Gutiérrez Ávila, Miguel Ángel. 1999. "Despotas y caciques: El proceso político en el municipio amuzgo de Xochistlahuaca, Costa Chica del Estado de Guerrero (1979–1999)." Master's thesis, Centro de Investigaciones y Estudios Superiores en Antropología Social, Mexico City.

Hale, Charles R. 1994. *Resistance and Contradiction: Miskitu Indians and the Nicaraguan State, 1894–1987*. Stanford: Stanford University Press.

———. 2002. "Does Multiculturalism Menace? Governance, Cultural Rights, and the Politics of Identity in Guatemala." *Journal of Latin American Studies* 34, no. 3:485–524.

Hall, Gillette, and Harry A. Patrinos, eds. 2005. *Indigenous People, Poverty, and Human Development in Latin America, 1994–2004*. New York: Palgrave Macmillan.

Harvey, Neil. 1990. "Peasant Strategies and Corporatism in Chiapas." In *Popular Movements and Political Change in Mexico*, edited by Joe Foweraker and Ann L. Craig, 183–98. Boulder: Lynne Rienner.

Hémond, Aline. 2002. "El proceso de definición de nuevas subregiones dentro del Estado de Guerrero: El caso del Alto Balsas." In *Moviendo Montañas . . . Transformando la geografía del poder en el Sur de México*, edited by Beatriz Canabal Cristiani et al., 129–46. Chilpancingo: El Colegio de Guerrero.

Hernández, Evangelina. 1994. "Consejo Guerrerense: Aún no es conveniente levantar el plantón." *La Jornada* (Mexico City), 8 March, 25.

Hernández Castillo, Rosalva Aída. 2001. *La otra frontera: Identidades multiples en el Chiapas postcolonial*. Mexico City: CIESAS/Miguel Ángel Porrúa.

———. 2002. "La política de identidades en México: Entre el esencialismo étnico y la descalificación total. Repensar el debate desde las mujeres." In *Moviendo Montañas . . . Transformando la geografía del poder en el Sur de México*, edited by Beatriz Canabal Cristiani et al., 147–62. Chilpancingo: El Colegio de Guerrero.

Hernández Castillo, Rosalva Aída, Sarela Paz, and María Teresa Sierra. 2004. "Introducción." In *El estado y los indígenas en tiempos del PAN: Neoindigenismo, legalidad, e identitad*, edited by Hernández Castillo, Paz, and Sierra, 7–24. Mexico City: Miguel Ángel Porrúa.

Hernández Navarro, Luis. 2003. "TLC: Lo menos por lo más." *La Jornada* (Mexico City). http://www.jornada.unam.mx/2003/ene03/030114/027apol.php?origen=opinion.html/ (accessed 6 February 2003).

———. 2005. "Neoindigenismo y autonomía." *La Jornada* (Mexico City), 15

March. http://www.jornada.unam.mx/2005/03/15/023a1pol.php/ (accessed 10 October 2006).
Hewitt de Alcantara, Cynthia. 1976. *Modernizing Mexican Agriculture: Socioeconomic Implications of Technological Change, 1940–1970.* Geneva: United Nations Research Institute for Social Development.
Hindley, Jane. 1996. "Towards a Pluricultural Nation: Indigenismo and the Reform of Article 4." In *Dismantling the Mexican State?* edited by Aitken et al., 225–43. London: Palgrave Macmillan.
———. 1999 "Indigenous Mobilization, Development, and Democratization in Guerrero: The Nahua People vs. the Tetelcingo Dam." In *Subnational Politics and Democratization in Mexico,* edited by Wayne A. Cornelius, Todd A. Eisenstadt, and Hindley, 207–38. San Diego: Center for U.S.–Mexican Studies, University of California, San Diego.
Horton, Lynn. 2006. "Contesting State Multiculturalisms: Indigenous Land Struggles in Eastern Panama." *Journal of Latin American Studies* 38, no.4:829–58.
Hu-DeHart, Evelyn. 1981. *Missionaries, Miners, and Indians: Spanish Contact with the Yaqui Nation of Northwestern New Spain, 1533–1820.* Tucson: University of Arizona Press.
Huntington, Samuel P. 1993. "The Clash of Civilizations?" *Foreign Affairs* 72, no. 3:22–28.
"Informe a la Asamblea de Representantes de Alcagro." n.d. Archives of the Consejo Guerrerense 500 Años de Resistencia Indígena.
INEGI (Instituto Nacional de Estadistica y Geografía). 2000. *General Census of the Population and Households.* Mexico City.
INI (Instituto Nacional Indigenista). 1982. *Memoria de actividades, 1976–1982.* Mexico City.
Jackson, Jean E. 2002. "Contested Discourses of Authority in Colombian National Indigenous Politics: The 1996 Summer Takeovers." In *Indigenous Movements, Self-Representation, and the State in Latin America,* edited by Kay B. Warren, and Jackson, 81–122. Austin: University of Texas Press.
Johnson, Jennifer L. 2005. "Appropriating Citizenship: Resources, Discourses, and Political Mobilization in Contemporary Rural Mexico." Ph.D. diss., University of Chicago.
———. 2007. "When the Poor Police Themselves: Public Insecurity and Extralegal Criminal-Justice Administration in Mexico." In *Legitimacy and Criminal Justice: International Perspectives,* edited by Tom R. Tyler, 167–85. New York: Russell Sage Foundation.
Kearney, Michael. 1996. *Reconceptualizing the Peasantry: Anthropology in Global Perspective.* New York: Westview Press.
Knight, Alan. 1986. *The Mexican Revolution.* 2 vols. Lincoln: University of Nebraska Press.
———. 1991. "The Rise and Fall of Cardenismo, c. 1930–c. 1946." In *Mexico Since Independence,* edited by Leslie Bethell, 241–320. Cambridge: Cambridge University Press.
———. 1998. "Populism and Neo-Populism in Latin America, Especially Mexico." *Journal of Latin American Studies* 30:223–48.
Legorreta Díaz, Carmen. 1998. *Religión, política, y guerrilla en las cañadas de la selva Lacandona.* Mexico City: Cal y Arena.
Leyva Solano, Xóchitl, and Gabriel Ascencio Franco. 1996. *Lacandonia al filo del agua.* Mexico City: CIESAS/Fondo de Cultura Económica.

Lockhart, James. 1992. *The Nahuas After the Conquest: A Social and Cultural History of the Indians of Central Mexico, Sixteenth Through Eighteenth Centuries.* Berkeley: University of California Press.

Lomnitz-Adler, Claudio. 1992. *Exits from the Labyrinth: Culture and Ideology in the Mexican National Space.* Berkeley: University of California Press.

———. 2001. *Deep Mexico, Silent Mexico: An Anthropology of Nationalism.* Minneapolis: University of Minnesota Press.

Mallon, Florencia. 1995. *Peasant and Nation: The Making of Postcolonial Mexico and Peru.* Berkeley: University of California Press.

Martínez-Echazábal, Lourdes. 1998. "Mestizaje and the Discourse of National/Cultural Identity in Latin America, 1845–1959." *Latin American Perspectives* 25, no. 3 (May): 21–42.

Martínez Luna, Jaime. 1993. ¿Es la comunidad nuestra identidad? In *Movimientos indígenas contemporáneos en México,* edited by Arturo Warman and Arturo Argueta, 157–70. Mexico City: CIIH/Miguel Ángel Porrúa.

Martínez Novo, Carmen. 2006. *Who Defines Indigenous? Identities, Development, Intellectuals, and the State in Northern Mexico.* New Brunswick: Rutgers University Press.

Martínez Rescalvo, Mario O. 1991. "Problemática agraria." In *La Montaña de Guerrero: Economía, historia, y sociedad,* edited by Martínez Rescalvo and Jorge R. Obregón Tellez, 297–319. Mexico City: Instituto Nacional Indigenista and Universidad Autónoma de Guerrero.

Martínez Rescalvo, Mario O., and Jorge R. Obregón Tellez, eds. 1991. *La Montaña de Guerrero: Economía, historia, y sociedad.* Mexico City: Instituto Nacional Indigenista and Universidad Autónoma de Guerrero.

Máttar, Jorge, Juan Carlos Moreno-Brid, and Wilson Peres. 2003. "Foreign Investment in Mexico After Economic Reform." In *Confronting Development: Assessing Mexico's Economic and Social Policy Challenges,* edited by Kevin J. Middlebrook and Eduardo Zepeda, 123–60, Stanford: Stanford University Press.

Mattiace, Shannan L. 2003. *To See with Two Eyes: Peasant Activism and Indian Autonomy in Chiapas, Mexico.* Albuquerque: University of New Mexico Press.

Maybury-Lewis, David, ed. 2002. *The Politics of Ethnicity: Indigenous Peoples in Latin American States.* Cambridge, Mass.: Harvard University Press.

Mejía Piñeros, María Consuelo, and Sergio Sarmiento Silva. 1991. *La lucha indígena: Un reto a la ortodoxia.* 2nd ed. Mexico City: Siglo Veintiuno Editores.

Meza Castillo, Miguel. 1995. *Historia de la organización campesina en Chilapa, Guerrero 1980–1992: Historia de la Sociedad de Solidaridad Social "Zanzekan Tinemi" de Chilapa, Guerrero.* Chilpancingo: Instituto de Estudios para el Desarrollo Rural Maya.

Middlebrook, Kevin J. 1995. *The Paradox of Revolution: Labor, the State, and Authoritarianism in Mexico.* Baltimore: Johns Hopkins University Press.

Middlebrook, Kevin J., and Eduardo Zepeda. 2003. "On the Political Economy of Mexican Development Policy." In *Confronting Development: Assessing Mexico's Economic and Social Policy Challenges,* edited by Middlebrook and Zepeda, 3–52. Stanford: Stanford University Press.

Migrar o morir: El dilema de los jornaleros agrícolas de La Montaña de Guerrero. 2005. Tlapa de Comonfort, Guerrero: Centro de Derechos Humanos de La Montaña Tlachinollan.

"Minuta de acuerdos, Copladeg-Consejo Guerrerense 500 Años de Resistencia Indígena." 1993. Archives of the Consejo Guerrerense 500 Años de Resistencia Indígena. 19 and 20 July.
"Minuta de la reunión celebrada entre las autoridades del Instituto Nacional Indigenista . . . y los miembros representantes del Consejo Guerrerense 500 Años de Resistencia Indígena, Negra y Popular." 1993. Archives of the Consejo Guerrerense 500 Años de Resistencia Indígena. 30 August.
Moguel, Julio. 1992. "El movimiento campesino ante la disyuntiva neoliberal." *Memoria* no. 47 (October): 39–42.
Monge, Raúl. 1995. "Figueroa desacata, desde febrero, una recomendación de la CNDH contra el policía Manual Moreno y este reapareció en la matanza de Coyuca." *Proceso* 975 (10 July): 13.
Montemayor, Carlos. 1997. *Guerra en el paraíso*. Mexico City: Seix Barral.
Morett Sánchez, Jesús Carlos. 2003. *Reforma agraria: Del latifundismo al neoliberalismo*. Mexico City: Plaza y Valdes Editores.
Muñoz, Maurilio. 1963. *Mixteca-Nahua-Tlapaneca*. Memorias del Instituto Nacional Indigenista, vol. 9. Mexico City: Instituto Nacional Indigenista.
Nahmad Sitton, Salomón. 1999. "La culminación del indigenismo y la inclusión de los pueblos indios en la nación." Unpublished paper.
———. 2004. "Los acuerdos y los compromisos rotos y no cumplidos con los pueblos indígenas de México." In *El estado y los indígenas en tiempos del PAN: Neoindigenismo, legalidad, e identitad*, edited by Rosalva Aída Hernández Castillo, Sarela Paz, and María Teresa Sierra, 81–113. Mexico City: Miguel Ángel Porrúa.
Nash, June C. 2001. *Mayan Visions: The Quest for Autonomy in an Age of Globalization*. New York: Routledge.
Nelson, Diane. 1999. *A Finger in the Wound: Body Politics in Quincentennial Guatemala*. Berkeley: University of California Press.
Nuijten, Monique. 2003. *Power, Community, and the State: The Political Anthropology of Organisation in Mexico*. London: Pluto Press.
Nuijten, Monique, and Gemma van der Haar. 2000. "The Zapatistas of Chiapas: Challenges and Contradictions." *European Review of Latin American and Caribbean Studies* 68 (April): 83–90.
O'Malley, Ilene V. 1986. *The Myth of the Revolution: Hero Cults and the Institutionalization of the Mexican State, 1920–1940*. New York: Greenwood Press.
Omi, Michael, and Howard Winant. 1994. *Racial Formation in the United States: From the 1960s to the 1990s*. Rev. ed. New York: Routledge.
Overmyer-Velázquez, Rebecca. 2003. "The Self-Determination of Indigenous Peoples and the Limits of United Nations Advocacy in Guerrero, Mexico (1998–2000)." *Identities: Global Studies in Culture and Power* 10:9–29.
Pallares, Amalia. 2002. *From Peasant Struggles to Indian Resistance: The Ecuadorian Andes in the Late Twentieth Century*. Norman: University of Oklahoma Press.
"Panorama siempre difícil para la Radio Ñomndaa." 2008. *El Sur* (Acapulco), 20 January. http://www.suracapulco.com.mx/nota1e.php?id_nota=31978/ (accessed 28 July 2008).
Pansters, Wil G., ed. 1997.*Citizens of the Pyramid. Essays on Mexican Political Culture*. Amsterdam: Thela.
Peña, Guillermo de la. 2002. "Anthropological Debates and the Crisis of Mexican

Nationalism." In *Culture, Economy, Power: Anthropology as Critique, Anthropology as Praxis,* edited by Winnie Lem and Belinda Leach, 47–58. Albany: State University of New York Press.

Postero, Nancy Grey. 2004. "Articulations and Fragmentations: Indigenous Politics in Bolivia." In *The Struggle for Indigenous Rights in Latin America,* edited by Nancy Grey Postero and Leon Zamosc, 189–216. Brighton, UK: Sussex Academic Press.

Postero, Nancy Grey, and Leon Zamosc. 2004a. "Indigenous Movements and the Indian Question in Latin America." In *The Struggle for Indigenous Rights in Latin America,* edited by Postero and Zamosc, 1–31. Brighton, UK: Sussex Academic Press.

———, eds. 2004b. *The Struggle for Indigenous Rights in Latin America.* Brighton: Sussex Academic Press.

Ramírez Celestino, Alfredo. n.d. *El espacio y el contexto histórico del Lienzo de Totomixtlahuaca.* http://www.celia.cnrs.fr/FichExt/Am/A_19-20_11.htm/ (accessed 8 August 2006).

Ramos, Alcida Rita. 1998. *Indigenism: Ethnic Politics in Brazil.* Madison: University of Wisconsin Press.

Ravelo Lecuona, Renato, and José O. Ávila Arévalo, eds. 1994. *Luz de la Montaña: Una historia viva.* Mexico City: Instituto Nacional Indigenista.

Roberts, Kenneth M. 1996. "Neoliberalism and the Transformation of Populism in Latin America: The Peruvian Case." *World Politics* 48, no. 1:82–116.

———. 2007. "Latin America's Populist Revival." *SAIS Review* 27, no. 1:3–15.

Rodríguez W., Carlos A. 1998. "Rancho Nuevo de la Democracia." In "Poder local, derechos indígenas, y municipios" (special issue). *Cuadernos Agrarios* 8, no. 16:120–27.

Roniger, Luis. 1994. "The Comparative Study of Clientelism and the Changing Nature of Civil Society in the Contemporary World." In *Democracy, Clientelism, and Civil Society,* edited by Roniger and Ayes Günes-Ayata, 1–18. Boulder: Lynne Rienner.

Rubin, Jeffrey W. 1997. *Decentering the Regime: Ethnicity, Radicalism, and Democracy in Juchitán, Mexico.* Durham: Duke University Press.

Ruiz Hernández, Margarito. 1999. "La Asamblea Nacional Indígena Plural por la Autonomía (ANIPA): Proceso de construcción de una propuesta legislativa autonómica nacional." In *México: Experiencias de autonomía indígena,* edited by Aracely Burguete Cal y Mayor, 21–53. Copenhagen: IWGIA.

Rus, Jan. 1994. "The 'Comunidad Revolucionaria Institucional': The Subversion of Native Government in Highland Chiapas, 1936–1968." In *Everyday Forms of State Formation,* edited by Gilbert M. Joseph and Daniel Nugent, 265–300. Durham: Duke University Press.

Sánchez, Consuelo. 1999. *Los pueblos indígenas: Del indigenismo a la autonomía.* Mexico City: Siglo Veintiuno Editores.

Sánchez Néstor, Martha. 2004. "Mujeres indígenas en México: Acción y pensamiento." Unpublished essay. 21 April.

Sariego Rodríguez, Juan Luis. 2000. "Políticas indigenistas y criterios de identificación de la población indígena de México." Paper presented at Dinámica de la Población Indígena en México: Problemáticas Contemporaneas, CIESAS, Mexico City.

Sarmiento Silva, Sergio. 1985. "El Consejo Nacional de Pueblos Indígenas y la política indigenista." *Revista Mexicana de Sociología* 3 (July–September): 197–215.

———. 2000. "El movimiento indígena y el gobierno de Vicente Fox: Una mirada desde Oaxaca." http//www.memoria.com.mx/142/Sarmiento/.

Schryer, Frans J. 1990. *Ethnicity and Class Conflict in Rural Mexico*. Princeton: Princeton University Press.

SEDESOL (Secretaría de Desarrollo Social). 2007. "Programa de Atención a Jornaleros Agricolas: Fourth Quarter Report." Mexico City.

SEDESOL/INI (Secretaría de Desarrollo Social/Instituto Nacional Indigenista). 1993. *Fondos Regionales de Solidaridad: Manual de operación*. Guías de Solidaridad. Mexico City.

Sieder, Rachel, ed. 2002. *Multiculturalism in Latin America: Indigenous Rights, Diversity, and Democracy*. Hampshire, UK: Palgrave Macmillan.

Smith, Peter H. 1991. "Mexico Since 1946: Dynamics of an Authoritarian Regime." In *Mexico Since Independence*, edited by Leslie Bethell, 321–96. Cambridge: Cambridge University Press.

So, Alvin Y. 1990. *Social Change and Development: Modernization, Dependency, and World-Systems Theories*. Sage Library of Social Research, 178. Newbury Park, Calif.: Sage.

Sollors, Werner, ed. 1989. *The Invention of Ethnicity*. New York: Oxford University Press.

Stephen, Lynn. 1998. "The Cultural and Political Dynamics of Agrarian Reform in Oaxaca and Chiapas." In *The Future Role of the Ejido in Rural Mexico*, 7–30. San Diego: Center for U.S.–Mexican Studies, University of California, San Diego.

———. 2002. *Zapata Lives! Histories and Cultural Politics in Southern Mexico*. Berkeley: University of California Press.

Tlachinollan, Centro de Derechos Humanos de la Montaña. 1998. *El laberinto de la guerra: Cuarto informe* (May 1997–May 1998). Diócesis de Tlapa, Guerrero.

———. 1999. *El imperio de la violencia y la impunidad: Quinto informe* (June 1998–May 1999). Diócesis de Tlapa, Guerrero.

Tully, James. 1995. *Strange Multiplicity: Constitutionalism in an Age of Diversity*. Cambridge: Cambridge University Press.

Urban, Greg, and Joel Sherzer, eds. 1991. *Nation-States and Indians in Latin America*. Austin: University of Texas Press.

Van Cott, Donna Lee. 2000. *The Friendly Liquidation of the Past: The Politics of Diversity in Latin America*. Pittsburgh: University of Pittsburgh Press.

———. 2003. "Indigenous Struggle." *Latin American Research Review* 38, no. 2 (June): 220–33.

Van Young, Eric. 1993. "Rebelión agraria sin agrarismo: Defensa de la comunidad, significado, y violencia colectiva en la sociedad rural mexicana de fines de la época colonial." In *Indio, nación, y comunidad en el México del siglo XIX,* edited by Antonio Escobar O., 31–62. Mexico City: Centro de Investigaciones y Estudios Superiores en Antropología Social.

Varese, Stefano. 1996. "The Ethnopolitics of Indian Resistance in Latin America." *Latin American Perspectives* 23, no. 2:58–71.

Vaughan, Mary Kay. 1997. *Cultural Politics in Revolution: Teachers, Peasants, and Schools in Mexico, 1930–1940*. Tucson: University of Arizona Press.

Vélez-Ibañez, Carlos G. 1983. *Rituals of Marginality: Politics, Process, and Culture*

Change in Urban Central Mexico, 1969–1974. Berkeley: University of California Press.

Villoro, Luis. 1996 [1950]. *Los grandes momentos del indigenismo en México.* Mexico City: Fondo de Cultura Económica.

Wade, Peter. 1997. *Race and Ethnicity in Latin America.* London: Pluto Press.

Warman, Arturo, et al. 1970. *De eso que llaman antropología mexicana.* Mexico City: Editorial Nuestro Tiempo.

Warren, Jonathan W. 2001. *Racial Revolutions: Antiracism and Indian Resurgence in Brazil.* Durham: Duke University Press.

Warren, Kay B. 1998. *Indigenous Movements and Their Critics: Pan-Maya Activism in Guatemala.* Princeton: Princeton University Press.

Warren, Kay B., and Jean E. Jackson. 2002. "Introduction: Studying Indigenous Activism in Latin America." In *Indigenous Movements, Self-Representation, and the State in Latin America,* edited by Warren and Jackson, 1–46. Austin: University of Texas Press.

Weyland, Kurt. 2001. "Clarifying a Contested Concept: Populism in the Study of Latin American Politics." *Comparative Politics* 34, no. 1:1–22.

Williams, Brackette. 1989. "A Class Act: Anthropology and the Race to Nation Across Ethnic Terrain." *Annual Review of Anthropology* 18:401–44.

Yashar, Deborah J. 1998. "Contesting Citizenship: Indigenous Movements and Democracy in Latin America." *Comparative Politics* 31, no. 1:23–42.

Zermeño, Sergio. 1997. "Society and Politics in Contemporary Mexico (Modernization and Modernity in Global Societies)." In *Citizens of the Pyramid: Essays on Mexican Political Culture,* edited by Wil G. Pansters, 183–208. Amsterdam: Thela.

index

Note: Page numbers in *italics* indicate illustrations.

acculturation, and ejido, 83
Agrarian Code, 41
agrarian myth
 folkloric poverty and, 173
 populism and, 8, 10
 Salinas administration and, 144–54
agrarian reform
 Cárdenas and, 79, 87
 end of, 34
 history of, 39–43
agriculture. *See also* agrarian myth; agrarian reform
 ejido lands and, 148
 in Guerrero, 25
 in Mexico, 43–46
Aguirre Beltrán, Gonzalo, 46 n. 6, 59, 60–61, 66–67, 83, 86–87, 122
Alemán Valdés, Miguel, 42
Alliance of Autonomous Peasant Communities of the State of Guerrero, 49, 50, 56 n. 13
Alonso, Marcos Matías, 22, 52 n. 11, 89, 90–91, 132, 171 n. 21, 180
Altepetl Nahuas, 90
Alto Balsas region, 50–58, 156–58
Amuzgos, 22 n. 17, 91–92, 186–88
ANIPA (Plural National Indigenous Assembly for Autonomy)
 council directors and, 125
 criticism of, 162–63, 176
 debate within, 1–2
 EZLN and, 177–79
 platform for national reform, 3
anthropologists. *See* Fabila, Alfonso; indigenistas
anti-dam campaign, 50–58
anti-quincentenary campaign, 33–34, 56, 98, 100
Antorcha Campesina, 120

Apetzuca, trip to, 116–17, 119–22, 123
Article 4, Mexican Constitution, 15, 18
Article 27, Mexican Constitution, 95–96, 137–38, 142, 169
assimilationist idea, 73–74
Atenco Vidal, Julio, 1–2, 176–77
authenticity
 hierarchy of, 20
 place and, 154–66, 170–71
Autonomous Department for Indigenous Affairs, 75, 87
autonomy, 3. *See also* political autonomy for indigenous peoples; self-determination
Ávila, Agustín, 156–58
Ávila Arévalo, José O. (Don Pepe), 158–59
Ávila Camacho, Manuel, 41, 75

Báez-Jorge, Félix, 143
banditry, 109 n. 12, 120–21, 129–30
Barrera, Abel, 117 n. 18, 121 n. 22, 146 n. 11
Barrios, Juan Carlos, 148–49, 150
Bartra, Armando, 21, 41, 42, 116, 119
Benito, 150, 162–63
bienes comunales, 25, 39, 83
Bonfil Batalla, Guillermo, 15–16, 17, 141, 143
Brass, Tom, 8, 10, 170

Cabañas, Lucio, 21
cabecera status, 115
caciques *(caciazgos)*, 76, 78 n. 13, 183–84
campesinos. *See* peasants
Cárdenas, Cuauhtémoc, 18 n. 11, 56
Cárdenas, Lázaro
 agrarian reforms of, 39–41, 79, 87
 Balsas River Commission and, 84
 indigenous peoples and, 75, 154–55

Cárdenas, Lázaro (*continued*)
    National Peasant Federation and, 35
cargo system, 93, 158, 159–60
Caso, Alfonso
    L. Cárdenas and, 84
    Fabila and, 76
    as indigenista, 17
    on indigenous peoples, 63, 65, 66, 67–68, 74
    INI and, 61
Caso, Antonio, 66
CCI (Indigenous Coordination Center), 61, 83–84, 85–86, 86
Chavarría Barrera, Armando, 187–88
Chiapas, 6–7, 95, 106–7. *See also* Zapatista National Liberation Army
Chilapa region, 48–49, 71
Chilpancingo, government buildings of, *186*, *187*
class and ethnicity, 20
clientelism, 105
CNC (National Peasant Federation), 42, 44, 82
comisarios, 91 n. 2, 92, 159–60
communication issues, 159, 183–89
Community Food Council, 49, 50
community members, views of council by, 109–14, 168–69
Community Police, 109 n. 12, 129–30, 169, 184
comunalista vision of autonomy, 3
CONASUPO–COPLAMAR, 46–48, 49
Constitution
    Article 4, 15, 18
    Article 27, 95–96, 137–38, 142, 169
Copanatoyac, 117–18
COPLAMAR (National Program for Depressed Areas and Marginal Groups), 45 n. 5, 46–48, 49, 144
council. *See* Guerrero Council 500 Years of Indigenous Resistance
Council of Nahua Communities of the Upper Balsas, 51, 52, 53–54
crisis
    in indigenous movement, 1–2, 4, 172
    revaluation of goals in time of, 15–16
    of Salinas administration, 18 n. 11
Cruz, Jon, 16–17
Cuamanotepec, community projects in, *114*
culturalism, 16–17
culture and politics, 117 n. 18

dam construction on Balsas, 36, 50–58
Dehouve, Danièle, 77 n. 12, 115–16

de Jesús Alejandro, Carlos, 125, 180
de Jesús Alejandro, Pedro
    Alonso on, 90, 91
    on ANIPA, 2
    anti-dam campaign and, 51
    career of, 22, 180
    on council, 175
    criticism of, 158 n. 18, 162, 163–64
    del Val and, 160
    as director, 12, 134
    on Nahuas of Alto Balsas, 56, 57–58
    speech of, 167
    takeover meeting and, 103
    trip to Rancho Nuevo and, 125, 126–27
Delegate Zero (Subcomandante Marcos), 170–71, 177–79
de los Santos, Marcelino Isidro, 127–28
del Val Blanco, José, 138–39, 154, 160–61, 169
Díaz, Porfirio, 39, 64
Díaz de Jesús, Marcelino
    anti-dam campaign and, 51, 52
    career of, 22, 101 n. 7, 165–66
    criticism of, 158 n. 18, 162
    del Val and, 160
    as director, 134
    indigenous identity and, 56–58
    takeover meeting and, 103
    trip to Rancho Nuevo and, 125
Díaz Ordaz, Gustavo, 84
Dionisia, 125–26, 127, 128
directors of council. *See also specific directors*
    accomplishments of, 134
    after demise of council, 175
    agrarian myth and, 8
    ANIPA and, 125
    careers of, 22
    concerns of, 168–69
    criticism of, 162–63, 175–76
    description of, 7
    as focus of study, 28
    INI takeover meeting and, 102–6, 133
    political parties and, 112–13
    PRD and, 185
    promises of Salinas and, 100–101
    representativeness of, 136
    salaries of, 101
    sense of entitlement and, 108–9
Dresser, Denise, 7
drug wars in Guerrero, 121 n. 22

Echeverría Álvarez, Luis, 44–45
economic reform, 137, 139–40

economy, indigenous, 69–72, 78
educational opportunities, 90–92, 161
ejido title to land
  agriculture and, 148
  Article 27 and, 95–96
  Ávila administration and, 41
  Cárdenas administration and, 40
  description of, 39
  Fabila and, 83
  government and, 96–97
  indigenismo and, 88
  regulation of, 25
Elías Calles, Plutarco, 40
Equihua, Martín, 54, 98–99, 101 n. 7, 103, 162, 164–66
Espinosa Velasco, Guillermo, 103–5
Estrada Guadalupe, Sabino, 52, 119
ethnicity, 20, 167–68. *See also* indigenous peoples; mestizos
Eufemia, 175, 179, 180–81
EZLN (Zapatista National Liberation Army)
  council compared to, 5, 109, 112–13
  Subcomandante Marcos and, 170–71, 177–79
  uprising of, 106–7

Fabila, Alfonso, 61–63, 71, 75–76, 79–83, 84
Felícitos, 130–32
Ferguson, James, 69, 72, 155, 160
First National Indigenous Congress, 143
Florencio, 57, 168, 169
Flores Félix, Joaquín, 55
Foley, Michael, 46
folkloric poverty
  definition of, 7, 60, 172–73
  function of, 173
  government and, 174
  indigenous women's leadership and, 182–83
  INI and, 148, 150, 152–53
  outmigration and, 27
  perpetuation of image of, 162, 189
food subsidy program, 46–48, 49
Fox, Jonathan, 48
Fox, Vicente, 176, 179–80, 185

Gamio, Manuel, 63–64, 65, 67, 75
Gates, Marilyn, 96
Gatica, Raúl, 3
gender issues, 92, 124, 160, 180–83
government
  council as client of and broker for, 94–97, 101, 109, 153, 168–69, 174

definition of, 5 n. 3
drugs and, 121 n. 22
Fabila on, 80
local, 159–60
municipal compared to state, 116–32
power relations and, 76–78, 169
relationship of council to, 99–102, 144
Guardino, Peter, 37
Guerrero. *See also* Nahuas of Guerrero
  anti-quincentenary campaign in, 33–34
  changes in, in 2005, 185–86
  Chilapa region, 48–49, 71
  description of, 20–22
  government buildings of, *186, 187*
  illiteracy rates in, 61, 62
  indigenous identity in, 58
  indigenous leadership in, 22, 24
  land ownership in, 24–25
  maps of, 23
  militarization of countryside in, 121–22, 184–85
  Montaña region, 25, 61–63, 71, 83–84, 117–18
  new municipalities in, 118
  outmigration from, 25–27
  violence in, 120–21, 128–30
Guerrero Council 500 Years of Indigenous Resistance. *See also* directors of council
  as client and broker, 94–97, 99–100, 101, 109, 153, 168–69, 174
  description of, 7–8
  EZLN and, 5, 106–7, 109, 112–13
  first decade of, 4
  formation of, 35, 54–55, 57, 132
  founders of, 2
  funding for, 147 n. 12
  legitimacy of, 135–36
  local needs and, 109–16, 133–34
  manifesto of, 97–99
  marches of, 106–7
  meeting of, 12
  peasant populist strategy of, 97–99, 133, 162, 174
  populism and, 10–11
  relationship with state, 99–102, 144
  takeover meeting of, 102–6, 133
  weaknesses of, 132–33, 175–76
  works of, 9
Guerrero Indigenous Women's Coordinating Committee, 180
Gupta, Akhil, 155, 160

Hale, Charles, 13, 19
Hall, Gillette, 183
Hermina, 112
Hernández, Violeta, 147, 150–52
Hernández Castillo, Rosalva Aída, 31, 136
Hernández Navarro, Luis, 142, 176
hierarchy, ethnic and racial, 22 n. 17, 80
Hindley, Jane, 6
Horton, Lynn, 19

ILO Convention 169. *See* International Labor Organization (ILO) Convention 169 on Indigenous and Tribal Peoples
Independent Peasant Organization of Indigenous Communities, 110
Indians
    as close and strange, 71, 73, 87
    as culturally deficient, 19
    defense of community by, 36–38
    elites among, 154–55
    legitimate, definition of, 154–66, 170–71
    mestizos and, 63–68, 69–70
    policy toward, 73–74
    as populist subject, 60
    prejudice toward, 76
    as representation for *lo mexicano,* 18
indigenismo
    criticisms of, 143
    definition of, 30
    Fabilo and, 62–63
    impulses guiding, 59
    INI and, 142–44
    legacy of, 170
    modernization and, 65–66
    multiculturalism and, 17
    origins of, 63–64
    promise of, 88
    Solidarity program and, 142
    tension between mestizaje and, 73
indigenistas
    beliefs of, 87–88
    definition of, 30
    industrialization and, 79
    politics and policy of, 59–60
Indigenous Coordination Center (CCI), 61, 83–84, 85–86, 86
indigenous identity. *See also* San Andrés Accords
    claims to, 98–99
    of Nahuas, 56–58
    nationalism and, 74
    neoliberalism and, 18–19, 36–38
    in U.S., 74–75

indigenous movement. *See also* Guerrero Council 500 Years of Indigenous Resistance
    basis for, 2–3
    crisis in, 1–2, 4, 172
    description of, 89
    in Guerrero, 4–5, 90–91
    history of, 42–43
    in Latin America, 13
    leadership of, 179–83
    mestizo intellectuals and, 54–55
    nationalist narratives of, 12–13
    neoliberalism and, 5 n. 4
    priorities of, 134
indigenous peoples. *See also* Indians; indigenous identity; political autonomy for indigenous peoples
    authority and authenticity of, 20, 154–66, 170–71
    discursive shift from "Indians" to, 19 n. 13
    government organization of, 42
    language of, 151 n. 14, 162–63
    nation-states and, 11–14
    rights movement and, 5–6
indigenous territory concept, 94
Indigenous Women in Struggle, 148–49
Indios nailons, 162
industrialization, 79
INI (National Indigenous Institute). *See also* Fabila, Alfonso; indigenistas
    centralization of power and, 76–78
    COPLAMAR and, 45 n. 5, 46–48
    council takeover of, 102–6, 133
    criticisms of, 158–59
    development model of, 72–73, 148–54
    Echeverría administration and, 45
    first anthropological study of, 59
    formation of, 42, 75
    funding from, 99–100, 101, 146 n. 11
    indigenismo and, 142–44
    indigenous economy and, 69–70, 72
    indigenous isolation idea and, 67
    Ministry of Education and, 87
    politics and, 84–87
    reform of, 179–80
    scholarships of, 161 n. 19
Institutional Revolutionary Party (PRI), 30, 81, 135
integrationist agenda, 89, 173
Intercultural Encounter of Indigenous Peoples, 115, 116, 166–68

International Labor Organization (ILO) Convention 169 on Indigenous and Tribal Peoples, 18, 52–53, 57, 94 n. 5, 98, 137–39
Isidro, 108–9, 125, 167
isolation of Indian communities, 68–73

José, 108
Juárez, Benito Pablo, 64
Judith, 54

Knight, Alan, 10

land. *See also* agrarian myth; agrarian reform; agriculture; Article 27, Mexican Constitution; ejido title to land
  conflicts between communities over, 3, 76, 80, 96
  history of privatization attempts, 37–38
language, indigenous, 151 n. 14, 162–63
La Parota dam, 185 n. 10
Las Palmas paperwork, 110–11
leadership. *See also* directors of council
  indigenous, 7, 22, 24, 179–83
  by women, 92, 180–83
legal systems, 82
Light of the Montaña Union of Ejidos and Communities, 50 n. 9, 159
localism
  overcoming, 166–69
  persistence of, 174–75
  problems of, 155–66
local needs, and council, 109–16, 133–34
local village politics, 80–83, 93
Lomnitz-Adler, Claudio, 16
López Bárcenas, Francisco, 3
López Portillo, José, 45, 144
Lourdes, 146, 148–49, 163 n. 20
lynching, 120–21

machete attack, 186–88
manifesto of council, 97–99
marches, and police brutality, 106–7, 110
Marín, Eligio Pacheco, 150
markets, 71–72, 72
Martínez Novo, Carmen, 19
Melchiades, 167
mestizaje, 60, 64–66, 65, 67, 73
mestizos
  council and, 54–55
  Indians and, 63–68, 69–70
  INI anthropologists as, 60–61
  prejudice of, 76
  village governments and, 93
  work ethic of, 26 n. 20
Mexican Association of Indigenous Professionals and Intellectuals, 43
Mexican Council 500 Years of Resistance, 33
Mexican Revolution. *See* Revolution
México profundo (Bonfil Battalla), 15, 141
Miguel García, Reynaldo, 3
militarization of Guerrero, 121–22, 184–85
Ministry of Social Development (SEDESOL), 99–100, 102
modernity, bridge to, 141–42
Moguel, Julio, 55
Molina Enríquez, Andrés, 64–65
Montaña region, 25, 61–63, 71, 83–84, 117–18
Morett Sánchez, Jesús Carlos, 41, 96
mulatto, construction of, in Latin America, 66 n. 5
multiculturalism, 15–20, 88, 173
Muñoz, Maurilio, 71, 84–85

Nación Amuzga, 186–88
NAFTA (North American Free Trade Agreement), 2, 6, 18, 25, 137, 142
Nahmad Sitton, Salomón, 77, 78, 84–85
Nahuas of Guerrero
  Altepetl Nahuas, 90
  A. Ávila and, 157
  in Chilapa region, 48–49
  in Copanatoyac, 117–18
  dam construction and, 35–36, 50–58
  ethnic hierarchy and, 22 n. 17
  identity formation among, 56–58
National Action Party (PAN), 40–41
National Coordinating Committee of the Play of Ayala, 48 n. 8
National Council of Indigenous Peoples, 45
National Human Rights Commission, 6, 137
National Indigenous Institute. *See* INI
National Indigenous Women's Coordinating Committee of Mexico, 180
national integration, myth of, 108
nationalism, 15–20, 74
nationalist, definition of, 5 n. 3
National Peasant Federation (CNC), 42, 44, 82
National Program for Depressed Areas and Marginal Groups (COPLAMAR), 45 n. 5, 46–48, 49, 144
nation-states, 5 n. 3, 11–14, 36–38. *See also* government

Nava, Roque, 103–4
neoliberalism
   anti-quincentenary campaign and, 33–34
   indigenous identity politics and, 18–19, 36–38
   multiculturalism and, 16, 88
   populism and, 5 n. 4, 8–11
   PRI and, 135
Néstor, 112, 132, 146–47, 153, 175–76
North American Free Trade Agreement (NAFTA), 2, 6, 18, 25, 137, 142

Oaxaca, 3, 79, 95, 96
Obregón, Álvaro, 38
Othón de Mendizábal, Miguel, 67
outmigration from Guerrero, 25–27
outside interests, 80

PAN (National Action Party), 40–41
participation
   COPLAMAR and, 144
   government and, 153–54
   INI model of, 148–54
   Solidarity program and, 140–42
Party of the Democratic Revolution (PRD)
   anti-dam campaign and, 52
   C. Cárdenas and, 56
   emergence of, and government funding, 55 n. 13
   Equihua and, 164–65
   in Guerrero, 21 n. 15, 185
Patrinos, Harry, 183
patriotism, 106–9
patron-client relationships, 105
peasant populist strategy of council, 97–99, 133, 162, 174
peasants (campesinos)
   agrarian reform and, 39–43
   definition of, 35 n. 1
   discourses of in 1800s, 37
   politicization of, 48
   Revolution and, 38–39, 60
   rights of, 34
   underdevelopment of, 43–46
place, and authenticity, 154–66, 170–71
Plural National Indigenous Assembly for Autonomy. See ANIPA
Pluriethnic Autonomous Region (RAP), 156–58
police brutality, 107, 110, 120–22, 184–85
political autonomy for indigenous peoples, 3 n. 2, 80–83, 93–97, 118–19
political parties. See also specific political parties

anti-dam campaign and, 51–52
council seen as, 112–13
funding from, 150
in Rancho Nuevo, 127–28
politics
   culture and, 117 n. 18
   INI and, 84–87
   local, 80–83, 93
populism
   of council, 97–99, 133
   multiculturalism and, 17–18
   neoliberalism and, 8–11
   during Salinas administration, 7, 10, 136
Portillo, Eduardo, 147
Pozas, Ricardo, 83
PRD. See Party of the Democratic Revolution
presidentialism, 136–37, 140–41
PRI (Institutional Revolutionary Party), 30, 81, 135
principales, 91 n. 2, 92, 159–60
PRT (Revolutionary Labor Party), 52, 119
Pueblo Hidalgo, 37–38

quincentenary celebration, opposition to, 33–34, 56, 98, 100

race, and governance, 80
Rancho Nuevo de la Democracia, 117, 124, 124–28, 133
RAP (Pluriethnic Autonomous Region), 156–58
Ravelo Lecuona, Renato, 158
Regional Indigenous Congress, 155
regional organization, logic of, 114–16
Regional Solidarity Funds, 7, 145–48, 173
regional vision of autonomy, 3
Renato, 54–55
research methods, 27–30
Revolution
   Fabila and, 82–83
   ideology of, 34
   industrialization and, 59–60
   mestizos and, 65
   myth of, 38–39
Revolutionary Labor Party (PRT), 52, 119
Ricardo, 168
rights movement, international, 5–6, 52–53, 55, 98, 135, 139–40. See also International Labor Organization (ILO) Convention 169 on Indigenous and Tribal Peoples
Roberto, 107–8, 133, 163
Roberts, Kenneth, 10

Rocha, Aceadeth, 183, 186, 188
Roniger, Luis, 105
Rostow, Walter, 79
Ruiz Hernández, Margarito, 1, 55
Rus, Jan, 80

Salinas de Gortari, Carlos
  administration of, 136–38
  human rights and, 6, 53
  legitimation crisis of, 18 n. 11
  nationalism of, 135
  populism and, 7, 10, 136
  promises of, 100–101
  Regional Solidarity Funds program of, 7, 145–48, 173
  Solidarity program of, 140–42, 169, 173–74
Salinas de Gortari, Raúl, 120
San Andrés Accords, 14, 93–94, 173, 178
Sánchez, Daniel, 28, 125, 163 n. 20, 187–89
Sánchez Capistrano, José Leonor, 90, 118–19
Sánchez Néstor, Martha
  author and, 28
  Benito and, 162
  career of, 180
  as director, 22, 134, 164, 168, 169
  on Equihua, 165
  on indigenous women leaders, 181–82
  photo of, 24
  trip to Rancho Nuevo and, 125, 127
San Luis Acatlán
  Community Food Council in, 50
  Community Police in, 109 n. 12, 129–30, 169, 184
  Light of the Montaña Union of Ejidos and Communities, 50 n. 9, 159
  outmigration from, 24
Sariego Rodríguez, Juan Luis, 77 n. 12
SEDESOL (Ministry of Social Development), 99–100, 102
self-determination
  council manifesto and, 98
  demands for, 93–94
  government affirmation of, 135–36
  local village politics and, 80–83
  processes of, 118–19
Seojtli Llankuik, 113–14
Smelser, Neil, 79
Solidarity program, 140–42, 169, 173–74
state, definition of, 5 n. 3
State Congress of Indigenous Peoples, 101
Stephen, Lynn, 95, 96
Subcomandante Marcos, 170–71, 177–79

takeover meeting of council, 102–6, 133
Tellez, Luis, 142
Tierra Caliente region, 26 n. 20
Tlachinollan, 159
Torreblanca Galindo, Zeferino, 21 n. 15
Totomixtlahuaca, 117, 128–32, 159
traitors, 154–66
travel, international, 163 n. 20
Tully, James, 171

United States. See also NAFTA
  comparison to, 13–14, 74–75
  Salinas administration and, 6–7

Van Young, Eric, 36–37
Vasconselos, José, 64, 65
Vásquez, Genaro, 21
Velasco, David, 172
Vélez-Ibañez, Carlos, 108
Veracruz, 79
Villa, Francisco "Pancho," 38
Villoro, Luis, 66–67, 68, 73, 143
violence
  drug wars and, 121 n. 22
  in Guerrero, 120–21, 128–30
  intercommunity, 3, 76, 80
  machete attack, 186–88
  police brutality, 107, 110, 120–22, 184–85

Warman, Arturo, 142–43
Watson, Alexander F., 6–7
Weyland, Kurt, 10
Williams, Brackette, 11, 13
Wittgenstein, Ludwig, 171
women
  community governance structures and, 160
  leadership by, 92, 180–83
  maternal mortality rate, 183 n. 7
  Mixteca, 124

Xochistlahuaca, 91–92, 155 n. 16, 183

Yvette, 149–50

Zapata, Emiliano, 38
Zapatista National Liberation Army (EZLN)
  council compared to, 5, 109, 112–13
  Subcomandante Marcos and, 170–71, 177–79
  uprising of, 106–7
Zolla, Carlos, 151–52
zones of expusion, 25–27

www.ingramcontent.com/pod-product-compliance
Lightning Source LLC
Chambersburg PA
CBHW031550300426
44111CB00006BA/248